C000231767

Routledge Rev.

Ayahs, Lascars and Princes

People from the Indian sub-continent have been in Britain since the end of the seventeenth century. The presence of princes and maharajahs is well documented but this book, first published in 1986, was the first account of the ordinary people in Britain. This book will be of interest to students of history.

Ayahs, Lascars and Princes

The Story of Indians in Britain 1700-1947

Rozina Visram

Routledge
Taylor & Francis Group

First published in 1986
by Pluto Press Limited

This edition first published in 2015 by Routledge
2 Park Square, Milton Park, Abingdon, Oxon, OX14 4RN
and by Routledge
711 Third Avenue, New York, NY 10017

Routledge is an imprint of the Taylor & Francis Group, an informa business

© 1986 Rozina Visram

Publisher's Note
The publisher has gone to great lengths to ensure the quality of this reprint but points out that some imperfections in the original copies may be apparent.

Disclaimer
The publisher has made every effort to trace copyright holders and welcomes correspondence from those they have been unable to contact.

A Library of Congress record exists under LC control number: 86212046

ISBN 13: 978-1-138-92120-7 (hbk)
ISBN 13: 978-1-315-68650-9 (ebk)
ISBN 13: 978-1-138-92121-4 (pbk)

Rozina Visram

Ayahs, Lascars and Princes

Indians in Britain 1700–1947

First published in 1986 by Pluto Press Limited,
The Works, 105a Torriano Avenue, London NW5 2RX
and Pluto Press Australia Limited, PO Box 199, Leichhardt,
New South Wales 2040, Australia. Also Pluto Press,
51 Washington Street, Dover, New Hampshire 03820 USA

7 6 5 4 3 2 1

90 89 88 87 86

Phototypeset by AKM Associates (UK) Limited,
Ajmal House, Hayes Road, Southall, Greater London
Printed in Great Britain by Guernsey Press Co. Limited,
Guernsey, C.I.

British Library Cataloguing in Publication Data
Visram, Rozina
   Ayahs, lascars and princes: Indians in Britain 1700-1947
   1. East Indians——Great Britain——Social conditions.
   2. Great Britain——Social conditions
   I. Title
   305.8'91411'041   DA125.S57

ISBN 0 7453 0074 X (pbk)
     0 7453 0072 3 (hbk)

Contents

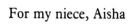

For my niece, Aisha

Preface

This book traces the history of Asian settlement in Britain from 1700 to 1947. It examines the nature of Asian migration, official attitudes to the Asian presence in Britain, the reactions and perceptions of the British people and the responses of the Asians themselves. The term 'Asian' as used here refers to the people from the Indian subcontinent. I have used the terms 'Asian' and 'Indian' interchangeably; I use 'black' in a political sense to refer to peoples of Afro-Caribbean and Asian origin. Contrary to common belief, Asians have been in Britain a long time, and have made a far greater contribution to the development of life here than is acknowledged.

Because of the nature of the source material available, the history of Asians in Britain inevitably becomes more a study of a few individuals than of communities. The book, however, does not wish to convey the impression that because a few Asians 'made it', life for Asians in Britain before 1947 was easy, and that they did not face problems similar to those faced by black communities in Britain today.

This book ends with Indian independence in 1947. This is for two reasons. One, in 1947, two sovereign states, India and Pakistan, emerged from the old Indian Empire (East Pakistan later became Bangladesh); after 1947 India cannot be treated as a single political entity. Two, after 1947, the patterns (and motivations) of migration from India change radically.

This book is very much a first study of the history of Asians in Britain before 1947. I hope that it will provide an inspiration for other, deeper studies of this very important topic.

Acknowledgements

The book was first conceived as a research project for the ILEA teacher-fellowship programme at the Centre for Multicultural Education, University of London Institute of Education. I owe a deep debt of gratitude to the Centre and to the ILEA for granting me time, administrative assistance and secondment to undertake this study.

I am grateful to the custodians and staff of the following libraries and archives who have met my requests for books, documents and records under their care with efficiency and courtesy: the British Library (both Bloomsbury and Colindale); the India Office Library and Records (IOLR); the Imperial War Museum; the Army Museum; the Marx Memorial Library and the Royal Commonwealth Society. Also the Tower Hamlets Local History Library; Finsbury and Islington Local History Library; Battersea Reference Library, Local History section (and especially R.A. Shaw); Camden and St Pancras Local History Library; Rose Lipman Library, Hackney, Archives Department and Brighton Reference Library. I am also grateful to the London City Mission for allowing me to consult their records.

Many other people have helped me with advice, suggestions and time. I would like especially to thank Victor Kiernan, P.K. Nayar, Chris Power, Sehri Saklatvala, Kathy Soud and Jatinder Verma.

I owe a particular debt of gratitude to the following: Steve Ashton of the IOLR for helping me find my way through the labyrinth of records at the library, for sharing his knowledge of Indian history with me, and for reading and commenting on my draft chapters; Peter Fraser, for his encouragement, interest in my work and for reading my draft chapters; Peter Fryer, for his interest in my research, for his most meticulous reading of my draft chapters and his constructive suggestions; George Shepperson, for his encouragement, valuable suggestions and for reading and commenting on the draft chapters. For any remaining errors and omissions the sole responsibility is mine.

Ayahs, Lascars and Princes

1. India and Britain

It is often forgotten that Britain had an Indian community long before the Second World War, and that the recent arrival of Asian people in Britain is part of the long history of contact between Britain and India. The arrival of Asians in Britain has taken place precisely because of these long-established connections.

Indian links with Europe go back 10,000 years. The East offered much which Europeans needed – spices, textiles and other exotic luxuries like carpets.[1] Traders travelled by the overland route through Constantinople and from there beyond, until Turkish hegemony effectively blocked this profitable trade route in the fifteenth century. There then followed a search for a sea route to India, and it was the Portuguese who came up trumps when Vasco da Gama arrived in Calicut, on the west coast of India, in 1498,[2] a few years before the Mughal emperors established their rule over India.[3] The Portuguese made Goa, on the west coast, their headquarters; and they were to remain there for over 400 years.[4] Not wishing to be left out of this lucrative trade, other European nations – the Dutch, English and French – followed in the wake of the Portuguese.

The East India Company was launched in England in 1599 by a group of London merchants, with a capital of £30,000. On the last day of 1600, Queen Elizabeth I granted the Company a charter which gave them the monopoly of trade with India and the East.[5] The Company's original goal was the spice trade of the East Indies. But the Dutch, who had beaten the English to that region, would brook no rivals, so the East India Company turned its attention to India for its field of commercial exploits.

In 1608, the first Company ship called at Surat on the west coast, and in 1612 the Mughal emperor, Jehangir, granted the Company the vital 'firman' (mandate), allowing it the privilege of Indian trade.[6] The seventeenth century saw a gradual expansion of factories round the Indian coast – Madras in 1640, Bombay (a wedding gift to Charles II from the Portuguese) in 1665, and Calcutta in 1690; and so the pattern of trade with India was built up.[7]

The East India Company operated from its headquarters in London. An imposing new building was erected in Leadenhall Street in 1726 as the permanent headquarters. To administer its vast interests, a Court of Directors of 24 members, elected for four years from the group of the original subscribers, was set up. Then there were the shareholders in the Company, and finally its various employees, both in London and in India. Labour was needed in London for its dockyards, warehouses, foundries, cordage works, saw mills and even slaughterhouses for cattle, which provided meat for the growing fleet of the East Indiamen which plied between India and England.[8] For the purpose of administration, the Company divided India into three Presidencies – Madras, Bombay and Bengal, independent of each other and answerable only to the Court of Directors in London. In each of the Presidencies, a president (also known as the governor), supported by a council of senior merchants, exercised control. Below these came a strictly defined hierarchy of the Company's servants: senior merchants, junior merchants, factors and writers, all recruited in England. Familiar British institutions, like the law courts, civic corporations, churches and theatres, were transplanted to the presidencies. And soon a growing band of attorneys, constables, churchwardens and artists went out to India to join the merchants and clerks. Their houses were separated from the 'Black Town', where the 'native' employees of the Company and the rest of the Indian population lived. As the East India Company was granted more trading concessions by the patronage of the Mughal emperors, so the Company's commercial enterprises expanded, and more recruits went out from Britain to swell the size of the British population living in India. After 1660, the Company recruited British soldiers and 'native sepoys'[9] to protect its commercial concerns in India.

Since the overriding interest of the Company was trade and the profit motive, it did little to interfere with traditional Indian society or engage in military adventures – all of which cost money. It concerned itself only with providing the framework of stability required for trade to flourish. In the early years, many employees of the East India Company stayed on in India for long spells. Communications were slow and opportunities for a run back to England less frequent, so many reconciled themselves to this long exile by developing an interest in the country and its people. Few women went out to India from Britain, and so there was much mixing between black and white.[10] But all this was to change in the second half of the eighteenth century.

By this time the Mughal Empire was very slowly beginning to crumble, faced by invasions from outside India, internal disputes and revolts from its Hindu subjects. In this fluid situation, it was the threat from a rival European nation that first stimulated the East India Company to embark on its expansionist forays into Indian territory. The French, who had been late arrivals on the Indian commercial scene – they began trading in 1664 – were by this time fast catching up in the share of profits from the Indian trade. And the British-French rivalry in Europe was dragged into India, where the French general Joseph François Dupleix faced Robert Clive, far away from the centre of European quarrels.[11] Having tasted victory against the French, Clive next turned to Bengal, which had succeeded in shaking off the authority of the Mughal emperor. Taking advantage of the friction which had developed between the Company and Bengal, Clive marched in, defeated the ruler of Bengal, Siraj-ud-Daula, in 1757, and made the East India Company ruler of Bengal in all but name. In 1765, the Mughal emperor recognized the Company as his diwan (minister), granting it the authority to collect taxes. Bengal became virtually a Company province and so began the plunder of

Bengal by the 'nabobs' who amassed vast fortunes which they
returned to spend in England.[12]

Robert Clive's conquest of Bengal heralded a change: not
only had the East India Company become effectively ruler of
Bengal, but it had laid the foundation of the British Indian
Empire. Although trade was still the Company's main objective,
the conquest of Bengal began a new phase in the administration
of its 'provinces'. By the Regulating Act of 1773 (the first time
that the British parliament had taken action to direct the affairs
of the Company in India), Warren Hastings became Governor
General, with authority to supervise the presidencies of Bombay
and Madras. Hitherto these provinces had been autonomous,
answerable only to the Court of Directors in London. Hastings
thus became not only governor of Bengal, but also Governor
General of all the Company's commercial provinces in India.
The administrative change that the Act implied was slow to
come, however. This was partly because of Warren Hastings.
He was a great admirer of Indian civilization, its artistic and
cultural heritage. He and other 'Orientalists' studied Indian
literature, languages, art and religion.[13] Hastings set up the
Asiatic Society in Bengal and a college of Arabic and Persian
studies. Hastings also believed that the East India Company
should govern India through the agency of Indians, and on
Indian principles. He therefore confined himself to cleaning up
the excesses of the nabobs, but otherwise left the details of
Indian administration without much change.

But change did come. The India Act of 1784 set up a dual
system of government. A tier of supervisory control was set up
above the Court of Directors of the Company in London.
Known as the Board of Control, this consisted of the President
and six commissioners. It was the Board of Control that now
appointed the Governor General in India; he was to be
answerable not only to the Court of Directors of the East India
Company, but also to the Board of Control in London. The
Company still retained the trading monopoly in India, but
Indian administration was recast. The Company's servants
could now hold either an administrative or a commercial post in

India, but not both as previously. More important, Indian administration was Europeanized; the top and middle rungs of power were now reserved for Europeans only, Indians being relegated to the bottom levels of public service. The style of administration changed as well. Cornwallis, who succeeded Warren Hastings as Governor General, believed that England ruled India for India's 'own good'. Unlike Hastings, he did not consider there was anything to admire in the ancient Indian civilization. And so he proceeded to govern India on European principles and values. This trend set by Cornwallis was to gather pace.

The nineteenth century reinforced this changing relationship. It also introduced a more expansionist phase in the Company's administration. In 1813, the East India Company's new Charter abolished its trading monopoly in India. This was the era when belief in free trade predominated. India was, therefore, opened up to *all* traders from Britain, who were eager to flood India with British manufactured goods. Free trade also implied a search for new markets in India, so the East India Company (which still retained administrative control of India, although it had lost its trading monopoly) embarked on a policy of conquest. The Company's expansionist policy was facilitated by the declining Mughal power. So with judicious self-interest, combined with military force – and all in the name of peaceful trade – the East India Company began the policy of playing off one prince against another, interfering in the internal affairs of the states, or lending 'help' to a 'friendly' state against its enemies. In this way British rule was extended over a large part of India. By the 1850s Britain ruled India.

Because it had been relatively easy to conquer India, and to do so in a short space of time, the British believed that the reason for this success lay in the superiority of Europe over Asia, and above all in the superiority of the British over all other peoples. Flushed with their success, they did not think that there could be other, more complex, reasons for it. The Christian missionaries, who after 1813 were free to go to India to spread the Gospel,[14] reinforced this view of the Indian subcontinent. Their

ideas were to influence the governing of India. The Utilitarians
and the Evangelicals considered the Hindu religion to be one
'grand abomination', and India to be full of 'dark and bloody
superstition'. They therefore regarded it as their 'moral duty' to
spread 'western enlightenment and reason' throughout India.[15]
They brushed aside the Orientalists' arguments that India was a
'moral and civilized' society and did not need the fare offered by
the missionaries.[16] And so began the 'reforming' phase of Indian
administration.

Those Indian social and religious practices which the British
regarded as 'barbaric' were abolished; land tenure was 'reorga-
nized', often with disastrous results for the social and economic
fabric of India. Indian classical education was reformed.
Macaulay believed the 'great object of British government
ought to be the promotion of European literature and science
among the natives of India'. And so, with his Education Minute
of 1835, he set in motion the anglicizing of Indian education.
Under the Governor Generalship of Lord Dalhousie reforms
gathered speed; Indian laws, customs and practices were all
remodelled on the English pattern. British technological and
material 'benefits' were grafted on to Indian society. More
Indian states were annexed.

The driving force behind this 'civilizing' zeal remained the
inherent belief prevalent in mid-Victorian England that the
British were culturally and racially superior to the mass of their
subjects in India and elsewhere in the Empire. As British rule
was consolidated over India, more 'sahibs' and 'memsahibs'
(their wives) arrived from England. Since communications had
improved, they tended to stay for shorter periods than their
predecessors. Not only did they believe themselves to be
superior, they made sure that the Indians acknowledged them as
such. Locked in this racist attitude, the British rulers isolated
themselves and their memsahibs in a rigid hierarchy of class
system, lording it over the conquered 'natives' with a high hand.
A correspondent to *The Times* wrote,

I must say that I have been struck with the arrogant and repellent manner in which we often treat natives of rank, and with the unnecessary harshness of our treatment of inferiors. The most scrubby mean little representative of *la race blanche* . . . regards himself as infinitely superior to the Rajpoot with a genealogy of 1,000 years.[17]

The Indian National Rising of 1857 was a shock to the British. In a bid to rid the country of foreign rule, Indians resorted to arms and fought ferociously for 14 months. The British retaliated with unprecedented savagery and the reprisals against the perpetrators of the so-called 'Mutiny' were terrible. But in many ways the Rising marked a watershed in British administrative practice in India (and in many other parts of the Empire, since the British never forgot the lessons of 1857). In the wake of the Rising, the East India Company's rule was wound up, and in 1858 India came under the direct rule of the British Crown. Queen Victoria's Proclamation of November 1858 declared:

We hold ourselves bound to the natives of our Indian territories by the same obligations of duty which bind us to all our subjects, and those obligations, by the Almighty God, we shall faithfully and conscientiously fulfil . . . We declare it to be our royal will and pleasure that none be in any wise favoured, none molested or disquieted, by reason of their religious faith or observances, but that all shall alike enjoy the equal protection of the law.

The Proclamation also laid down the principle of non-interference with the religious beliefs and practices of the Indians. But in granting this 'benevolence' to her Indian subjects, Queen Victoria was at pains to point out that 'in their prosperity will be our strength; in their contentment our security'.

In 1858 Indian administration came directly under the control of Whitehall with the Secretary of State for India and his Council responsible for the affairs of India.[18] The Governor

General, as the direct representative of the monarch, took on the additional title of Viceroy. They were answerable to the British parliament where ultimate authority resided. In 1877 Queen Victoria assumed the title of Empress of India or Kaiser-i-Hind.

The Indian National Rising also put an end to the aggressive policy of imperial expansion and headlong reform of Indian society on western lines. The British propped up the power of the princely states and the landed classes, rewarding loyalty and thus building up a stratum of society with a vested interest in the Raj. All the same, the steady growth in western education and western institutions continued. Roads, railways and irrigation schemes were extended. At lower levels of administration they employed Indian bureaucrats who collaborated in the maintenance of the Raj. The policy of racial separateness became even more rigid and elaborate. 1857 convinced the British that they 'belonged to a race whom God has destined to govern and subdue'.[19] The majesty of government, the pomp and protocol surrounding the Viceroy grew more complex: all designed to dazzle the ruled and maintain the authority of the rulers.

The government became more autocratic and centralized. Power, at all levels, was concentrated in the hands of the rulers. When the first slow steps at representative government came it was at the local government level only, 'allowing the Bengali Baboo to discuss his own schools and drains'.[20] This was the 'concession' granted to educated Indians in the government of their own country in the 1880s. However, by the last decade of the nineteenth century educated Indians, the product of British education, became critical of the 'un-Britishness' of British rule. The Indian National Congress, moderate in its sentiments, demanded a share in the government of India.

Surrounded with pomp and prestige and convinced in the words of Lord Curzon, the Viceroy from 1899 to 1905, that Indian improvement could only be realized through 'the unchallenged supremacy of the paramount power',[21] the British government carried on ruling India. Indian self-government – if it was considered at all – seemed a very distant and remote possibility. However, events like the partition of Bengal in 1905 and the First World War changed the nature of nationalists' aspirations. Self-government became the goal. The British government responded to this both by granting concessions in order to silence agitation, and by imposing restrictions and repression. The 1920s and 1930s saw the momentum for Indian independence gather pace, and finally in 1947 India regained its independence. Two new sovereign states were born out of the old Indian Empire.[22]

One of the major legacies of the British control of India was the planting of peoples of Indian origin all over the British Empire, including Britain itself.[23] India was considered to be a reservoir of cheap labour. After African slavery was legally ended in 1833, 'indentured' labourers were recruited from India to work on plantations in Mauritius, Guyana, Trinidad, and Jamaica. This was slavery in a new guise: many laboured under conditions no less degrading than slavery.[24] Thereafter wherever need arose, Indian labour was employed. Indians worked in the plantations and mines in Ceylon, Malaya, Burma, South Africa and Fiji. Indian labour provided the manpower to build the East African Railway. Indian sailors worked the British merchant navy. Indian soldiers not only helped to maintain the British Raj in India, but were used as cannon fodder overseas in colonial wars of conquest to extend its frontiers.

Indians were brought to Britain too. They did not come as 'indentured' labourers, but the principle of cheap labour applied here as well. Many Indian servants and ayahs (nannies or ladies' maids) were brought over by British families returning from India. Indian sailors were employed by the East India Company to work on its ships. Some of these servants and sailors settled permanently in Britain.

One of the results of the policy of introducing western education in India was that, from about the middle of the nineteenth century, many Indian students began arriving in Britain, some on scholarships, to study law or medicine or to prepare for other professions. Some came to take the examination for entry into the Indian civil service since this examination could only be taken in London. Some Indian students settled in Britain after qualifying, to practise as doctors, lawyers or in other professions. Some Indian business firms opened branches in England. Nationalist politicians came to London, the centre of power, to argue the cause of Indian freedom. Indian princes and maharajahs visited England, not only as guests of the Crown on formal occasions, like the coronations, but also to pay their 'respects' to the monarch or for pleasure. London, as the metropolitan capital, attracted many visitors from India. Exhibitions of Indian arts and crafts were displayed in England too. The Asian presence in Britain therefore goes a long way back and forms a prelude to the post-independence migration of Asians to Britain.

2. Chattels of the Empire: Servants and Ayahs

This chapter looks at the position of the servants and ayahs who, as the chattels of the Empire, were brought over to Britain entirely for the convenience of their masters and mistresses as cheap labour.

The custom of importing Indian servants and ayahs into Britain probably began in the early eighteenth century, if not earlier. In India the British employees of the East India Company had created luxurious lifestyles for themselves, adapting Oriental conditions to suit their tastes and conveniences. Many servants – each with a specific duty – waited on them;[1] their households exuded an aura of grandeur and comfort. On their return to England many a Company nabob and army officer, like the 'Sugar Barons' of the West Indies, lived in splendour on their estates, recreating something of the life of India in the midst of the rolling English countryside.[2] References to Indian servants abound in the literature of the period.[3] Warren Hastings, the Governor General and his wife (the former Baroness von Imhoff) came back with two Indian boys and four maids. Sophie von la Roche, a German, has given us a description of the two boys, who were 'thirteen to fourteen' with 'longish faces, beautiful black eyes, fine eyebrows, sleek black hair, thin lips, fine teeth, a brownish complexion and kindly intelligent faces'. The boys spoke only 'East Indian'. The four maids, we are told, had to be sent back because they 'refused to work any harder than in India, and wanted to lead exactly the same life'.[4] This is hardly surprising. In India there were more servants to lighten the load of work. A Captain Baker of the East India Regiment brought back with him to Cork,

Ireland, Deen Mahomed, who was later to be famous as Sake Deen Mahomed, 'Shampooing Surgeon to George IV'. Such fame was achieved very rarely, and by very few.[5] Many Indian servants in Britain simply eked out their anonymous existence. Writing to Fanny Burney in 1789, Mrs Lock described the arrival at Godalming, Surrey, of 'several post chaises containing East Indian [British] families with their negro [Indian] servants, nurses and children'. Their 'inhuman voices and barbarous chattering' had disturbed her, but she had felt sorry 'to see these poor negro women taken away from their own country'; later her servant had 'met one on the stairs in tears'.[6]

Not only higher officials from the British East India Company, but lesser men, petty clerks, factors and women came back from India with their Indian servants. A Mrs Gladwin, on her return from Bengal on account of ill health, had been accompanied by two maids, who, it was later alleged, had poisoned her.[7] Often children sent back to England for their education were accompanied by Indian servants.[8] The trend of bringing servants home to Britain, begun in the time of the East India Company's rule, continued after 1858 when the government of India came under the direct control of Whitehall; and as communications became easier and more families travelled back and forth, so more Indian servants came to England.

Reasons for bringing back servants to Britain

These servants were brought over for many reasons. A reluctance to leave behind a favourite, faithful servant; a wish to recreate the nostalgic splendour of Indian life in England; to minister to the needs of the family and children during the long and arduous sea voyage back – an ayah was considered to be an expert at this; or merely as a status symbol or curiosity. The 'gentleman Attorney' of Calcutta, William Hickey, brought back with him a 'little pet boy, Nabob', a Bengali lad, whom he dressed 'very smart as a hussar'. Hickey emphatically mentioned that 'as a servant he was not of the least use to me'. The entire Hickey family took a great liking to Nabob and he became 'a little pet with all the ladies', since he was an 'interesting looking handsome boy'.[9] For whatever reason, Indian domestics provided a cheap source of labour and, like African servants, Asian valets and footmen came to be quite in vogue for fashionable British families in the eighteenth century. With 'full-blooded' Asians available, there was no longer any need to dress African servants in Oriental costumes.

Many advertisements of the time bear testimony to this preference. A footman's place was being sought by a 22-year-old 'black man from Bengal' brought to England by a gentleman in whose service he had been for 15 years. He wished to serve any 'person of quality on reasonable terms'. Another 'East Indian' advertised for a place with 'a single gentleman, or as a footman in a small family'. He appeared to be quite accomplished: he could 'shave and dress hair, read, write and understand common accounts, clean plate and furniture well, and do anything in that capacity as he [had] been brought up to it all his life, would look after a saddle horse or two.' Another who had lived for seven and a half years with his previous master was looking for a place as a footman; and yet another who could 'speak English, read and write a little and willing to travel with a small family to any part of England' was seeking a footman's place.[10]

Many families going out to India advertised for Indian servants, preferring to be accompanied by Indian rather than European servants.[11] After all, the expense of taking out English servants was quite high; and besides, European servants did not always prove very reliable.[12] Some servants, especially females, went off to get married, while others deserted to set up in business. Their unfamiliarity with the climate, the country and customs proved quite a trial. Indian domestics, on the other hand, not only had become accustomed to English whims and ways but also knew India.

Some Indian servants, it would appear, were slaves and so were disposed of publicly. An advertisement in 1709, in the fashionable Steele's and Addison's *Tatler*, read:

A Black Indian Boy 12 Years of Age, fit to wait on a
Gentleman, to be disposed of at Denis's Coffee-house in
Finch-Lane near the Royal Exchange.

A female advertising for a return passage in 1775 had this to say:

Any lady going to the East Indies, having occasion for a
maid servant may be advantageously supplied with one
who is lately come from thence; she is a Slave Girl, and the
mistress who brought her over having no occasion for her
will give her over to any Lady to attend her in the passage to
India and to serve her for three years after the arrival there
without wages, provided the lady engages at expiration of
the Term to give her freedom. She is a good servant,
perfectly good natured, and talks English well. She may be
heard of by sending a line to —.[13]

'Hue and cry' advertisements chronicle the plight of these
Asian slaves. In 1688 the *London Gazette* offered 'a guinea
reward' for a 'black boy, an Indian, about 13 years old, run away
the 8th inst. from Putney with a collar about his neck with this
inscription "The Lady Bromfield's black, in Lincoln's Inn
Fields" '. Another advertisement in 1737 was searching for an
'East India Tawney Black', while another in 1743 tried to find a
'Run-away Bengal Boy'. In 1772 Thomas Hornsey, 'a black, a
native of the Coast of Malabar' had run away from his master.
The runaway in question was said to have 'long hair', was
'well-made, likely featured' and spoke English well. The notice
warned that anyone who harboured him would be prosecuted,
while two guineas were offered as a reward for returning him.[14]

Slavery in Anglo-Oriental society in India was accepted as a
normal state of affairs. Slave boys and girls were employed as
pages and ladies' maids. Slave notices also appeared in many
Calcutta newspapers: 'Two Coffree boys, who play remarkably
well on the French Horn, about eighteen years of age, belonging
to a Portuguese Paddrie lately deceased. For particulars enquire
of the Vicar of the Portuguese Church.'[15] 'Coffree' was a term
used for African slaves. The East India Company itself traded in

slaves, making enormous profits, supplying slaves from Africa to its west coast settlements in India, and was only prohibited exportation of slaves by the 1789 Proclamation.[16] But African slaves were expensive in India. They cost usually about ten times as much as local boys and girls from Dacca, so most English families preferred to obtain Indian servants. Conversion to Christianity, it was believed, gave the slaves certain rights – they were no longer mere property.[17]

The treatment of Indian servants in Britain

Most Asians, however, were free men and women; but their treatment was no better than that of other black servants in England. There are instances of cruel treatment, of absconding servants; occasionally they were dumped even before reaching England, or given away as gifts. In 1795 the *Morning Chronicle* carried this notice from a Mrs Ramus:

> Whereas a Black Servant Boy, a native of Bengal, called by the name of HYDER did on the 18th of this inst February, leave the services of Mrs Ramus, no: 58, Baker Street, Portman Square, and had taken with him his livery and other apparel, the property of his mistress – This is therefore to forewarn all persons from hiring the said Hyder, or harbouring him in any manner as they will be prosecuted for the same as the law directs.
> NB. The said Hyder is about 14 Years of age, is about 5ft or 5ft 6ins high, thin made, and upright, talks broken English and is pretty fluent in the Moorish language. If the said Hyder will return to his place in the country of a week, and behave himself properly in the future, he will be received and nothing more be said; but if not, whoever will give Mrs Ramus the information where he may be met with shall be handsomely rewarded.[18]

And we hear of another 'East India Black from Bombay' who had run away after 'committing an Act of Bestiality with a Mare'.[19] We are not told why the first of these two servants had run away. But it is not difficult to guess the reason. Many servants who could no longer endure the mistreatment ran away, often with their 'livery' etc., as they considered this their entitlement. In 1800 a lady was to appear before the Surrey Quarter Sessions charged with the cruel treatment of her maid while the husband 'who had brought the poor girl from her native country' was absent from home.[20]

William Hickey had been given his 'pet boy' as a present by Auriol, who subsequently, after Hickey's return to India, claimed him back on the grounds that he had only 'lent him' the boy.[21] Another case brought to light in 1855 was that of a poor 'little native of India' who had been induced to run away with a sailor, who had hidden her and a companion on board a ship bound for England. But, once in England, the girl had been taken to 'the most disreputable house in Ratcliffe Highway' in the East End of London, and in less than a fortnight the man who had brought her over had deserted her. She had then been cast out into the street. She had ended up in the Whitechapel workhouse where she had remained for two months.[22] In 1872 the British consulate in Brindisi, Italy, informed the India Office in London that a certain Mrs Murray 'in a state of intoxication' had dismissed her servant at the railway station just as the train was about to depart – and this despite the fact that a written agreement had been made with Mahommed Ali in India, stipulating that he was to attend Mrs Murray and child for the duration of the voyage to England and, if she wished it, to attend on her and her child in England and then to return with her to India. He was to be paid 200 rupees for the voyage and one rupee a day for board throughout his stay in England. Mr Murray had also agreed to pay his passage back. But the unfortunate Mahommed Ali never saw England.[23]

In fact these Asian servants and ayahs had no security; they were brought over entirely for the convenience of their masters and mistresses. They were engaged to attend to the needs of the family during the long and tedious sea voyage; in most cases no contract of employment existed and not even a provision for a return passage was made. Once in England they were discharged and left to fend for themselves, either by looking for employment in Britain or by being taken on by some family going back to India. No one thought about what would happen to the Asian servants in the alien environment of Britain while they awaited a reengagement. No wonder there were so many looking for a passage back to India:

> WANTS PLACES: As a servant to a family going to Bengal, a native of that country, where she lived two years with the Lady she is going to leave, who brought her to England, and has kept her here for eight years; she does not quit her place for any fault, but because it no longer suits the Lady to keep her; She can speak French tolerably, having accompanied her mistress to France, and remained there twelve months; can dress hair, cook plain victuals, make bread, wash well, and will endeavour to make herself useful to any lady who may be going to India, or with children. Her mistress with whom she still lives till she can otherwise be provided for, will recommend her.[24]

Not every Asian servant was kept on for so long. Another 'black woman, a native of Bengal' wished to return 'under the protection of any Lady going to India' whom she was willing to attend without wages or without any charges to her mistress as she was desperate for a passage back to India. And yet another woman from Bengal was ready to serve 'as a servant to a Lady' in return for a passage to Bengal; she could dress hair and 'be serviceable on board of ship'.[25] Not only female but also male servants advertised themselves thus.[26] While awaiting reengagement many lived in squalid lodging houses and were grossly exploited. It was believed that while these lodgings for the ayahs were usually 'far more respectable' than for the lascars in Ratcliffe Highway, they too were highly overcrowded. For instance, in one lodging house it was found that 'there were between 50 and 60 ayahs'; and another lodging housekeeper assured Colonel R.M. Hughes, Secretary to the Strangers' Home in Limehouse, London, that 'on one occasion there were no less than 32 in her house'. Joseph Salter, the Missionary to the Asiatics and Africans, found 28 ayahs in one house; and according to him it was by no means unusual to find men also lodging in the same house. This house in question was never free of them, the 'boxes of the ayahs generally formed their bedstead, and they [were] all placed close together, to prevent them rolling out'. The rent paid by the ayahs for such a lodging was 16 shillings a week.[27]

A scheme was proposed in 1898 for bringing over Indian women between the ages of 13 and 40 or 45 for service as domestic servants in Britain. This was the brainchild of a Mrs Warr of Surrey who was so impressed with her Indian manservant, 'a half-caste' whose father was in the siege of Lucknow, that she tried to enlist the help of the India Office in her plans. She proposed that to start her off, the India Office should send her 'free of cost' two or three young women who were willing to be taught domestic service. She would find them employment immediately on their arrival, and if the Indians were found to be capable, she would bring them over by 'the score and by the hundred before three months elapsed'. The motive for this scheme, it would seem, was not merely hard cash, but philanthropy, as the lady was at pains to point out that 'I can earn something not only for myself but set going something that will last while England stands and create *good* feeling as well.' The India Office were discouraging in their reply, dismissing the scheme as impracticable as the Indians did not speak the language, and at any rate they were not willing to lend official support to such a scheme.[28]

Since many Indian servants were discharged without ceremony after their arrival in England, it was not uncommon to see destitute Indians begging in the streets of London. Writing to the *Public Advertiser* in 1786, 'Truth' pointed out that:

When a family return from India, they generally bring over with them one or more female blacks to take care of the children, under a promise to send them back to their native country free of expense – Many, no doubt have honesty or humanity enough to keep their word; but the number of

those poor wretches who are daily begging for a passage
back, proves that the generality of those who bring them
over leave them to shift for themselves the moment they
have no further occasion for their services. Many of them, I
am informed, have been in England two or three years; and
some them must for ever remain here, unless the Company
will generously give them a passage to India; and as it will
be an act of humanity, I hope the Directors will give orders
that as many as possible may be accommodated in the ships
now preparing to sail.[29]

In reply 'Orientalis' disputed 'Truth's' facts, asserting that all
black servants both male and female brought over from India
'within these late years' had been sent back 'greatly to the
honour of their masters'. He concluded that the writer of the
letter 'perhaps mistakes West Indian for East Indian Blacks'.[30]
All foreigners look the same, it would appear.

Notwithstanding the protests of gentlemen like 'Orientalis',
the evidence disproved 'the honour' of those who brought Asian
servants back with them to England. In a letter to *The Times* in
1852, an Indian gentleman, writing anonymously, confessed
that he was 'not a little surprised' on his arrival from India to see
in the streets of London several Indian beggars, who were 'a
great annoyance to the Public, but more so to the Indian
gentlemen who visit England'. He found the cause of their
begging in the streets to be the death of those who had brought
them over and, being left unprovided for, and unable to find
employment, the only alternative open to them was begging. He
suggested a reintroduction of the system of deposit to stop the
'annoyance' and to rescue the Indian beggars from the 'want of
care and the effect of climate'.[31] In fact, it was not only this
anonymous Indian gentleman who worried about the plight of
his own countrymen and women brought to England and then
discarded and left destitute; so also did the East India Company,
as far back as 1782, though for a very different reason. In a
directive to the President and Council at Fort St George,
Madras, the Directors admonished that:

> Notwithstanding our orders that security should be taken
> for the return of Black servants to India, yet several have
> been left destitute here, who came to England on foreign
> ships, or for whom no security has been taken; and the
> Company thereby have been put to considerable expense.

To save itself from financial commitments on behalf of
destitute Asian domestics, the Company recommended discouraging the practice of sending black servants to Europe.
Failing that, the Company suggested obtaining sufficient security
for their maintenance while in Britain and their return to India.
The Directors of the East India Company in London concluded
by declaring, 'We have come to a Resolution that if the commanders still receive any persons on board their ships without
permission of our governors and Councils and the certificate
before mentioned they will incur our severest displeasure.'[32]

Despite this 'resolution' and 'severest displeasure' of the
Directors, the plight of the stranded servants did not improve. In
1835 the Court of Directors again brought to the attention of the
Governor General in Council the question of Asians brought to
England – servants, sailors, and other workers – without any
adequate provision for their return and then discarded. They
considered resorting to legislative powers for protecting these
unfortunate beings. But this concern, like the earlier one, was
really prompted by financial considerations rather than just
humanity, since according to the Directors, the Company
incurred a 'great expense' helping 'all classes of East Indians'
who were left destitute in Britain.[33] The Directors were
reluctant to use their profits for the relief of such cases.

Nothing much had come of this initiative beyond the fact that
persons taking Indian servants with them to England were
required to deposit a sum of money with the Treasury to secure
the return passage of an Asian servant. To begin with, the
deposit had been fixed at £100, but later this sum was lowered to
£50 or 500 rupees. But the custom soon lapsed; the last deposit
was made in 1844.[34] As far as the sailors were concerned the
1855 Act solved that 'problem'.[35]

Official attitudes to servants and ayahs in Britain

Even after 1858, when the control of the Company was wound up and India came under the direct control of Whitehall, no initiative was taken to improve the position of Asian servants taken to England and then left to become destitute if they failed to secure employment. The attitude of the Secretary of State for India and his Council at the India Office in London was ambivalent. £200 per annum was given to the 'Strangers' Home' for the maintenance and repatriation of the sailors, the lascars.[36] But as for other Asians – and they only came to the notice of officialdom as a 'problem' when they became destitute – the view of the India Office was that the government of India was not legally responsible for destitute Asians in England. In exceptional cases this stringent view was relaxed and Indian taxpayers' money ('the revenues of India' – in the official language) came to the rescue, but only piecemeal attempts were made to tackle the 'problem' at source – to secure better treatment for the servants and ayahs.

In August 1868 a particularly tragic case was brought to the notice of the Secretary of State for India by Colonel R.M. Hughes, the Honorary Secretary to the Directors of the Strangers' Home for Asiatics, Africans and South Sea Islanders. The case involved 11 Asians from Oudh, in northeast India, four men, three women and four children, who, not as servants but as part of a troupe of 18 strolling players, had been brought over from Bombay at the end of 1867 by Messrs Edward and George Hanlon. The Asians spoke no English, and they had originally been engaged under a written contract to perform for three months only at Suez and then to be returned 'to their homes in India' at the expense of the Hanlons. However, from Suez the players had been taken to Cairo, Alexandria, then on to Malta and France, and finally the party had arrived in England.

The troupe had been promised – only verbally – that they would be provided with board, lodging, allowances and a return passage to India after three months' performance in England. After appearing at the Crystal Palace and other places of amusement in London, the troupe had moved on to Manchester and Liverpool, where the Hanlons had been arrested for debt and jailed in Lancaster Castle. The troupe had then been taken on to Norwich by a Mr Weldon; but disagreements had broken out. The players, in the meantime, had been ill-treated and had received none of the profits of the 'exhibition'. Seeing no prospect of a return to India, 11 of the 18 came to London, arriving at the Great Eastern Station, Shoreditch. Here, out of pity, two men took them to the Bishopsgate police station. But the police refused to help them. After a night in a stable, they finally arrived at the Strangers' Home.

Not only had there been a breach of contract, but the players had received no money and had suffered great hardship. And so to 'seek for justice' and 'to get home' they had thrown themselves on the mercy of London. Colonel Hughes took a serious view of the case because contracts, whether made in writing or not, if not honoured, brought 'discredit on the British name'. And, more seriously, as he further pointed out, it led to the streets of the metropolis being 'inundated' with destitute Asians, and the workhouses, jails and hospitals becoming full of 'numerous' Asian occupants who had been cast adrift and left unprovided for. The India Office agreed with this view. The Directors of the Strangers' Home were also of the opinion that there was a need for measures to be adopted in India to prevent poorer classes of Asians from being brought over to the United Kingdom, unless the government sanctioned the migration of Asians to Britain under similar rules as those which were in force for the emigration of 'coolies' to Mauritius or the West Indies.[37]

When Messrs Hanlon were finally contacted for an 'explanation' of their conduct, pending an appeal to the India Office, they shrugged off any direct responsibility:

> Nor do we consider our contract with them broken – their performances were not hitherto a success and the annoying proceedings which occasioned our incarceration here [Lancaster Castle], is entirely owing to a liability incurred

on their account . . . and if these eleven will join them [the rest of the party], . . . we shall be happy to remit their fares and expenses, for the purpose as we hope to have them more directly under our supervision and care.[38]

No mention here of the inhuman treatment of the Indians, living off their earnings or regret at bringing 'discredit on the British name'. The Oudhians were not taken in this time and refused to rejoin the rest of their party. They were finally sent back – as a special case – at the expense of the India Office.

Cases like this, and more pertinently the fact that 'revenues of India' had to foot the bill, prompted the Secretary of State for India to alert the Governor General to consider the adoption of adequate measures to ensure the provision of a return passage for all 'natives' engaged in India for service out of the country.[39] The aim was to stop 'evils' like the case of the 11 Oudhians being repeated. In India, however, the majority of the local government administrations felt that interference by legislation was uncalled for as they considered the provisions of the Emigration Act of 1846, especially Section 3 of the Act, to be an adequate safeguard since the Act decreed that 'England is not a place to which emigration (for the purpose of labouring for hire) from British India is lawful; consequently any person who takes strolling players or men following similar professions to England violates the law, since these men labour for hire in the full legal sense of the term.'[40]

But it was not difficult to evade the law by passing off the hired Indians as menial servants or seamen – precisely the class of people who were most easily exploited! As for reviving the deposit system, this was ruled out on the ground that it would cause great hardship to the British. No redress here for the Asian servant who was treated like a mere object to serve the needs of the sahibs. However, as a precaution, the government of Bengal instructed the collector of customs at the port of Calcutta to explain to Indian servants 'the nature of their position' and to help them to secure 'a satisfactory arrangement' for their return passage. It was then decided to issue similar notifications at all Indian ports.[41] And here the government of India felt they had adequately discharged their duty.

It was then left to some Asians in England to take up the cause of these servants. In his letter dated 17 January 1869, Syed Abdoollah (Professor of Hindustani at University College, London), drew the attention of the India Office to the treatment meted out to the Asian servants and the great suffering endured by them owing to their ignorance of the language. He reckoned that during the 'last year 900 destitute Asiatics' had been wandering about the streets. He suggested a return to the deposit system as it would 'save the lives of some thousands' who were brought every year not only to Britain but to 'all European countries'.[42] The India Office dismissed Syed Abdoollah's long letter as confused and exaggerated and his remedy as unsuitable on the grounds that all Asians brought to England were not servants.[43]

The fact remained that not all Asians that were mistreated were servants. Asian seamen (lascars), as we shall see later, were another category, as were the 'topazees'. These were sweepers or cleaners employed on emigrant ships carrying indentured Indian labourers to the West Indies or Mauritius. They were engaged by the agents of various colonies for six months only at 13 rupees per month. Their contract did not provide for a return passage. Often the topazees fell prey to fraud and did not receive the wages due to them. Once discharged in the colonies, they had no further claim on the colonial government and no redress. Because they came from the lowest Indian caste, they were unable to find any employment in the West Indies or to work their passage back to India. Some managed somehow to reach England where as paupers and beggars they came to the notice of the Strangers' Home.[44]

However, at official level, the root cause of the 'problem of the destitute Asians' – the system itself – remained unchanged. The Directors of the Strangers' Home devised their own means of ridding the country of destitute Asians. They used the 1823 Merchant Shipping Act to put pressure on the parties involved to make arrangements for the 'relief and return to India' of

servants and followers found destitute in England.[45] Since the
1823 Act had been replaced by the 1855 Merchant Shipping
Act,[46] was such pressure legal? The view of the legal adviser at
the India Office was that since the statutes dealt with merchant
shipping, the provisions applied only to seafaring men and not
landsmen, as the Directors of the Strangers' Home had taken
the term 'other natives' to mean. The Directors were therefore
in their zeal stretching the law beyond its legal limits. But the
question still remained: who was then responsible for the return
of Asians who were not lascars and who became destitute in
England?[47] From time to time destitute Asians were brought to
the notice of the India Office; for instance, in 1870 S.B. Ivatts
wrote from Dublin on behalf of Sheikh Ahmed, brought over a
few years previously by an officer in the Royal Navy. After his
master's death Ahmed had, to ward off starvation, taken to
selling curry powder and doing occasional work for English
families who had been out to India. But he was desperate to
return to India.[48] The case of a destitute servant of the Nawab
Nazim of Bengal, who lived in Tottenham, was reported to the
India Office: in this case, the Nawab took the responsibility for
his servant.[49] Following the Proclamation of the Queen as
Empress of India in 1877, a new class of distressed Indians
appeared on the scene, whom Sir Gerald Fitzgerald, the
Political Aide de Camp (ADC), dubbed the 'petitioner class'
and which he believed to be on the increase. These were mainly
small-scale farmers from the Punjab who came to petition the
Queen about their land claims.[50]

The India Office held strictly to the view that according to the
law they were responsible only for 'indigent lascars' and they
therefore contributed £200 a year to the Strangers' Home for
destitute seamen.[51] But what of servants: were the people who
brought them over held responsible? It would appear not.
When J.H. Bowen, a Weymouth solicitor, wrote to the India
Office inquiring whether his client, a major in the Indian Army,
could be held responsible by any law which compelled Europeans
to send back Indians brought over by them, the India Office did
not consider it their duty to advise solicitors 'upon points of

law'. An internal document reiterated the point that 'there is no absolute law compelling persons who bring native servants to England to send them back'. However, the India Office did consider that people bringing them should send them back.[52]

The Political ADC, Sir Gerald Fitzgerald, initially appointed to act as a *'mehmendar'* ('host') to the Indian princes and who had responsibility for the 'destitute Indians' devolved on him, believed the 'petitioner class' to be the main 'problem'. He did not consider the poor law arrangements to be adequate or fair to those parishes which found themselves saddled with destitute Asians in no way connected with that parish. In his opinion the system was uneconomical since Asian paupers, unlike ordinary paupers, were unable to maintain themselves even in the summer months and, even if 'sheltered for 20 years' they were no more likely to be able to return to their own country at the end of that time than they had been on the day they entered the poor house.[53] Fitzgerald therefore proposed extending the powers of the law (section 2 and 3 of 8 and 9 Vic Cap. 117) to embrace India. In this way Asians would be compelled to return to their place of settlement, India. However, this neat solution would have required the Treasury to enter into an arrangement of reciprocity, as under the European Vagrancy Act Englishmen found destitute in India were already being sent back to Britain by the government of India at the expense of the Indian taxpayer.

Before approaching the Treasury, it was decided to find out the extent of the 'evil': the accounts department was asked to furnish the India Office with returns showing the total cost and the number of Englishmen sent back from India over the 'last ten-year period', and the same information was requested for the Asians returned from Britain to India. Colonel Hughes, too, was asked to send figures over the past 20 years of destitute Asians, not seamen, repatriated by the Strangers' Home itself or by putting pressure on private individuals. The returns furnished by both parties are revealing. According to the accounts department, a total of £273 had been paid out for passages of Asians sent from England to India for the ten years 1869–79; while over the same period, £1,380 had been spent to repatriate

Englishmen from India at the Indian taxpayers' expense. According to Colonel Hughes's semi-official letter, 200 destitute 'natives, not seamen' had been sent back through the liability of the 1823 Act; of these 150 had been sent back between 1858 and 1868.[54]

So much for Sir Gerald Fitzgerald's assertion that it was the 'petitioner class' which was flocking to England to take advantage of the role of the Queen as Empress of India, thus glorifying her as the 'fountain of justice' for the simple villager from India.[55] In the end, it was decided that the 'evil' was not of such a serious proportion as to demand 'legislative remedy'.[56] Hence, as far as the India Office was concerned, the 'evil' or the 'problem' as they saw it was the number of destitute Asians who became a 'burden' on the rates of the parishes, and not the whole system which allowed Asians to be transported from India without adequate safeguard for their dignity or wellbeing.

The question was revived again in 1886 with the setting up of a tripartite committee comprising the India Office, the Colonial Office, and the Local Government Boards[57] on the lines previously suggested by Sir Gerald Fitzgerald, as by this time the number of 'pauper' Asians was deemed to have increased even further.[58] According to the India Office, there were three arguments for setting up the committee: first, the Asian poor suffered hardship in the workhouse because their language was not understood, they could not practise their religion and the food did not suit them; second, the presence of Asians interfered with the enforcement of discipline in the workhouse, causing inconvenience to the authorities who in any case could not find suitable employment for Asian paupers. The burden on the rates was, consequently, considerable. And, lastly, the poor law authorities shifted the burden onto the revenues of India, and the India Office was reluctant to use Indian taxpayers' money to relieve Asians found destitute in Britain.

What was needed, therefore, were powers of deportation, in some ways similar to powers which enabled the Poor Law authorities to remove paupers in England to their place of settlement within the United Kingdom.[59] On 16 July 1888, the committee met to consider the general issues connected with powers of deportation.[60] Should the parishes be responsible for deportation? Should Imperial taxes bear the cost of such forcible removal of Asians to India? Or should the term 'place of settlement' be extended to include India – and so facilitate the removal of pauper Asians back to India? The committee decided to sound out Local Government Boards to see how far they considered pauper Asians to be a 'burden' on them and the rates before deciding what further steps should be taken.[61]

When the returns came (for the year 1886), 11 'natives of India' appeared to have been relieved by the various work-houses of the metropolis. Some of the local authorities concerned were: Camberwell, where two women, one of whom had been there for five years, had died in the workhouse infirmary; Chelsea had taken in one East Indian cook; St George's relieved one Asian for two days; Hackney sheltered one Indian ayah; one Hindu male stayed in Kensington workhouse for three days; Marylebone had admitted another Hindu man; and finally Whitechapel had looked after one high-caste Hindu for a fortnight.[62] The figures certainly do not bear out the view that the Asian poor were a growing 'problem'. In this context, it is interesting to find that in his report for the year 1884, Sir Gerald Fitzgerald admitted that it was 'rare to see a native of India destitute in the streets . . .'[63] Henry Mayhew, too, in an earlier survey of the London poor, had found only 19 'East Indians' to have been sheltered by the Household Poor Society during the winter of 1848-9.[64] Therefore, it would appear that, despite being transported to an alien environment and then discharged, the Asians survived. Using their initiative and resourcefulness, they got themselves a reengagement or looked for service in England; and, failing that, turned to small-scale entrepreneurial enterprises. They did not as a rule become a 'burden'. In time small settled communities of Asians grew up in Britain.

The 'petitioner class' was discouraged from coming to England by measures to tackle the 'problem' at source. Instructions were sent to the local provinces in India to issue notifications in the 'vernacular languages' warning claimants that appeals for the decisions of the Indian courts did not lie in England. Prospective petitioners were informed of the risk of going to England on meagre resources and of becoming destitute. And finally, to make absolutely sure that the 'problem' did not recur, the provinces were warned that if 'any men of this class should be repatriated by this Office, the expense incurred on their behalf shall be debited to the Provinces to which they may belong'.[65]

As for the Asian servants, the India Office once again resorted to making requests for 'specific measures' to ensure the provision of a return passage for 'the menial servants'.[66] And there the matter rested. But such requests remained pious pronouncements only; cases of Asians being mistreated and brought over for the gain of other individuals continued as before.[67]

The position of the ayahs, too, was very curious. As travelling nannies they formed the most valuable adjunct to the whole life style of the Raj between Britain and India. Essential for the memsahib's household in India, they were considered indispensable for the long voyage home – either the trusted family ayah or an experienced travelling ayah. Once on board, the ayah took complete charge of the children, the baggage and the memsahib. Good ayahs were not only meant to be clean, honest and trustworthy with children, but capable as nurses and excellent sailors too. Once in England, their services were over and they were discharged to await a return engagement. The waiting period could be a few days, a few weeks or even months. They found temporary lodgings; and, as we have seen, these were usually overcrowded and expensive.

In time, however, a sophisticated network was formed – equal to any modern-day employment agency. The ayahs found shelter in the East End of London in what came to be called the Ayahs' Home, run by Mr and Mrs Rogers at 6 Jewry Street, Aldgate. Later the London City Mission took over the running of the Home and in 1900 it was moved to 26 King Edward Road, Mare Street, Hackney, a working-class district in East London, with a superintendent, usually with experience of Christian work in the East, in charge of the home.[68] It had about 30 rooms, furnished in eastern style and bearing regional names – 'Chinese', 'Javanese' or 'Indians'. Every year up to 100 ayahs stayed there: ayahs from Calcutta, Madras, Bombay, Colombo, Rangoon, Penang, Java, Singapore, Aden and even Japan. It was to the Ayahs' Home that families going out to the East came to engage the services of these nannies. Some of the ayahs travelled between Britain and India many times. For instance, Mrs Antony Pereira, a grandmother, herself married at the age of 16, made the journey between India and Great Britain – and once even to Holland – 54 times.[69]

Not all the ayahs stayed at the Ayahs' Home; Joseph Salter, the Missionary to the Orientals and Africans in London, reckoned that every year between 100 and 200 ayahs visited London.[70] Attempts were made to convert them to Christianity; sometimes small groups from the Ayahs' Home were invited to tea at the Asiatic Rest run by Salter.[71]

Since there was 'never much trouble' in the case of the ayahs, no official interest was taken in their welfare.[72] As long as the Raj lasted, these 'human birds of passage' continued to minister to the needs of the memsahibs and their children during the long sea voyage between Britain and India.

Abdul Karim, Queen Victoria's 'munshi'

The Empress of India, Queen Victoria, had several Asian servants. Two of them, Mohammed Bux and Abdul Karim, arrived for service at Balmoral soon after the Golden Jubilee in 1887. Sir Henry Ponsonby, the Queen's secretary, commented that 'she was as excited about them as a child would be with a new toy'.[73] Mohammed was large, bearded and quite dark; Abdul Karim on the other hand was 'much lighter, tall and with a fine serious countenance'.[74] He was only 24 years old. Dressed in scarlet and gold in the winter, and in white during the summer, Mohammed and Abdul Karim waited on the Queen at table, standing motionless behind her chair.

Abdul Karim, however, soon pointed out to the Queen that he had been a clerk in Agra (earning ten rupees a month) and that serving at table was therefore beneath him. The Queen in 1889 promoted him to be her 'munshi' or teacher and he began to teach her Hindustani – with the religion and customs of India on the side. The Queen, although not able to devote 'as much time [to] it as she would like',[75] worked hard and was delighted with her progress. She wrote: 'I am learning a few words of Hindustani to speak to my servants. It is a great interest to me for both the language and the people, I have naturally never come into real contact with before.'[76] Soon she was able to greet the visiting maharanis in Hindustani.

Queen Victoria was very pleased with 'her munshi', and wrote to the Viceroy, Lord Lansdowne, for a suitable grant of land for her 'really exemplary and excellent young munshi' who was 'quite a confidential servant (she does not mean in a *literal* sense, for he is *not* a servant)'. He was 'most useful to her with papers, letters and books etc.' The Queen waxed enthusiastic: 'It is the *first time in the world* that any Native has ever held such a position and she is very anxious to mark this permanently.'[77] Hence the request for a grant of land.

However, the Queen's patronage and attempts at improving race relations set alarm bells ringing. It was one thing to elevate Abdul Karim to the status of 'munshi' since, as Frederick Ponsonby (Sir Henry Ponsonby's second son) pointed out, 'there was nothing wrong about this because he was a Mohammedan, and a munshi, or teacher, is not very high up in the Indian world.'[78] But then, in 1890, Von Angeli was commissioned to do a portrait of the munshi and in 1894 Abdul Karim rose to the position of the Queen's 'Indian Secretary', Companion of the Order of the Indian Empire (CIE).

The court retaliated by questioning the munshi's social origins – a very acute weapon for the class-conscious Victorians, although it may not have cut much ice with the monarch herself:

That division of classes is the *one thing* which is most dangerous and reprehensible, never intended by the law of

nature & which the Queen is always labouring to alter . . .
The present Archbishop of York's Father was a butcher, &
so on.[79]

Frederick Ponsonby, who had been in India prior to taking up
his appointment in the Queen's household, informed her that
the munshi's father was 'only an apothecary at the Jail at
Agra'.[80] The Queen did not forgive Ponsonby for a long time!

To make out that the poor Munshi is so *low* is really
outrageous & in a country like England quite out of place . . .
She has known 2 Archbishops who were sons respectively
of a Butcher & a Grocer . . . Abdul's father saw good &
honourable service as a Doctor & he [Abdul] feels cut to the
heart at being thus spoken of.[81]

The Queen therefore did her best to promote her 'excellent
and much esteemed munshi and Indian Clerk',[82] but court
members resented the 'social and official position accorded to
him in Court Circulars and in all occasions by the Queen',[83] and
snubbed him wherever possible. They were convinced that
although the munshi was 'a thoroughly stupid and uneducated
man', he was also dangerous as he 'saw confidential papers
relating to India, in fact to all state affairs'. He was also friendly
with Ruffudin Ahmed, a law student in London, who supplied
'the brains that were deficient in the munshi'[84] and who was an
'untrustworthy adventurer'.[85] Although Lord George Hamilton,
Secretary of State for India, did not consider the munshi to be
'as dangerous as some suppose', he had his movements in India
watched. Reports were compiled on him by the Thuggee and
Dacoity Department.[86] (The department also investigated anti-
British agitation.) The Secretary of State for India also asked the
Viceroy, Lord Elgin, for information concerning the munshi's
background and especially his 'exact social position at time of
engagement'.[87] But none of this yielded anything of importance.
The munshi's father, although of humble origin, was in
subordinate medical service as a hospital assistant with a salary
of 60 rupees. He was 'respectable and trustworthy.'[88]

But members of the Queen's household went even further. After the munshi and Ahmed arrived at Cimiez – he had been left out of the official party after the Queen was given an ultimatum: the munshi or the household – Frederick Ponsonby wrote to India for 'cuttings from the Native or European papers' since it would 'be the greatest use to be able to quote Indian papers'.[89] He hoped to get some gossip about the munshi to damn him in the Queen's eyes. In the end it was left to 'two old Indian officers in her court' to speak 'plainly' to the Queen about the 'social and official position' accorded at court to the munshi. And he was relegated to his 'proper place'.[90] The Queen informed Lord Salisbury:

> With reference to the subject on which Lord Salisbury has been so kind and just – the Queen would just wish to assert that *no* political papers of any kind are ever in the hands of the munshi. even in her presence. He only helps to read words which she cannot read or merely ordinary submissions on warrants for signature. He does not read English fluently enough to be able to read anything of importance.[91]

After the death of Queen Victoria in 1901, King Edward VII ordered that all the papers of the munshi were to be burnt. A bonfire took place at Frogmore Cottage, one of the munshi's houses. Abdul Karim returned to India and lived at Karim Lodge in Agra till 1909, when on his death all the remaining papers were burnt, except for a few letters in Queen Victoria's handwriting which the wife of the munshi was allowed to keep as a memento. The munshi episode is yet another illustration of the relationship of race and class in the age of Victorian imperialism – of keeping 'natives' and lower classes (for instance, the Queen's Scottish Highland servant, John Brown) in their 'proper place'.[92]

3. Sailors who Filled the Gap: the Lascars

Lascars and Chinese seamen were employed on the ships that sailed between Britain and the East.[1] Britain owes a debt to these sailors for carrying here the wealth of the East which helped to build up British maritime wealth and prosperity – a fact acknowledged by contemporaries but often forgotten today. At a meeting held on 28 March 1855 to launch the appeal to found the Strangers' Home for the lascars, it was emphatically pointed out that these sailors were 'brought in the service of our merchants to navigate our ships, and to contribute to swell the tide of wealth poured upon our shores'.[2] For the shipowners, the lascars were cheap, being paid between one-sixth and one-seventh of the European rate of pay.

Section 7 of the Navigation Act of 1660 laid down that the master and at least 75 per cent of the crew of a British registered ship importing goods from Asia had to be British, so before 1780 lascars did not serve in very large numbers. In fact, until 1802, successive British governments forbade the employment of lascars on ships sailing west of the Cape of Good Hope.[3] But these regulations were not always adhered to as lascars were needed to fill the gap in time of war when European crews were taken on by the Royal Navy or when British crews deserted.[4] For instance, during the Revolutionary and Napoleonic Wars the number of lascars arriving in London was as follows:[5]

1804	471	1809	965
1805	603	1810	1,403
1806	528	1811	929
1807	1,278	1812	1,193
1808	1,110	1813	1,336

The Articles signed with the crew serving on the Sloop *Tryal* show that there were definite rules governing the employment of the lascars.[6] First, the men were paid a fixed monthly wage for the duration of the voyage from the port of sailing in India to London. Second, while in London the crew received bounty money and maintenance money pending a return voyage to India; third, the Articles provided for the return passage to the port of origin in India. Finally, the crew had to promise not to stay over in England once the passage for their return had been obtained. Despite these rules, lascars often found themselves sold short. Recruitment in India for the crew was through the intermediary of the Ghaut Serang (agent-recruiter), while it was the Serang (boatswain) who exercised discipline and control over the men on board and on shore.[7]

Lascars were often mistreated on board ship – and their only remedy then was to desert, giving up their wages and risking destitution in an alien land. Mirza Abu Talib Khan described how the ship on which he was travelling to Europe was delayed on the way because 'sixteen of our best lascars being much disgusted by the treatment received on board this ship, deserted and hid themselves in the woods; and it was discovered that the remainder of the crew only waited the approach of the night to follow the example of their comrades.'[8] Incidents of this kind were not uncommon; Joseph Salter, the Missionary to the Orientals and Africans, recorded some harrowing tales of mistreatment. In one case the entire lascar crew of Muslims deserted after the ship docked in the Thames. Their complaint, confirmed by the European members of the crew, was that they 'had been hung up with weights tied to their feet, flogged with a rope'; they were forced to eat pork, and 'the insult carried further by violently ramming the tail of a pig into their mouths and twisting the entrails of the pig round their necks'. One lascar tried to escape this vicious treatment by jumping overboard: he drowned. In another instance Salter met lascars who had been flogged: one had his teeth missing after being hit with a chain; another could not walk straight.[9] The most gruesome story concerned nine lascars who had died because of wounds inflicted by the captain; their bodies were then thrown overboard. Others arrived in England in a state near to death. In court the sad tale of Abdullah was narrated: he had been flogged, tied to the windlass and doused with salt water. Abdullah died.[10] Salter found it strange that there were people who seemed to think that 'the coloured part of mankind exists only to be used like brute beasts, and to have the most insulting names language can supply heaped upon them'.[11] Hilton Docker, the doctor appointed by the Company to look after the medical needs of the lascars and Chinese, recorded having noticed marks on the backs of some lascar crew he had examined after their arrival in port.[12]

Their misery did not end when they arrived in Europe. In 1782, complaints reached the East India Company that the lascars were being cast adrift in Europe. In a letter addressed to the President and Council at Fort St George, Madras, the East India Company in London complained that several lascars had found their way to the London office having been 'reduced to great distress', and the Company had had to provide them with relief 'from motives of compassion and Humanity as well as policy'. But the East India Company was not too happy about this expense which according to them 'ought not to be borne by the company'.[13]

In 1784, a pamphlet protesting about the beggars of Westminster commented:

> Do not deem me so uncharitable as to conclude I wish to steel your heart against feeble but interesting efforts of those poor sons of misery, who strangers to the climate, to the manners, and to the people of this country, have traversed the town naked, penniless and almost starving in search of subsistence. Their situation is as singular as it is deplorable; they have been brought into this country as the friendly assistants of natives . . . While the dispute lasted as to who should maintain them they have been left a prey to melancholy and distress. The dispute, you know, has been between the husband of the ships and the Directors of the East India Company.[14]

This is a reference to the East India Company's reluctance to bear responsibility for the stranded lascars.

Their plight was further highlighted in March 1785 when a letter appeared in the *Public Advertiser* in which the writer, 'an old man just arrived from the country', expressed shock 'at the number of miserable objects, lascars, that I see shivering and starving in the streets'. He could remember 'subscriptions set on foot for the French prisoners, for the Hessians', but the neglect of the lascars seemed to him 'a striking instance of the hard-heartedness and insensibility that distinguish the present times'. He implored some 'persons of sense and worth' to 'promote a subscription' for the relief, as he put it, 'of a race of human beings, who, though different in colour, religion, and country from ourselves, are still our fellow-creatures, and who have been dragged from their warmer and more hospitable climates by our avarice and ambition'.[15]

In November 1785 Soubaney and four other lascars brought an action against William Moffat of Queen Square, 'managing-owner' of the ship *Kent*, for the balance of their wages, owed to them 'since July 1784'. In court Moffat claimed that he was joint owner with two others, Timothy Curtis of Homerton near Hackney, and James Hunt of Newman Street, Oxford Street, who were responsible for the payment. In support of his pleas, he produced an affidavit. The jury did not believe Moffat and the lascars won their case. They were each awarded £20.10s.[16]

In December 1785, 'Truth', writing to the *Morning Chronicle*, pleaded for the 'unfortunate natives of the Eastern clime', the lascars, who were often found wandering about the streets of London deprived of the common necessities of life. He, like the earlier writer, believed that they justly deserved public charity, as,

Enticed, perhaps, from their native country where the climate is mild and tepid . . . brought to one more cold . . . without clothing proportional to conciliate them thereto . . . Considering them as foreigners, independent of any service they have rendered us by navigating our vessels trading to the East Indies, I think they have a claim to our patronage and hospitality, in the condition in which they are at present permitted to roam about this opulent city, unnoticed and unrelieved without a coat to shield them from the extremity of the weather, a shoe to preserve their feet from disaster, or even money to purchase sustenance sufficient to allay the gripping pangs of hunger.[17]

Concern about the lascars led early in 1786 to the setting up of a 'Committee of Gentlemen' to organize emergency relief. The Committee soon, however, widened its scope to help other black people in need. Later it was announced by the Committee that 320 people had been found, including 35 who were from the East Indies. The Committee changed its name to the 'Committee for the Relief of the Black Poor' and a fund was started, not only for temporary relief, but to stop such distress recurring in the future. Later, plans were made for a settlement in Sierra Leone. Of the original eight 'Headmen' or 'Corporals' selected by Jonas Hanway the philanthropist, one was a 29-year-old Bengal-born lascar, John Lemon. He was a hairdresser and cook, and had arrived in Britain on a naval ship.[18]

The problem of responsibility for the lascars

How had this state of affairs arisen? Who was responsible for the lascars? The East India Company did not own any of the ships; they hired them from a consortium of shippers and, before 1795, the onus of maintaining lascars and Chinese seamen in port was vested in the shipowners. They were allowed by the East India Company £1 per ton for the maintenance of lascars and Chinese in England, and for their return passage to India or China.[19] Once the ship arrived in London, the seamen were discharged and left for some months pending a return passage. Ignorant of the language and customs of the people, the lascars and Chinese fell prey to the more wily inhabitants of the slums of Wapping and Shadwell in the East End of London. Robbed of their money and clothes, some arrived in the lodging houses of St Giles as beggars.

As complaints multiplied – from the lascars themselves that the owners did not care for them, and from the public that the lascars were not kept under restraint – the East India Company was forced to take charge. They claimed that regardless of expense, their concern for the lascars had been prompted only by the thought of 'the comfort of the natives and convenience of the public'.[20] Considering earlier grumbles about having to spend money on the relief of distressed lascars, this was indeed a change of heart. The Company was now trying to appear as a concerned and caring body – not merely preoccupied with balance sheets and the profit motive. So from 9 December 1795 the Court of Directors took over themselves the maintenance of lascars and Chinese and no longer paid the £1 per ton to the owners of freighted ships.

Arrangements were then made for the board and lodging of lascars and Chinese. Whatever the Company may have claimed later in its report to the Commissioners for the Affairs of India, these boarding houses were usually of the worst kind. Owners of various different premises were contracted to house lascars and Chinese: for instance, from March 1797 to early 1798 the premises of Susannah Smetza in Kingsland Road, Shoreditch, were used at the rate of 10s.6d per week. Then from 1798 to the end of 1799, they went in nearly equal numbers to Mrs Smetza and the lodgings of Mrs Coates in Hackney Road. By 1801 three premises had been converted for the reception of sailors – Kingsland Road, Shoreditch, Hackney Road, and the premises of John Anthony in Shadwell. However, following complaints from the magistrates of the City of London 'of the nuisance occasioned by the men living so near the city as Shoreditch', they were all transferred to Shadwell. Finally with the death of John Anthony, the depot was moved and the business transferred to Abraham Gole in Ratcliffe Highway. From 1798, William Docker was officially appointed medical attendant and after his death in January 1807 his brother, Hilton Docker, took over.

Lascars and Chinese brought to England in ships not in the

service of the Company were maintained and returned by the owners themselves; if they neglected their obligations the Company took over and charged expenses for maintenance to the owners. The Company claimed that despite this safeguard, lascars from these ships often deserted in London and when found wandering in the streets were taken to East India House. The Company then had to support them since they often could not find out the name of the ship on which they had been employed. It claimed that the bill amounted to £500 per annum.[21] This arrangement was legalized in 1814 by the Act which gave the Company the power to provide for the lascars and to recover expenses from negligent shipowners.[22]

However considerate in theory, practice was different. As the number of lascars increased during the Revolutionary and Napoleonic Wars, overcrowding and indiscipline occurred; fights broke out among lascars and some got sucked into the criminal underworld of the East End. There were many complaints of neglect. The death rate was high, especially in winter. It was estimated by some that before 1810, 130 lascars died in Britain each year (making 2,600 in 20 years). According to the lascars themselves the figure was double that. During the severe winter of 1813, nine deaths occurred on one single day.[23]

The lascars were ill-treated and ill-fed. A Society for the Protection of Asiatic Sailors set up in February 1814[24] began systematically to collect evidence of the living and working conditions of the lascars. The Committee met a cook who had been flogged; the marks on his back made the Committee conclude that 'the lacerations must have been very deep'.[25] When the East India Company officials were informed of lascars' complaints of their treatment, the Directors 'resolved to send the grumblers off by the first ship'.[26] William Allen, one of the Society's members, applied to the Directors for an order to enable them to visit the barracks to see for themselves; the Company granted this after some hesitation.[27] The Society's members found the place somewhere near Wapping, and found two or three hundred of them . . . people were ill-fed and badly treated by a person (a superior lascar) who had command of them, both as to food, clothes and settling disputes among them. He frequently whipped them . . . The buildings . . . were like warehouses, very dirty, and . . . without pavement – the floor consisting of earth . . . There were two or three large cupboards of the height of sentry boxes.

When they commanded these to be opened, 'out came a living lascar'. The Committee were informed that he had been 'put into confinement for quarrelling and bad behaviour'.[28] The Society for the Protection of Asiatic Sailors sent the evidence they had collected to the Cabinet, the Directors of the Company and the Board of Control for the Affairs of India.

The visit 'of several gentlemen'[29] to the lascar premises worried Hilton Docker, the doctor. In letters to the Court of Directors, Docker was at pains to assure the Company officials that he

did not doubt the benevolent intentions of the gentlemen who have undertaken the enquiry but I apprehend that personal ignorance of the characters of the Native seamen will make them very liable to be imposed upon particularly as their information is mainly if not entirely collected from the discontented and criminal of which description there always be a great number in many hundred men that annually arrive in this country.[30]

Docker also tried to cover himself, and by extension to exonerate the Company, since according to him the findings of the Society 'were not warranted by any imperfection existing in the present system'.[31] Finally, with the publication in *The Times* of the letter by the Society for the Protection of Asiatic Sailors,[32] Docker regarded it his duty to refute the 'false representations in this mischievous appeal to the public' by addressing a long memorandum to the Court of Directors on 14 December 1814.[33] Not surprisingly, the opinions expressed by

Docker formed the main thesis of the argument of the Directors to the Commissioners for the Affairs of India.

Several important issues emerge from the various memorials of Docker to the Court of Directors. In November 1809, justifying his medical expenses to the Directors, who considered them too high, Docker had pinned the blame for the health of the men on the climate and the promiscuous nature of the men. But he had also firmly pointed to the 'confined and unwholesome situation of the premises' and 'the very great number which is generally (now 724) at the worst season of the year crowded in them'. This, according to Docker, was not conducive to the health of the lascars. But after the complaints by the 'benevolent gentlemen' he attributed the ill-health of the sailors to the 'innate sloth and filthy habits of the men' which 'defy every attempt to remedy it'.

As for punishment, Docker thought that the Society had exaggerated 'both the number of punishments and the severity of them'. Docker firmly held to the view that if the Serang was not allowed to use his authority to discipline the lascars, then the lascars would have no security for the little property that they possessed. And 'the evil' would not stop among the lascars. The public at large and 'more particularly the neighbouring inhabitants [would] feel the consequences of these men sometimes nearly 1,600 in number being without prompt control . . .'[34] So in Docker's reasoning the indiscipline was the result not of the overcrowding – 1,600 men – but due entirely to the character of the men who if 'let loose' would harm the local people. And hence the need for tight control by the Serang. Like most Victorians who considered Orientals to live in 'darkness and ignorance', Docker believed that the lascars and Chinese 'have not an idea of the comfort beyond what they enjoy in this country and that a vast majority of them would be sensible of the Honourable Company's protection and grateful for its benefits, if no influence was used to impose the opposite in their minds'.[35] So it was the busybodies that were stirring up 'trouble'; the Company's arrangements were adequate and the lascars themselves were quite content with their situation.

To help cure lascar and Chinese demoralization induced by the long waiting period before they received a reengagement on eastbound ships, it was suggested by many, including the Society for the Protection of Asiatic Sailors, that temporary employment for the first few weeks should be provided. Docker, and later the Company, pointed out that the experiment of providing employment in the Rope Ground had not been a success because the men had no inclination to work and they lacked sufficient strength compared to the Europeans. But the main reason was

> There being always in the metropolis a far greater number of English and Irish labourers than find constant employment, consequently the employing of these men would be to the prejudice of our native population. Hence both policy and humanity are against the adoption of a measure which, while it tends to relieve a race of foreigners who have no families in this country, to partake of the benefits from the only unavoidable evil to which they are exposed, namely the effects of climate, would expose several hundreds of our native population, with their numerous families, to the complicated evils of climate, want and nakedness.[36]

To emphasize the fact that it would be detrimental to employ lascars and Chinese when the indigenous population had more of a claim on local jobs, it was pointed out that a Chinese sailor employed as a lumper (stevedore) on board the ship to which he belonged had been beaten up by the Irish and obliged to desist from working. But no such arguments were put forward when employing lascars and Chinese as cheap labour on ships.

Finally, as for the complaint about the absence of sick wards, this was excused on the grounds that it was the sick themselves who objected to being separated, and if they were separated it was found impossible to get adequate attention paid to them by their own companions. The men also preferred to lie on the floor and did not use the hammocks provided for them.

So, in the end, to exonerate themselves from the allegations of the Society for the Protection of Asiatic Sailors, Hilton Docker and the Company had laid the blame for the state of affairs at the door of the lascars themselves, their habits and customs, rather than on the overcrowding, the negligence and stringent book-keeping of the Company.

A parliamentary inquiry on lascars

However, as a result of the agitation by the Society for the Protection of the Asiatic Sailors, a Parliamentary Committee of Inquiry was appointed to investigate the working of the 1814 Act and to see whether there was a need for further regulations concerning the lascars and Chinese. The Committee made a surprise visit to the barracks where lascars were and came to the conclusion that they were overcrowded since at times 1,000 to 1,600 sailors were accommodated in premises which were not intended for such a large number. They found the rooms to be dirty, with no bedding or furniture; the lascars slept on the floors. There were no fireplaces and the men were only given one blanket each. The sick had neither separate quarters nor a hospital; and during their visit the Committee even saw several sick sailors lying on the floor covered only by a blanket in a room which opened onto the yard. The Committee did not regard as valid the Company's excuse that the men objected to being separated. The diet was considered inadequate as too much salt fish was provided although 'fresh fish are so abundant in London as to be the cheapest article of animal food'.[37] The Committee concluded that although lascars might have enjoyed a decent standard of living on board the ship (even their music was played to keep up their spirits),[38] they were grossly neglected while on shore. The Committee was informed by the Directors of the Company, as a defence, that if bedding was provided the lascars sold it; and that during the winter stoves were supplied. As for the death rate, the Company did concede that during the severe winter of 1813–14 five had died in 24 hours during one very cold day; while at least two per week was the usual average.[39] The Committee also visited the apartments of the Chinese which they considered to be 'clean and airy' and comfortable. They attributed this to the 'different characters of the nations and the habits which distinguish them'.[40] Although the Committee had commented on the overcrowding in the barracks of the lascars earlier on in the report, it too contradicted itself later on in its report, and took refuge in stereotyped national characteristics of the lascars and Chinese. In doing that, the Parliamentary Committee tried to ignore the obvious: since more lascars were employed by the East India Company, the number in any apartment was much higher too. It was estimated that of the sailors employed in the British merchant service 60 per cent were 'natives' of India, 20 per cent were from Malaya, and only 10 per cent from China.[41]

The Committee in their report considered that since the number of lascars coming to England had grown, the method of contracting individuals to house lascars and Chinese had become outdated. They therefore saw the need for purpose-built housing for lascars and Chinese. They also considered the location of the existing barracks 'in the midst of the populous part of the town' undesirable and so recommended siting new lodgings away from the town, but nearer the docks. They recommended a superintendent with experience of the East to be put in charge. Since one of the greatest defects in the existing system of managing the lascars and Chinese on shore, according to the Committee, was the absence of a 'regular authority' to 'prevent the lascars from wandering away from the barracks', they suggested 'regular superintendence' by the East India Company, vested with legal powers, for caring for and policing the lascars while on shore. Finally the Committee emphasized that such an authority was needed to enforce the return of the lascars to their country of origin. To facilitate their repatriation, the Committee recommended that shipowners keep regular returns of the number of lascars brought to England and the numbers shipped back. The owners would face a penalty if they left any lascars behind.[42] In this way it was hoped to rid the country of any Asian sailors who stayed on in Britain.

Following the recommendations of the Committee of Parliament, the Commissioners for the Affairs of India approached the Directors of the East India Company to find out if they would take over the responsibility of managing the proposed housing for lascars. The Company was their first logical choice because of their Imperial role in India and so had the obligation as the government of India to protect the 'subjects of our Dominions'.[43] However, the Directors of the Company showed reluctance to take charge as they felt that once peace returned after the Napoleonic Wars they would not need to employ lascars. Next the Commissioners turned to the East India Dock Company. By this time the Commissioners for the Affairs of India had received proposals for the establishment of hulks in the river Thames for the accommodation of the lascars arriving in England. Hulks were considered ideal as they would isolate the lascars from the rest of the population. But the Dock Company, too, while agreeing with the view that there was a need for 'some proper authority' to impose 'coercive measures' because of the 'depravity that attaches to [lascars'] characters', declined to take charge on the grounds that they were 'wholly unconnected with any ships trading to and from India'.[44]

In the end the only result of the enquiry was the 1823 Merchant Shipping Act.[45] The main aim of the Act was to facilitate the repatriation of lascars and other sailors from the East. The Act had four main provisions. First, it made it compulsory, on pain of a penalty of £10, to furnish the customs officer with a list of every 'Asiatic sailor, Lascar or Native of the East' employed on board the ship. Second, the master or owner of the ship was liable to a penalty of £30 for any 'native of Asia, Africa or South Sea Islander' brought to the United Kingdom and then left behind. Third, the East India Company was again made responsible for the repatriation of such 'natives' left behind and was to charge the owners with the cost of shipment and maintenance. Finally, the poor law authorities were empowered to claim from the East India Company any relief afforded by them to destitute sailors left behind by the shipowners.

Despite parliamentary intervention, the condition of the lascars did not improve. They remained the most despised group of aliens in England. They were considered 'naturally indolent'[46] and 'entirely destitute of moral capacity', with 'habits which are so repugnant to all Englishmen's ideas of comfort'.[47] Even the Christian missionaries who showed concern, especially after 1813, about their spiritual and material welfare, considered them 'extremely depraved':

> They are the senseless worshippers of dumb idols, or the deluded followers of the licentious doctrines of a false prophet; ... ignorant, darkened, and deceived through the blindness which is in them... They are enemies to God by wicked works; they are practically and abominably wicked. They are a prey of each other; and of the rapacious poor, as well as the most abandoned of our abandoned country-women. They have none, or scarcely any, who will associate with them, but prostitutes, and no house that will receive them, except the public house and the apartments of the abandoned.[48]

This view of the lascars was reemphasized in 1817 when a magistrate informed a committee of parliament, following licensing scandals in the Tower Hamlets, that 'little good can be done by taking away the licences of the houses in Shadwell for this reason, that the population consists entirely [an obvious exaggeration] of foreign sailors, lascars, Chinese, Greeks, and other filthy dirty people of that description.'[49] Some considered lascars fair game: they were cheated, given spurious coins. Some women – prostitutes and thieves – made their living by 'plundering coloured sailors of their money and clothes'.[50]

The founding of the Strangers' Home

The lascars were not only the most despised group, they also still suffered appalling hardships when on shore. Neglected and destitute, some turned to vagrancy and crime, ending up in prisons. Some were even transported to Australia.[51] Their hardship was compounded further when, following the grant of a new Charter in 1833, the East India Company lost its

commercial privileges and became the administrative agent of
the British Crown in India. Its barracks at St George's-in-the-
East were then wound up.[52]

Once again the plight of the lascars became an issue when in
1842 a letter was published in the *Sailors' Magazine*. Reproach-
ing shipowners for neglecting their legal duty to provide for the
lascars while on shore, the writer commented:

> Last winter their circumstances were truly deplorable;
> hundreds of them were allowed the most scanty and
> miserable provisions from their respective ships; were left
> to sleep in the open air or beneath some defenceless
> covering, with scarcely an article of clothing; while in every
> part of the city they might be seen engaged in sweeping the
> crossings of the streets for a few chance pence.[53]

By this time 3,000 lascars were arriving in Britain every year.
Many were housed in lodgings 'unfit for human habitation'[54]
into which they were 'herded like cattle – six or eight in a single
room or cellar without bedding, or chairs, or tables'.[55] Others,
fleeced of their possessions, ended up in 'abodes of infamy and
vice' as no-one else would take them.[56] Those who fell ill were
sent to hospitals or workhouses where they lay 'for weeks in a
most desolate condition, without being able to communicate
their wants to any around them'.[57] They lost their ships and
were stranded, some resorting to begging, thus adding to 'Asian
mendacity'. The death rate of lascars was appallingly high – by
one count it was estimated that at least 10 per cent of all those
who landed in England died here.[58] The coroner of East
Middlesex admitted that, during the five months from
November 1854 to March 1855, he had held 19 inquests on
lascars, and these were only the cases brought to the notice of the
police. Many more deaths went unreported.[59] The coroner had
felt so strongly about the wretched condition of the lascars that
in 1854 he had written to Lord Palmerston, then Secretary of
State for the Home Department, who had merely passed the
matter on to the India Board and the Lords Commissioners for
the Admiralty. Since nothing had happened, the coroner had

then communicated with the East and West India Dock
Companies and the local marine board. But bureaucracy had
taken over and the government had done nothing.[60]

Christian conscience was stirred, especially as the lascars
were leaving England with 'feelings of undisguised distrust
towards Englishmen'[61] and returning to their own countries
with the impression that 'the Englishmen, from all they have
seen, are as vicious or even worse than their own countrymen'.[62]
When Henry Venn, the Secretary of the Church Missionary
Society, took the initiative, various missionary societies met to
launch an appeal for a home for 'Asiatic' and African sailors.
The Maharajah Duleep Singh provided the first £500, and the
fund was begun. On 31 May 1856, in a colourful ceremony with
the representatives of the East and West gathered in Limehouse,
Prince Albert laid the foundation stone for 'The Strangers'
Home for Asiatics, Africans, South Sea Islanders and others
occasionally residing in the Metropolis'.[63] In June 1857 the
Strangers' Home in West India Road, near the Church of St
Andrews, Limehouse, was officially opened. (The Home was
demolished in 1937 and West India House erected on its site.)

During the years of its existence the Strangers' Home served
a triple purpose. First it was a lodging house for foreign sailors,
providing board and lodging on the 'most economical terms'
(about eight shillings a week).[64] Second, it was a repatriation
centre, providing employment on ships returning to the East for
any wandering Asian sailor. And finally, it was used as a centre
for propagating the Christian gospel among the sailors, so that
'the heathen' would not 'leave a Christian land without being
brought into contact with its Christianity'.[65] Joseph Salter of the
London City Mission was appointed by the Directors of the
Strangers' Home to spread the Gospel.[66]

The Strangers' Home was the first institution of its kind for
'Asiatic' and African sailors to be established in England.
Commenting on this feat, the *Illustrated London News* was of the
opinion that since in the seaports of India, Ceylon, China and
Australia there were comfortable homes for British seamen
provided for in part by the contributions of the 'natives' of those

countries, it was 'high time that such an institution should be
established in England, frequented as our ports have been for
many years past by thousands of Asiatics and other natives of
the East'.[67] Later a Sailors' Home was also established in
Liverpool.

The Strangers' Home provided many facilities for the sailors
who stayed there, either at their own expense, or at their
employers'. They could deposit their valuables for safekeeping,
remit their earnings to India, and use its library, which had a
collection of Christian books in various Asian and African
languages. The dormitories, named after the principal donors,
both 'Christian and Hindoo', had room for 220 beds; the large
hall was capable of accommodating 200. There were store
rooms, pantries, laundry rooms, bathrooms, lavatories and a
dining hall. The Lascar Shipping Office, which kept a register
of unemployed sailors, was attached to the Home.[68]

Not all lascars stayed at the Strangers' Home; as more ships
plied between the East and England, many were kept on board
their ships. It was estimated that in the first ten years 2,870
'Asiatics, Africans and South Sea Islanders' were boarded in the
Strangers' Home; 785 destitute lascars had been taken into the
Strangers' Home. Some of these had been shipwrecked, but
many more were 'principally beggars taken off the streets of the
metropolis, outports or provincial towns'. They were all found
employment or a passage on ships bound for India.[69] After the
first 16 years of the Home's existence Joseph Salter reckoned
that 6,400 had been boarded there, while 1,300 'destitutes' had
been sheltered and found employment;[70] the Home's own
statistics for the period between June 1857 and December 1877
showed that 5,709 sailors had registered as lodgers, and 1,605
'destitute cases' taken off the streets.[71]

Two developments made it easier to repatriate the lascars.
The first was the Merchant Shipping Amendment Act of 1855
which not only obliged the East India Company as the rulers of
India 'to take charge and provide for' and repatriate all 'persons
being lascars or other natives of the territories under the
government' of the Company. But more pertinently, contracts

made with 'natives in India' for a voyage out were deemed to have contained a further contract binding them to serve in other ships returning to India.[72] The law was further strengthened with the opening of the Strangers' Home, as it provided a clearing house facility with a shipping office attached to it, and a register of all unemployed or wandering Asian sailors. Jobs enabling them to work their way back to India were found for them. When in 1858 the Company was wound up and the government of India came directly under Whitehall, the responsibility for repatriating Asian sailors became that of the India Office, and £200 was contributed annually to the Strangers' Home for temporarily maintaining the lascars before finding them employment on ships bound for India.

As the number of lascars engaged for service to the United Kingdom grew in the 1870s with the coming of the steam-powered liners,[73] lascar desertion remained a problem. Bearing in mind that lascar terms and conditions of employment on these ships were far below those of white sailors,[74] it is not surprising that lascars sometimes deserted. In 1871, therefore, lascar transfer officers were appointed by the Board of Trade at all major English ports. Their duty was to send Asian crews under escort to London to await India-bound ships.[75] And then in 1894 another law reiterated the fact that lascar contracts bound them to return to India even if at the start of the voyage they had not done so.[76]

However, despite these laws, lascars and Chinese sometimes jumped ship in London to escape the treatment they received on board. In time a small community of Asian sailors grew up in Britain, especially in the East End of London and other important seaport towns like Liverpool. Some lascars and Chinese married European wives. A few even set up lodging houses for lascars and Chinese. Salter considered these to be 'gambling and opium dens'.

How many?

The number of lascars – and of African and Chinese sailors –
employed on British-registered ships grew as more ships were
built in India. After the 1840s the big steam-powered liners of
the Peninsular and Oriental lines, the Clan Line and the British
India Steam Navigation Company, began making up to three
voyages a year between England and India. Lascars were
regularly employed by these shipping companies, not simply
because they were cheap, but because they were good, efficient
sailors. More docks were opened up in London – the Victoria
and Albert Docks, the Royal Docks at Tilbury – and the liners
began calling at all these. The missionary bodies did not lose the
opportunity provided by this growth in shipping traffic to open
up new pastures in which to convert 'the heathen'. In 1896 the
Lascar Mission, a branch of St Luke's Church, was founded to
work among the Asian sailors in Canning Town.[77] The London
City Mission opened its Lascar Institute at Tilbury.[78] Liners
also called at Southampton and Liverpool, and so lascars were
found among the population of these ports too. During the First
World War more lascars were needed by the merchant shipping
companies as European crews were wanted for the British navy.
And so the numbers grew.

How many lascars arrived in the United Kingdom each year?
Official statistics are not available prior to the last decade of the
nineteenth century. However, the Parliamentary Committee of
Inquiry of 1814–15 had estimated the number of lascars to be
'not less than 1,000 or 1,100'.[79] Figures of admissions to the
Dreadnought Seamen's Hospital provide another estimate of
the proportion of lascars to other sailors employed on British
Empire ships.[80] Colonel Hughes, writing in 1855, suggests that
'at the lowest computation' the British merchant service
employed '10,000 to 12,000 lascars' for service in the East
Indian, Chinese and Australian trade. 'About half' of these were
brought to the United Kingdom every year. He further
suggested that of these 60 per cent were 'natives of India', 20 per
cent Malays 'or natives of the Straits of Malacca, Java etc.',

10 per cent Chinese and 10 per cent from East Africa and
Arabia.[81] Joseph Salter gives two sets of interesting statistics in
his annual reports for 1873 and 1874. He visited 40 ships in
1873, with a total of 3,271 sailors on board; he also visited at the
same period 362 sailors at the Strangers' Home, 70 ayahs, 40
visitors to England and 30 residents in London, making a grand
total of 3,773. In his analysis by 'ethnic' origin, he found the
highest number to be from India, and mainly Muslims: 1,653
East Indians; 1,200 East Africans; 400 Egyptians; 180 Chinese;
150 Malays; 70 West Africans; 50 Turks; 40 Burmese/Japanese
and 30 South Sea Islanders. In 1874, his total jumped to 7,815.
Of these he found '4,685 East Indians; 400 Hindu, Portuguese;
1,440 Arabs; 220 Chinese; 200 Manillas; 225 Turks; and 85
Malays'. He also visited 440 on shore.[82] After the 1890s statistics
from the annual statement of Trade and Navigation provide a
more official guide to the numbers arriving in Britain (see
Appendix 3).

The number of lascars employed on British ships depended
not only on the number of the ships and the growth of British
trade with the East, but also on the availability of the lascar
sailors themselves. In a good agricultural year the number
volunteering for work on ships obviously went down. The
attitude of British trade unions was another factor. Because
lascars were cheap, shipping companies preferred to employ
them: the unions considered this a threat to the livelihood of
British sailors and so tended to look unfavourably on the
employment of lascars. For instance, during the early years of
the twentieth century, under the leadership of Havelock
Wilson, the National Sailors' and Firemen's Union adopted a
hostile attitude to lascar employment.[83] And finally there is the
problem of 'ethnic origin' implied in the word 'lascar'. Although
originally the term was applied to sailors from India, at times
'lascar' was used loosely to denote 'Oriental' or 'Asiatic' sailor,
and could also denote Arabs and Africans. So we have to be
careful in drawing conclusions from even the official figures.

Lascars were recruited from East Bengal, the Punjab and the
west coast of India stretching from Ahmedabad and Surat to

Bombay, Goa and Cochin in the south. They were mainly peasant farmers.

The practice of employing lascars in British merchant fleets has continued well into the twentieth century. Lascars, therefore, have been a familiar sight in many west European ports for over two centuries. Many have settled in the port cities of the west.

4. Towards an Asian Community in Britain: Individuals and Interests

By the middle of the nineteenth century there were already in Britain the beginnings of an Asian population. In the last two chapters we saw how Asians from the subcontinent of India came to Britain. Servants, ayahs and the lascars all formed part of the growing international community, not only in the docklands of London, but in other seaports as well – such as Southampton and Liverpool. Asians also lived in some provincial towns. Joseph Salter, who spent much of his time attempting to convert lascars to Christianity, did not confine his efforts to work on board ships and in London hospitals and prisons, but also worked among the resident Asian population of London and other cities since, according to him, 'a wandering life is an essential characteristic of the Asiatic'.[1] During the summer and autumn months some left their families in London, Liverpool and Birmingham and went around the country in search of work. In 1867 Salter visited Brighton, Southampton, Birmingham, Manchester, Liverpool, Edinburgh and Peterborough, meeting Asians in all these places.[2] In 1869 he travelled to Glasgow, Stirling, Leith, Edinburgh, Sunderland, Durham, Hull, Liverpool, Manchester, Birmingham, Bath, Bristol, Southampton, the Isle of Wight and Brighton. He met 81 Asians including four at Edinburgh, 18 at Liverpool, 14 at Manchester, three at Bristol and two in Cardiff; in Birmingham he met three lodging house keepers catering for Asians.[3]

Although the early community was a migratory one, some Asians settled permanently in Britain; some married English or Irish wives, and gradually became absorbed into the general population. The roots of the early Asian community lay in the servant and lascar class, but there were other 'pioneering' Asian immigrants – teachers of Asian languages, doctors, barristers, merchants and traders, all offering something unique to the British way of life. Some members of the nobility, exiled from India as the Raj conquered their kingdoms, lived in Britain. No official statistics are available to indicate the size of the Asian population in the early period as early census returns do not record the population by ethnic origin. The Asian community, however, was much smaller than the other black communities in Britain.[4] And because of the nature of the documentary material available to us, we know more about the lives and work of particular individuals than about the 'community' in general.

The Asian poor in Britain

Pierce Egan, describing life in London's low gin-shop, 'All-Max', painted a picture in which

> colour or country [was] considered no obstacle . . .
> Everybody free & easy, – lascars, blacks, jack tars, coal
> heavers, dustmen, women of colour, old and young, and a
> sprinkling of remnants of once fine girls . . . were all jigging
> together.[5]

But the reality was not quite like this; the alien population of Britain was tolerated, after a fashion, but racial prejudice abounded. In 1816, for instance, the African and Asian guests at a pub dinner given by the members and friends of the African and Asian Society found themselves set apart from the other guests by a screen placed across one end of the room. William Wilberforce presided at this occasion.[6] Joseph Salter, too, found much prejudice against lascars in the East End of London. As Missionary for Orientals and Africans with the London City Mission, he decided to set up the Asiatic Rest where the sailors could meet, read, write letters and receive Christian teaching. He found that when local inhabitants realized that the premises were required for lascars, he encountered much opposition and his proposed scheme was considered a 'disgrace to any neighbourhood'. In refusing to grant permission to use his rooms, the landlord of 'The Pig and Cabbage' painted a picture of 'noisy Malays, Chinese with long pig tails, coal black Africans and dusky lascars sitting on the steps, climbing on the wall, and swinging on the railings, singing "Hallelujah", and shouting "Amen" till midnight, relieved not unfrequently by a free fight'. The landlord was emphatic in his refusal and would 'not disgrace the locality with such a nuisance'.[7]

Since it was usual to identify Christianity and the Protestant ethic with civilization, progress and moral values, Christian missionaries and other Englishmen who had been to India reaffirmed the jaundiced view of the Asian 'heathen'. Indians were considered 'uncivilized' and full of darkness and superstition.[8] Missionaries also considered the Hindu 'obsequious, deceitful, licentious and avaricious' and 'destitute of all that is good and distinguished by almost all that is evil'.[9] Longer association with India did not alter this view. Writing in 1902, a missionary was still of the opinion that 'the Hindu is inherently untruthful and lacks moral courage'.[10] 'The educated Indian' was regarded with patronizing superiority and considered rather comic for his literal English, intonation and verbosity. 'Baboo Jabberjee' was a figure of fun.[11] These views, formed in India, were taken back to England.

In his survey of the London poor of the 1850s, Henry Mayhew met Asians engaged in various forms of street trading and some beggars. He considered the selling of religious tracts to be a 'line peculiar to the Hindoos';[12] of the 40 or so individuals whom he believed to be engaged in this trade about half were 'men of colour'.[13] Besides selling Christian tracts, some were engaged in sweeping crossings. There were also street musicians and street traders, the most famous being the street herbalist, Dr Bonkanki.[14] Mayhew generally regarded Asians as pretty poor specimens of humanity – unscrupulous and a prey on the local population. He referred to the Hindu beggars as

Those spare, snake-eyed Asiatics who walk the streets, coolly dressed in Manchester cottons, or chintz of a pattern commonly used for bed-furniture, to which the resemblance is carried out by the dark, polished colour of the thin limbs which it envelops. They very often affect to be converts to the Christian religion, and give away tracts; with the intention of entrapping sympathy from old ladies . . . Or they will sell lucifers, or sweep a crossing, or do anything where their picturesque appearance, of which they are proud and conscious, can be effectively displayed. They are as cunning as they look, and can detect a sympathetic face among a crowd . . . From the extraordinary mendacity of this race of beggars – a mendacity that never falters, hesitates, or stumbles, but flows on in an unbroken stream of falsehood, – it is difficult to obtain any reliable information respecting them.[15]

Salter, too, reemphasized this stereotype by suggesting that 'artifice and deception' were the 'common modes of procedure with the cringing mendicant from the sunny land'. He considered Asians to have 'an eye as keen as the eagle to detect a sympathetic nature . . .'[16] And yet both Mayhew and Salter met many Asians who were engaged in honest trade and, when they could find employment, eager to work.

Mayhew related two interesting cases of the Asian poor. The first one was that of a 'tom-tom' player, a 'very handsome man, swarthy even for a native of Bengal' who was accompanied by his six-year-old son. The son assisted his father's profession by dancing while the father played the drum and sang. The man, a Muslim, was born in Calcutta, and had been brought to Britain as a servant by an army officer who had taken him to Scotland with him. Within seven months of their arrival the 'master' had died, and the 'tom-tom' player had moved to London, where he had lived for five years. Unable to obtain 'service', he had turned to the 'tom-tom', playing it in the streets of London. In the early days, he had earned good money – up to 6 shillings a day. But when the novelty wore off his takings dwindled, and so to supplement his income he took to modelling and earned a 'few shillings from two or three picture men, who draw me'. His outlook was 'anything for honest bread'. Life in London, he found, was hard; he had had to put up with many insults and racist name-calling ('black dis or de oder' as he put it). Sometimes he got beaten up in the streets: a magistrate punished one rough who gave him a blow that had left a mark on his chin. He was married to an Englishwoman who had been a servant; she could sew but was unable to get work. He met many Asians who had come to England as lascars but had deserted because of 'bosen and bosenmate, and flog'. They begged or swept the streets but they 'never pickpocket'.[17]

Joaleeka was the other Asian interviewed by Mayhew. He, too, had been a servant. He had learnt English from the Europeans he had worked for in India and had been employed as an interpreter. A 'great native prince' on a visit to England had brought him over as part of his retinue to act as an interpreter for the household servants. They had put up at an hotel in Oxford Street where Joaleeka had formed a liaison with an English servant girl who worked at the hotel. Having 'broken his caste' in this manner, he decided not to return to India. He ran away and was sheltered by another Englishwoman until the prince had returned to India and he felt safe. He later married his benefactor and became a Christian. She taught him to beg. When Mayhew met him he was living in Drury Lane with an Irish wife to whom he had been married for six years; they had three children. He did various jobs; he swept the crossing for two years and often worked as an interpreter. His only complaint was that his wife got 'drunk too often'.[18]

Salter also gave an account of many Asian poor he had met; some were beggars, but many more were men of enterprise, earning their living by various trades. One sold curry powder in the suburbs. Another, a Hindu, was a professional player on the 'tum-tum'. He wore his 'native garb' and carried his 'noisy instrument' round his neck. When he played his 'eastern melody he seemed to catch the inspiration of a dancing dervish', performing 'antics which only Asiatic exhilaration can produce'! Dermian was another musician who travelled round the country, singing and dancing. Dressed in white and with his long hair, Salter considered Dermian looked attractive.[19]

Then there was Ringa Swamee, another Hindu from Madras, who had come to England as a servant to an English 'sahib'. After working for him for 15 years, he had been left destitute through the death of his master. He was married to an English wife, had a small daughter and made a living by begging.[20] Abdool Rhemon had come from Surat in 1830. He had started by sweeping a crossing at St Paul's, then had been employed by the Nepalese ambassador for some years. Finally he had set himself up in business, keeping two lodging houses for lascars. According to Salter, these were kept for 'degrading purposes'.[21] Francis Kaudery, from Goa, had been in England since 1855; he worked as a steward at the 'Royal Sovereign', a public house in Bluegate Fields, Shadwell, which catered for lascars.[22]

Another Asian was Ameen Adeen from Bombay. He had come to Britain in 1843, and worked at various jobs. For some time he had been employed at Harley House, London, as part of the retinue of the Queen of Oudh.[23] Then he had turned to street hawking. But Salter believed him to be hawking 'spurious jewellry'.[24] James Abdoolah from Bombay was only 30 years old and had settled in England in 1842. He was married and had a little daughter of eight. He worked as a servant to a major of the Bombay Artillery.[25]

Jhulee Khan was considered a success, dear to Salter's heart. Originally from Calcutta, Jhulee Khan had come to England as a lascar in 1841. He jumped ship and began earning his living in 'taprooms' of England and Scotland, 'with his fiddle playing horn pipes and singing English songs'. In 1857 he became a Christian, having been influenced by an Englishwoman living in Tottenham. He then took to singing hymns in London streets. Finally he was baptized as John Carr and in 1866 returned to India with his wife and five children to work as a missionary.[26]

A long-time resident in Edinburgh was Roshan Khan, well known in that capital city as a supplier of 'savory pipes'. He went to the fairs and races, and on Fridays he sold his pipes in the High Street, near Castle Hill. He lived with his wife and two children in Gilmour Close, Grassmarket.[27] Khuda Baksh, an old man, lived in Cannongate: he had been in Europe a long time, earning his living from basketry work.[28] Musicians were not the only entertainers of Asian origin in Britain. In 1790, an 'east Indian Gentoo', a conjurer, was practising his art at Bartholomew Fair. His collection of tricks included cards and thought reading.[29] A snake charmer entertained his audience in Limehouse, London.[30] In 1886 five Punjabis arrived in England with a performing bear, hoping to make a living. Their venture lasted only a few months, however, and they had to return to India.[31]

The presence of a visiting sailor community as well as a resident Indian population in Britain meant that colourful Asian festivals and burials formed part of the British social scene. These were a source of curiosity, both to the media and the local populace. The *Gentleman's Magazine* tried to interpret some of these ceremonies for its readers.[32] In 1889 an Islamic mosque – the first in Britain – was opened at Woking.[33]

The Parsis, too, had a cemetery and a chapel at Brookwood, Woking. They had first started to visit Britain in 1742, but it was only after the 1850s that they arrived in any significant numbers. In 1861 the Religious Society of Zoroastrians was founded in Britain and it acquired a burial ground at Woking.[34]

Mixed marriages and association between white women – 'fallen women' – and Asian men were usually frowned upon by the British. Many were concerned about the 'innocent offspring' of these cross-cultural marriages, looking on them with 'anxiety and pity', as they showed so distinctly the evidence of their 'foreign parentage' – 'the dark little face with the woolly hair of Africa curling above the smiling eyes, or the features, perhaps not so dark, with the luxuriant hair of Hindoostan'.[35] These relations between Asians and white women strengthened British prejudice and the generally accepted notion that the 'dark races' were inferior and uncivilized:

It would surprise many people to see how extensively these dark classes are tincturing the colour of the rising race of

children in the lowest haunts of this locality: and many of
the young fallen females have a visible infusion of Asiatic
and African blood in their veins. They form a peculiar
class, but mingle freely with the others. It is an instance of
depraved taste, that many of our fallen ones prefer devoting
themselves entirely to the dark races of men, and some who
are to them have infants by them.[36]

Not all Asian migrants in nineteenth-century Britain were
servants and sailors. Some small entrepreneurs from India came
to seek their fortunes in Britain – itinerant surgeons, eye
doctors, and ear doctors, who went around the provinces and
London undertaking to cure the blind and the deaf in the
cheapest manner.

The most famous in this category were a group of oculists,
'eye specialists', who came in the 1890s; they based themselves
in various towns – London, Norwich, Swansea and Edinburgh.
Some advertised themselves with sophisticated handbills
carrying testimonials of their success. Four set up in the Poplar
and Whitechapel areas of London. They had had a flourishing
practice in Egypt, but were persuaded by some 'adventurers' to
come to Britain to better their prospects. They were disappointed
in this and eventually returned to India.[37]

Another group of five, with Kream Bocesh as the leader,
practised for some nine years in Bradford. Some of their
treatment went horribly wrong. They were convicted in
September 1893 and charged with 'obtaining money by false
pretences and unlawful and malicious wounding'.[38] Their trial
in Richmond attracted much interest and publicity. They were
acquitted on a point of law. The common serjeant, in his
summing up, concluded that as no deaths had been caused by
the treatment of their patients' eyes, their action did not amount
to criminal damage. In the end, they too departed for India as
they had exhausted their money during the trial and were
destitute. To save further embarrassment, the India Office gave
them money for a return passage to India, on condition that the
money was repaid in Bombay.[39]

The Richmond trial dealt a heavy blow to the reputation of Indian oculists in Britain. Ali Buksh and his younger brother had done reasonably well in Swansea for two years; but after the Richmond case their custom fell away and they faced ruin. Their local MP agitated on their behalf to get them a passage back to India, even raising the matter in parliament since the India Office refused to come to the aid of Asians who, in their opinion, 'had come to better themselves'. Eventually charity came to their rescue and they were provided with a return passage.[40]

Asian professionals

At the other end of the scale were the Asian middle classes – teachers, doctors, lawyers and businessmen. Some, against all odds, managed to gain renown during their time.

A teacher of the 'Persian and Arabick' languages, Monshee Mahomet Saeed from Bengal, advertised for pupils in 1777. He himself could 'speak and write English tolerably'.[41] We do not however know how successful he was in his field. Syed Abdoollah, another linguist, settled in England in the 1850s. He was a Professor of Hindustani at the University College, London. Professors were paid very small salaries in those days. Later, he set himself up as a Hindustani tutor or 'coach', preparing students for the Indian civil service examination. He was said to be making a good living at this.[42] He was present during the laying of the foundation stone for the Strangers' Home for Asiatics and Africans in Limehouse in May 1856. He also interested himself in the welfare of the Indian community in Britain, writing to the India Office from time to time (see p. 24).[43] He had an English wife.

Another Asian who taught at University College, London, in the 1860s was Ganendra Mohan Tagore, a Bengali. He was Professor of Hindu Law and Bengali Language. He himself had been educated in Britain. He lived with his Bengali wife and family.[44] G.M. Tagore was a close friend of F.H. O'Donnell, the Irish MP (see p. 78).

Aziz Ahmad lived in Hillhead, Glasgow, with his Scottish wife and three children. He had come to Britain in the 1880s to train as a missionary for India, but he found that only Europeans were appointed for service in India. He settled in Glasgow, a disappointed man, supporting himself by lecturing on Islam and 'kindred subjects'. In 1897, he attracted the attention of the Thugee and Dacoity Department, which also investigated anti-British agitation in India, for his articles in some Indian newspapers which were considered 'objectionable and seditious'. The Glasgow police department was asked to investigate him but found him 'quiet and respectable'; his visitors were mainly lascar seamen.[45]

One of the most colourful and well-known early Asian migrants was Sake Deen Mahomed, 'the Shampooing Surgeon to George IV'. Born in Patna, Bihar, in 1759,[46] Sake Deen Mahomed was the younger son in a family of two children. His father, 'descended from the same race as the Nabobs of Moorshadabad', was a captain in a battalion of sepoys commanded by Captain Adams, and died in battle in 1769, when Sake Deen was 'about eleven years old'.[47] Sake Deen went to school in Patna; however, his early ambition was to enter a 'military life'. In 1769 he agreed to join Captain Baker as his follower. Captain Baker was an officer in the East India Regiment commanded by Colonel Leslie.[48] Sake Deen Mahomed then followed the fortunes of Captain Baker in the army, rising to Market-master, Jemidar (ensign) and finally Subidar (captain) in Captain Baker's battalion. While in the army, Mahomed took part in the storming of Gwalior, the Battle of Ramnagaur and five other engagements in the year 1780.[49] When Captain Baker decided to return to Britain, Sake Deen Mahomed resigned his commission to accompany him, because, as he put it, he had 'a desire of seeing that part of the world'. They sailed from Calcutta and arrived at Dartmouth in England in September 1784.[50]

Sake Deen Mahomed settled in Cork, Ireland, with the family of a younger brother of Captain Baker, his former master. Here he went to school to improve his English. While at school, he met a 'pretty girl' of 'respectable parentage' with whom he eloped to another town. Once married, they returned to Cork.[51] It was at this time, too, that he had his first book, *Travels*, published.[51] In 1801, he arrived in Brighton.[52]

Brighton was a growing and fashionable health resort at this time – its population of about 2,000 in 1750 had grown to 7,400 in 1801 and would be 65,000 by 1850. Two of the many developments that contributed to this growth were the discovery of sea bathing (and drinking) by Dr Richard Russell, and the patronage of the Prince of Wales. As the idea of sea bathing for health reasons became popular, many indoor baths – both hot and cold sea-water baths – were established by the enterprising for those unable or unwilling to expose themselves to the cold air.[53] Following the patronage of the Prince of Wales, the rich and the elegant came to Brighton to be cured of their rheumatic aches and pains and enjoy fashionable society.

Here on the seafront Sake Deen Mahomed introduced his Indian Vapour Baths and Shampooing Establishment – a luxury then not known in England. Mahomed, whose interest in this cure dated back to his early days in India, had studied the properties of the cure.[54] He was convinced that with some improvements, what in the East was regarded as a restorative luxury would in England prove to be a powerful remedy for many diseases.[55]

At first he met with scepticism and little success as his baths operated on different principles from the popular hot and cold sea-water baths. Unwilling to try out a new and alien system, the Brighton public regarded the vapour baths and Mahomed with a suspicious eye. Determined to prove the superiority of his cure, Mahomed decided to treat some patients without payment, and met with complete success in curing ailments where other remedies had failed.[56] This aroused interest in his method of treatment, won over the hesitant, and brought him the fashionable clientele of Brighton, guaranteeing the survival of his baths and eventually making him famous. Eager to try out new cures, those suffering from muscular ailments flocked from not only Brighton but all of Britain and even Europe. The rich and the

fashionable indulged themselves in the Oriental luxury of a
sweet-smelling herbal vapour bath – with herbs brought
'expressly from India'.[57]

In the nineteenth century the term 'shampooing' (from the
Hindi *champi*, meaning 'to massage') did not mean washing
hair. At Mahomed's Vapour Baths and Shampooing Establishment the patients first lay in a steaming, aromatic herbal bath;
having sweated freely, they were then placed in a kind of flannel
tent with sleeves. They were then massaged vigorously by
someone outside the tent, whose arms alone penetrated the
flannel walls.

Mahomed's Baths became the most famous in Brighton.
Many eminent men and women were among his patients.[58]
Admiring patients declared their undying gratitude to Mahomed
for curing them; many signed testimonials in recognition of his
remedies. In 1820 a list of *Cases Cured by Sake Deen Mahomed*
appeared, written by the patients themselves.[59] Amateur poets
composed verses in praise of him and local papers carried letters
of recommendation for his treatment. One grateful patient even
credited the growth of Brighton to Mahomed's reputation for
curing disease![60] The King honoured him with the appointment
of 'Shampooing Surgeon to His Majesty George IV', with the
task of superintending the Royal Baths at the Pavilion.[61]

In 1822 Mahomed wrote up his own most important medical
work, largely consisting of cases successfully treated by him.[62] It
contained accounts of cures for asthma, contractions, paralysis,
rheumatism, sciatica, lumbago and loss of voice. The book also
includes a 'few complimentary notices which have been taken at
different times, of my humble endeavours to mitigate the sum of
human suffering, and relieve the afflictions of my fellow
creatures'.[63] The book had its third edition in 1838.

This was no mean feat for a 'Native of Hindoostan'.
Struggling against many odds – prejudice against his race, and
prejudice against the medical properties of his cure[64] – he had
succeeded in gaining recognition from the British public. Like
any successful businessman, Mahomed had to rely on his
instinct for publicity, and he cashed in on it not always too

scrupulously, it would appear.[65] He seems to have achieved some miraculous cures – patients who had given up all hopes of walking again pronounced themselves cured after a course of treatment at the baths. The vestibule of his establishment was 'hung with the crutches of former martyrs to rheumatism, sciatica and lumbago', which Mahomed's 'vigorous and scientific shampooing' had cured.[66] Visitors to the baths were given a tour through these 'testimonials' as Mahomed called them.

He may have been a self-publicist – and he had to be to succeed – but there is no doubt of his skill. The medical profession of the time was impressed by his claims and treatment. Dr John Gibney, an Edinburgh graduate and the senior physician at the Royal Sussex County Hospital, sent patients to Mahomed and wrote two short works on bathing, the second of which, published in 1825, owed much to Mahomed's work. In 1825 a rival shampooing establishment, Molineaux's, was set up, and in 1868 the Turkish Bath Company built the Brighton 'Hammam' or Turkish Bath – all owing their inspiration to Mahomed's success.[67] In 1830, Mahomed himself opened a second establishment in London, at 7 Ryder Street, St James's. His son Horatio was the proprietor. Horatio Mahomed, too, was an author in his own right.[68]

In 1843 Sake Deen Mahomed retired from active work: a son, Arthur, took over the running of the Brighton establishment, while another son, Frederick, and his wife Sarah, ran a fencing academy in Brighton.[69] During his active career, Mahomed had received much help from his wife, Jane, and many patients expressed special gratitude to 'Mrs Mahomed' for the 'courtesy and kindness . . . invariably met with' during their 'attendance at their establishment'.[70] Mahomed was a generous and kind-hearted man, always willing to help the poor and needy, either by giving them free treatment or by donations of money.[71] He died on 24 February 1851 at Frederick's home, 32 Grand Parade, Brighton. A simple tombstone in St Nicholas's church-yard commemorates this colourful citizen of Brighton.[72]

Frederick Akbar Mahomed, MB, FRCP, the grandson of Sake Deen Mahomed, exceeded his grandfather in the contribution he made to medicine. He was born in Brighton on 11 April 1849.[73] After private education, he began his medical studies at Sussex County Hospital and then at Guy's (1869–72), where he carried off many prizes. In 1872, having qualified as a Member of the Royal College of Surgeons, he took up his first appointment as Assistant Medical Officer at the Highgate Infirmary. In April 1873 he was elected Resident Medical Officer to the London Fever Hospital. Two years later, in February 1875, Akbar Mahomed became medical tutor and pathologist at St Mary's Hospital. He obtained his MD from Brussels in 1875, and in 1877 he was elected Medical Registrar at Guy's Hospital. Akbar Mahomed was aware that to obtain further promotion, it was necessary for him to have a British university degree. He therefore registered at Caius College, Cambridge, in October 1877, and to fulfil the minimum residential requirements, travelled to Cambridge by the last train every day after a heavy day's work at Guy's, returning to the hospital the following morning. In 1880, Akbar Mahomed was elected Fellow of the Royal College of Physicians and in 1881, the year he took his MB from Cambridge University, he became assistant physician at Guy's, being the first member of the staff to be recommended by his colleagues for the post.

Because of his interest in scientific and social medicine, Mahomed also took up appointments of physician at the London Fever Hospital, physician to the Edinburgh Assurance Company and Sanitary Inspector to the Welford Milk Farms.[74]

He wrote many articles – all of which made important contributions to research – on questions relating to kidney diseases and hypertension.[75] But his life's main interest and work lay in 'collective investigation' – common practice in the medical world today. He pioneered the system of gathering information on diseases by means of printed questionnaires sent out to doctors throughout the country. He was employed by the British Medical Association to visit the main towns to organize the collective method of the registration of diseases. To extend the system, he attended the International Medical Congress at Copenhagen in 1884.

Mahomed was a tireless and enthusiastic worker; he died of typhoid fever in November 1884 at the age of 35. He is buried in Highgate Cemetery. His untimely death, in the words of his professor at Cambridge, was a great loss 'nationally, and internationally – great to science and the profession of medicine, great to the British Medical Association, great to the hospitals and school with which he was connected'.[76]

The tradition of Indian doctors practising in Britain goes back a long way. Dr Fram Gotla came to Britain in 1891 after a brilliant career at Bombay University. He intended to return home after further qualification and experience, but he stayed on, working as a physician in London. At the start of the First World War he was one of the signatories to the letter sent by Mahatma Gandhi in London offering the services of Asians resident in Britain to the military authorities.[77] Dr Gotla was an influential member of the Parsi community in London in the 1920s and 1930s. Another distinguished doctor, Dr K.M. Pardhy had gone out to South Africa as a civil surgeon with the Indian contingent during the Anglo-Boer War in 1899. He saw service in Natal, the Transvaal and the Cape. After six months he was sent to England as a medical officer with the English soldiers; he arrived in Britain in 1900. He obtained his MRCS and LRCP and in 1904 took up the appointment of House Surgeon at the Royal Cornwall Infirmary in Truro, staying there for three years. In 1910, he was elected Fellow of the Royal College of Surgeons and in 1911 became a house surgeon in Birmingham. While in Birmingham he helped found the British India Association. Dr Pardhy was a man of many other talents: he was a good sportsman. He played hockey for Cornwall, and cricket and tennis for other English clubs. In 1910 he won a gold medal for wrestling in the Midlands championships. He married an Englishwoman and had two children.[78]

Asian businessmen, too, were engaged in commercial enterprise in nineteenth-century Britain. Some had come as employees of British-Indian firms, others represented great Indian companies. One of the earliest Asian commercial ventures was the firm of Cama and Company, established in

London in 1855, with a branch in Liverpool. Dadabhai Naoroji, later to be the first Asian MP, came to Britain as a partner in this firm. In 1860, he established his own cotton business: Dadabhai Naoroji and Company.[79] The firm of Tata and Company was established in Manchester and London. Sir Ratan Tata who lived in York House, Twickenham, was in charge; Shapurji Saklatvala, to be the first Asian Labour MP in the British House of Commons in 1922, was a departmental manager.[80] By 1914 several Asian businesses operated in Britain as can be seen by the signatures on Gandhi's letter of 1914.[81]

Early Asian migrants to Britain were not all male. Indian ayahs, as we have seen, were brought to Britain. Other Indian women, too, lived in Britain. When Mirza Abu Talib Khan visited London in 1800 he met 'two or three Hindoostany ladies'. He visited Noor Begum, the wife of 'General De B___ e from India', with whom she had come to England in 1797. They had settled in London. Later 'General De B___ e' had deserted Noor Begum to marry a young French girl. But Noor Begum continued to live in England with her two children.[82] Other Europeans who had married Indian women while in India had returned to live in Britain with their Indian wives and children.[83]

Some professional Asians may have done well and even risen to fame, but they were still viewed with condescending patronage in some quarters, and there remained racial prejudice against them. The Edalji case in the Great Wyrley mystery is a case in point.

A Parsi named Shapurji Edalji, a convert to Christianity, became in the 1870s the vicar of Great Wyrley in Staffordshire. He was married to an Englishwoman, Charlotte Stoneham, and they had three children. Their eldest son, George Edalji, a sedate lawyer, practised as a solicitor in Birmingham. George had been a brilliant law student, had won prizes from the Law Society and had written an authoritative handbook on railway law. In 1903, he was arrested and sentenced to seven years' penal servitude for maiming horses in the neighbourhood. The trial had been conducted on what was obviously a trumped-up charge. Although there was evidence to the contrary, the police of Staffordshire and the people of Great Wyrley were convinced that George Edalji made nocturnal sacrifices to his alien gods – and this despite the fact that the Edalji family were Christians.

The people of Great Wyrley had not accepted the Reverend Edalji: how could a Parsi, an Asian, become the vicar of a Christian church? The family suffered many malicious 'jokes' and from 1892 to 1895 had been subjected to hoax letters and many other nuisances. But the chief constable of Staffordshire, 'who thought Black Men less than the beasts'[84] refused to take any action, claiming that the Reverend Edalji's son, George, was the author of the anonymous letters against his own family.

And now, in October 1903, George was found guilty of horse maiming. While George was serving his prison sentence, anonymous letters and horse killings continued. Finally, after agitation by R.D. Yelverton, a former Chief Justice of the Bahamas, and others, George Edalji was released from prison in 1906, when he had already served three years of the prison sentence. But although he was freed, he remained under police surveillance and was not pardoned. It was then that Arthur Conan Doyle took up his case and conclusively proved that George Edalji could not have been guilty. He sent his findings to the *Daily Telegraph* and the Home Office. The Home Office then appointed a committee to reexamine the case. The committee concluded that George Edalji had been wrongly convicted of horse maiming, but despite the three years he had spent in prison, he never received any compensation. (He was still considered to have been guilty of forging the letters.)[85]

Asian nobility

Duleep Singh,[86] the son of Runjit Singh, the founder of the Sikh nation, was born on 4 September 1838.[87] In 1843, he was officially proclaimed Maharajah of the Punjab; but he did not enjoy this status for long. The Punjab was annexed by Lord Dalhousie in 1849, after the Second Sikh War, and Duleep Singh, still a child, was forced to renounce all claims to his kingdom and to surrender the famous Koh-i-noor diamond to Queen Victoria as a 'gift'. He was however allowed to retain the title of 'Maharaja Duleep Singh Bahadoor' and received a regular stipend from the East India Company.[88] Lord Dalhousie, the Governor General, considered this a good bargain as the prince would 'die in his bed like a gentleman', which he would not have done had he been allowed to continue as the ruler of the Punjab.[89] So at the age of 11 Duleep Singh lost his kingdom and his estates to the British and was separated from his mother. He was exiled to Futteghur, and Dr John Login, a Scottish doctor, and his wife took over his education and guardianship.

In March 1853, Duleep Singh officially embraced Christianity, and in April 1854 the Court of Directors of the East India Company finally granted permission for him to visit England which was to be his home for the greater part of his life.

Queen Victoria was impressed by the 15-year-old Duleep Singh – his youth, his good looks and especially the fact of his being a Christian, 'the first of his high rank who has embraced our faith' – all created a favourable impression and Queen Victoria took him under her wing.[90] He was invited to Osborne and accorded the rank equal to a European prince. All this distinction was considered not good for a deposed Indian prince and bound to give him ideas.[91]

Meanwhile the Maharajah's education continued under Dr Login. He was found to be quite industrious at his studies and truthful. The Queen considered this to be an exception in an Oriental. She concluded that Christian influence must have helped him to overcome the 'natural indolence . . . inherent in all Easterners'.[92] Duleep Singh made progress in German and photography.

In 1857, it was officially agreed by the Court of Directors of the East India Company that Duleep Singh was of age and so could manage his own affairs. He was given an allowance of £25,000 a year. However, being used to Eastern princely splendour, he considered this sum to be inadequate; he wished it to be raised to £35,000. Sir Charles Wood, secretary of state for India, commented that the sum was far above the average income of the nobility in Britain – reckoned to be about £10,000. So Duleep Singh had to be content with the stipend, at least for the time being.[93]

In 1863 Duleep Singh acquired Elveden Hall on the border of Norfolk and Suffolk for £105,000. Built in the 1760s, it was originally owned by Admiral Keppel. The exiled Maharajah transformed it into an Indian palace and settled down to playing the role of the Norfolk country squire, with game-shooting parties, receptions and support to local charities. Nicknamed the 'Black Prince' by the locals, the Maharajah and his wife Bamba became great socialites. All the great names of the day came to Elveden Hall as Duleep Singh's shooting guests: the Prince of Wales, Lords Kimberley, Dacre, Ripon, Atholl, Balfour of Burleigh, Abinger. Duleep Singh was rated the fourth best shot in Britain.[94] He was elected to the Carlton Club in March 1873 and even entertained the idea of standing for parliament. But he was discouraged from doing so on constitutional grounds.

Money problems, however, soon loomed large as his extravagant style of life forced him into debt. So began his wrangles with the India Office. His attempts to recover some of his private estates in the Punjab did not make him popular in British eyes. Convinced that injustice had been done to him as a child, he turned to studying the 'Punjab Question'. He wrote a long letter to *The Times* in 1882[95] explaining the wrong done to him and denouncing the greed of the then British administrators. The financial wrangles with the India Office did not produce any results either. Finally, Duleep Singh renounced Christianity, reembraced Sikhism and in 1886 prepared to travel to India to claim his lands.[96] He was arrested in Aden, and went to live in Paris.[97]

Maharajah Duleep Singh died, an exile, in Paris in October 1893; his body was brought back to England and buried at Elveden. Elveden Hall was sold in 1894 to the First Earl of Iveagh. One of the daughters of Duleep Singh, Sophia, visited the wounded Indian soldiers who fought on the Western Front during the First World War, and merited a mention in the 'report' from the censor's office.[98]

Princess Gouramma, born in February 1841 and the daughter of the ex-Maharajah of Coorg, was brought up in England and given education befitting an 'English child'. She was converted to Christianity and baptized in July 1852 at St James's Chapel, with Queen Victoria as her godmother.[99] Lord Dalhousie considered it 'a great mistake' to have royalty present at the ceremony and to have named Princess Gouramma 'Victoria' after the Queen.[100]

It was hoped that Princess Gouramma and Maharajah Duleep Singh would be sufficiently attracted to each other to make a match of it; but nothing came of this. Princess Gouramma lived as the ward of Colonel and Lady Catherine Harcourt at Buxted Park in Sussex. Miserable, lonely and far away from her friends, she fell in love with a young under-butler and contemplated elopement. The plan was frustrated. Finally she was introduced by Duleep Singh to Colonel John Campbell, Lady Login's brother. He was 30 years her senior and a widower with several children. Their marriage took place in July 1860. The Queen expressed satisfaction at the 'comfortable', if not 'brilliant', future of her goddaughter.[101] Princess Gouramma gave birth to a daughter and died of consumption in London at the age of 23.[102]

Another Indian prince – the Nawab Nazim of Bengal, whose territories (at Murshidabad) had been annexed by the British – also lived in England for some time. The Nawab arrived in England in 1870, initially to appeal to the House of Commons for an increase in his family allowance. In 1876 he moved to Edmonton, north London, and lived with his retinue at Pymmes House.

Nawab Nazim, too, became a favourite of Queen Victoria. But he fell out of favour with the government of India for leading in England what they termed 'a life of debauchery' and for marrying 'an Englishwoman of low extraction'. The government considered it 'very inexpedient . . . to encourage Englishwomen of mean extraction to ensnare Indian noblemen'.[103] The Nawab had also by this time run up many debts. After many years of lobbying and with the support of some MPs

- especially the Irish MPs - the Nawab's affairs were settled. He was allowed to abdicate in favour of his son, and granted £8,000 a year, which was considered sufficient for his personal maintenance. But he was not allowed to return to India. In 1880, he left England for Kerbala, the holy Muslim city in the Middle East (today in Southern Iraq).

This then was the cross-section of the Asian population in pre-First World War Britain. Whatever their profession and their contribution to British society, and despite their small numbers, their experiences of British society were in one important respect similar. Racial prejudice, indifference or at times grudging acceptance characterized their presence. In this respect, the reception given to more recent arrivals from India has its roots in the treatment accorded to these earlier settlers.

5. Early Challengers to the Empire

The movement for Indian freedom was not confined to India. From its earliest days, Britain, the centre of Imperial power, formed one of the platforms of the movement, and from this vantage point Indian nationalists and their British allies launched their campaigns to free India. Diverse means were employed to educate parliament and the British public about the nature of British rule in India and about Indian aspirations for political advancement.

Rajah Rammohun Roy, a Bengali, regarded as the 'father of Indian nationalism', was the first Indian to involve himself in political activity in Britain.[1] His memorandum submitted to the Parliamentary Committee on Indian Affairs while he was in England has been described as the 'first authentic statement of Indian views placed before the British authorities' by an Indian.[2] Both Roy and Dwarkanath Tagore saw the need for an association which would act as a pressure group in Britain on behalf of India. In July 1839 some sympathetic Englishmen formed the British India Society which aimed at 'bettering the condition of our fellow subjects the natives and inhabitants of British India'.[3] The Society had the further aim of 'advancing the prosperity of our own country',[4] the implication being that British and Indian prosperity were intertwined. The inaugural meeting of the Society, held in London, was attended by Englishmen, Anglo-Indians, and some Indians.[5] During its existence, the British India Society put pressure on the East India Company, brought together 'the friends of India', and, more important, stimulated political agitation in India.[6]

The next association of this kind was the London Indian Society set up in March 1865. This was to be 'a centre of action and communication in England for the promotion of native interests'. Dadabhai Naoroji and some 'principal Indian gentlemen' - students and businessmen living in London - were its leading lights. At its meeting at University Hall, Gordon Square, the Society unanimously decided that its English sympathizers were to serve in an honorary capacity only; otherwise 'Indian interests and Indian sentiments would be completely lost'.[7] The Society was short-lived, being absorbed in the East India Association, formed in 1866. Again, Dadabhai Naoroji was one of the principal founders of this movement, which was open to Britons and Anglo-Indians as well as Indians. In the East India Association's early years, its Indian members, with the active co-operation of some liberal-minded Britons and Anglo-Indians, played an active role in educating public opinion on Indian affairs. Many papers critical of official policy in India were read before the Association by Naoroji and others. Deputations met to lobby MPs on Indian matters. However, the more conservative-minded Anglo-Indians regarded the pro-Indian sentiments of the Association as 'the most dangerous fallacies'.[8] They considered Naoroji's views 'extreme',[9] and were able to blunt the influence of the radicals. By 1881 the Anglo-Indians had turned the Association into a debating forum for themselves.

A London-based society, the London Indian Society, consisting mainly of students, was formed in 1872 with Dadabhai Naoroji as President. It aimed 'to bring into closer union the Indians residing in England, and to furnish an opportunity for the interchange of thought and feeling on all matters connected with India'.[10] The London Indian Society carried on effective propaganda on behalf of India for more than 50 years. It was to this society that Frank Hugh O'Donnell, the Irish MP, made approaches with his plans for forming an Irish-Indian organization for bringing the grievances of India before parliament.

Many Indian nationalists took a great interest in Irish political developments as they saw close parallels between Irish and Indian experiences. The emergence of the Irish Home Rule Movement and the Irish Parliamentary Party in the 1870s excited and influenced many Indian nationalists. But the Irish nationalists, preoccupied with their own concerns, were slower to take an interest in India. However, by the mid 1870s, Indian nationalists and Irish MPs began to develop an alliance. Indian nationalists, disappointed in the East India Association, were looking for a new voice that would speak on behalf of India in parliament. The Irish MPs, for their part, were embarking on a policy of filibustering, and found Indian issues handy for their tactics of obstruction in parliament. It was F.H. O'Donnell who first saw the advantage of Indian nationalists and Irish MPs working together. He was a close friend of G.M. Tagore. This friendship enabled O'Donnell to appreciate Indian affairs and come into contact with other Indian nationalists.

The idea was also floated of adopting four Indians to represent Irish constituencies in parliament and to speak for Irish Home Rule on all Irish questions. In return, Irish MPs would lend them their support on all Indian legislation. But nothing came of this.[11]

In their efforts to campaign for India, the nationalists in Britain did not confine themselves to addressing meetings and writing speeches. They tried also to seek election to parliament, so as to put forward the 'native view'[12] in the corridors of power. The first Asian to try to do this was Lalmohun Ghose who unsuccessfully contested Deptford as a Liberal candidate in 1883.[13] Rajah Rampal Singh of Kalakankar entertained the idea of standing as a Conservative candidate; but the first successful Asian candidate was Dadabhai Naoroji, 'the Grand Old Man of India'.

Dadabhai Naoroji

Naoroji was born in Bombay on 4 September 1825, the only child in a poor Parsi priest's family. Encouraged to study by his mother, he was one of the first Indian students to graduate from Elphinstone College in Bombay; later he became the first Indian to be appointed Professor of Mathematics and Natural

Philosophy at Elphinstone College. In London, he later held the post of Professor of Gujerati at University College, and was a member of that College's senate.

Besides pursuing an academic career in India, Naoroji threw himself into the service of his country and championed a wide variety of causes. He campaigned for social and educational reforms, especially the cause of female education: he is known as 'the father of girls' schools'.[14] He founded many scientific, literary and cultural societies, and contributed learned articles to many journals and newspapers. He spoke English, Gujerati, Hindustani, Persian and French. In 1852 he set up the Bombay Association to voice the political aspirations of the Indian peoples. In 1873 he served for a year as diwan (minister) for the state of Baroda, and in 1875 he was elected member of the Bombay municipal corporation and town council. Lord Reay, Governor of Bombay, appointed him a member of the Bombay Legislative Council in 1885. After the Indian National Congress was founded, Naoroji was elected its president for three sessions – 1886, 1893 and 1906.[15]

Naoroji's academic career ended in June 1855 when he came to England as a partner in the Indian commercial firm of Cama and Company. He resigned in 1858 and a year later set up his own cotton company.[16] This business career was, however, secondary to his life's main mission to voice the political and economic grievances of the millions of Indians suffering under British rule and to try to change that relationship. His business served as a centre from which Indians he encouraged to come to Britain could take the Indian civil service examination. The holding of the examination in London was discriminatory, since it effectively barred all Indians from competing except those who could afford the fare to London. Naoroji agitated for a change in this system. As already seen, he was the driving force behind the setting up of the London Indian Society and the East India Association. He also founded the London Zoroastrian Association for the wellbeing of the Parsis living in London, and was its president from 1861 to 1907.

Educating public opinion about India meant not simply

reading papers at the gatherings of the East India Association and writing articles in the newspapers. Naoroji also had to defend Indian equality and refute those who argued for the inherent inferiority of the character of 'Asiatic races'. But his main theme in his speeches and writings was Britain's economic exploitation of India. He argued that the former invaders of India, such as the Mughals, did not export India's wealth abroad: not only did they become part of India, they also employed Indians in the running of the country. However, under British rule India was saddled with an expensive civil administration, employing highly paid European personnel. Indian taxpayers also paid for maintaining the British Raj in India and for the army's deployment beyond India's frontiers. The country's trade and industry was developed to suit the British economy. The peasant was being used as a milch cow to pay for British rule of India. In short, Naoroji's main thesis was that England drained India of £30-£40 million annually, causing poverty, famine and misery. This was his famous 'drain theory', later developed in his important work *Poverty and Un-British Rule* (1901).[17] What was more unjust was that the Indians from whom these taxes were extracted had no say in the expenditure of 'a single farthing' as their voice was not represented in parliament. It also concerned Naoroji that the wealth taken from India did not benefit the 'working men of Britain' but filled the 'pockets of the capitalists and higher classes'.[18]

Naoroji also canvassed for the 'Indianization' of government service. Under the British Raj, Indians were totally excluded from a share in the administration of their own country, despite the 1834 Act and the 1858 Proclamation which had pledged that the subjects of the Crown, regardless of 'race or creed', would be 'freely and impartially admitted to offices' in government services. But Naoroji pointed out that the promise remained unfulfilled. Every ploy was used to debar Indians from government service. The examination for entry into the Indian civil service was held only in London. Of those Indians who tried, most failed, even though many had high qualifications.[19]

This grip on Indian administration was further demonstrated by the furore over the Ilbert Bill in 1883. Before that date no Indian magistrate could try a case involving a charge against a European. In 1883, Lord Ripon, the Viceroy, introduced the Ilbert Bill designed to remove this 'invidious distinction' and to establish the principle of equality before the law. Under the Bill, Indian judges could try Europeans in courts outside the three presidency towns. But the Bill roused such strong passions among the European community in India that it had to be modified.

Naoroji and the early Congressmen firmly believed in a British sense of justice and fair play. They demanded reforms like the expansion of the Legislative Council to admit Indian members thus giving them 'a real voice' in the administration of their country. They demanded that civil service examinations be held simultaneously in India and England; they asked for Indians to be given commissions in the army. And above all, they wanted the drain on Indian finances to be reduced.

Naoroji's speeches and writings attracted the support of many influential Englishmen – radicals like John Bright, of the Anti-Corn Law League; Henry Fawcett, a retired judge; Charles Bradlaugh, freethinker and politician; Allan Octavian Hume, son of the radical politician; Sir William Wedderburn, a retired civil servant; and W.S. Caine, well-known temperance reformer and MP. H.M. Hyndman, the British socialist leader who was to edit the journal *Justice*, became a firm champion of India, as did radicals like Keir Hardie and the future Labour MP Ramsay MacDonald. After the Indian National Congress was founded in India, in 1885, the need for a similar organization in Britain was felt to be imperative. And so, in July 1889, Naoroji and W.C. Bonnerjee, with the support of Wedderburn, Hume and William Digby, a journalist, set up the British Committee of the Indian National Congress. This Committee aimed to 'rouse the English working classes, to whom political power had so largely passed, to a sense of the duties which England owes to India',[20] and it dedicated itself to Indian reforms. Public meetings, petitions and resolutions were organized; news items were sent to the press to draw attention to India. In 1890 the Committee published its own journal, *India*, which continued to be its voice for over 30 years.

In the end Naoroji was convinced that, if Indian reforms were to be a reality, he would need to be elected to parliament to speak on behalf of the silent millions of Britain's Indian subjects. Ignorance and apathy ruled Indian affairs, not only at the level of public opinion but also in parliament, where even the Indian finance bills were 'huddled over in an evening to empty benches'.[21] This was the measure of interest in India, that brightest jewel in the British crown.

As far back as 1872, Naoroji had thought about entering parliament. Only in 1886 did he seriously start canvassing for a British constituency. With his radical leanings, the Liberal Party was the obvious choice. As a realist, Naoroji was aware that he would need a good deal of preparation on local issues, if he was to be adopted by an English constituency.[22] The art of public speaking, too, would be an asset. So he started to prepare himself for this new responsibility. Holborn, in central London, adopted him unanimously and he contested the seat in 1886. But Holborn was a strong Tory seat; it was also strongly opposed to home rule for Ireland. Naoroji, a supporter of Gladstone's policy for Irish Home Rule, could never win the seat. Undaunted, he threw all he had into the contest. In the end, though he lost, he did better than expected, polling 1,950 votes to his opponent, Colonel F. Duncan's 3,651.[23] His next chance came in 1892 when he stood for Finsbury Central, also a working-class constituency.[24] With a majority of five over his Tory opponent,[25] he won this seat, thus becoming the first black MP to sit in the House of Commons.

A predominantly white working-class electorate had returned an Asian to parliament: a historical achievement for Dadabhai Naoroji. How was this possible? What was the attitude of the British public towards black candidates?

Naoroji's candidature roused strong passions; his achievement gave rise to racist attacks and even opposition from his own party. The views of the Conservative Party and rightwing opinion in the country were predictable. The first racist shot came in fact from the Conservative Prime Minister, Lord Salisbury, who voiced the unspoken thoughts of many Tory minds. Explaining the overwhelming victory of the Conservative candidate at Holborn, Lord Salisbury declared:

> But then Colonel Duncan was opposed to a black man, and however great the progress of mankind has been, and however far we have advanced in overcoming prejudices, I doubt if we have yet got to that point when a British constituency will take a black man to represent them . . . at all events he was a man of another race who was very unlikely to represent an English community.[26]

The theme of *colour* was taken up throughout the country as that great British establishment, the press, spoke out on behalf of the 'silent majority', the British people.

To have debarred a British citizen merely on the grounds of colour was considered by some 'liberal' opinion not only to be in utterly bad taste, but also, coming from a prime minister, positively scandalous. The *Newcastle Leader* reminded the noble lord that 'by far the larger proportion of the British subjects are black men' and to condemn a man for the colour of his skin was 'to revive the very worst days of the old brutality'.[27] The *Star* indignantly pointed out that if skin colour was to be the criterion for holding office, then 'surely Lord Salisbury of all men should not be the Prime Minister', as Naoroji, the Parsi, was lighter-skinned than Lord Salisbury. In defending the Asian candidate, the *Star* was of the opinion that such remarks, in the long run, were bound to be counterproductive for Britain, as Indian eyes would be opened to the fact that their 'progress and emancipation' could only be achieved by their own exertions, and could not depend on 'the tender and slender mercies of this or that English party, which, when it suits them, do not hesitate to level against their leaders such brutal insults'.[28]

Fear that such slurs would fan the flames of Indian demands for freedom and so 'cost' Britain 'dear India', was also expressed.[29] One newspaper, the *Accrington Times*, tried to remind Salisbury that India had a flourishing civilization long before Britain had emerged from 'the darkness of primitive savagery'.[30] Some genuinely felt that Indian representation in parliament would be 'extremely valuable and useful, for there is no doubt that we greatly neglect India in parliament'.[31] The *Warrington Examiner* declared unequivocally that

> In India there are 250 millions of people; and it is a monstrous doctrine that they are not to have as much as one representative in the House of Commons. The right policy is to strengthen Parliament by admission of men who know something of the pressing wants of people who were advanced in civilization . . . They do not ask for Home Rule yet; but they do demand, and have a right to demand, that they shall have some voice in the government of their country.[32]

The London *Graphic* was emphatic that men like Naoroji, who knew both India and England, should be given the opportunity of putting forward the claims of their fellow citizens in parliament; while the London *Daily News* declared that men like Naoroji should be in parliament because it was desirable that a 'reliable, well-informed, and strong man should speak for the reformers of India with authority', and who better than the Parsi, who was the 'trusted representative' of the 'great Indian National Congress'?[33]

But such sentiments were counterbalanced by equally strong passions about the suitability of a man of 'another race' representing 'English communities'.[34] It was considered unwise to let a man from the 'conquered country',[35] or, in the words of the *Hawk*, a 'Baboo from Bombay',[36] enter the British House of Commons. Lord Salisbury considered such candidates to be 'incongruous', since, as he put it, the British House of Commons 'with its traditions and understandings . . . is a machine too peculiar and too delicate to be managed by any but those who have been born within these Isles'.[37] Lord Salisbury seemed to have forgotten that whites born in Australia and the USA, not to say in India, were in parliament at the time he was speaking.

Sir Lepel Griffin, Chairman of the East India Association
and one-time Chief Secretary in the Punjab, writing to *The
Times*, hit out at Naoroji, declaring that he had nothing to
recommend him to an English constituency except for a 'gift of
fluency common to all Orientals'. In Sir Lepel Griffin's words,
Naoroji was

> an alien in race, in custom, in religion; destitute of local
> sympathy or local knowledge, no more unsuitable repre-
> sentative could be imagined or suggested. As to the people
> of India, Mr Naoroji no more represents them, than a
> Polish Jew settled in Whitechapel represents the people of
> England. He is a Parsee, a member of a small foreign
> colony, probably Semitic in origin, settled in the west of
> India. The Parsees are the Jews of India; intelligent,
> industrious, and wealthy . . . But they are quite as much
> aliens to the people of India as the English rulers can
> possibly be.[38]

The right wing of the Tory Party relied on the time-honoured
and tested doctrine of 'divide and rule'. The Parsis were
branded as 'foreigners'[39] in India and, as settlers of 'comparatively recent times', they were 'not the native proper of India'
and so could not be a 'fit exponent of the thoughts, intentions
and feelings of India'.[40]

What of the Liberal Party? Were they above such petty
prejudice, having adopted first Ghose then Naoroji? No, even
they were divided and did not lend Naoroji the whole-hearted
support that he deserved.

Although influential Liberal friends were anxious to have an
Indian in parliament, caution prevailed. John Bright warned
Naoroji that constituencies preferred 'local men or men of
distinction'. Others advised him to try a Scottish seat as the
Scots had the reputation of being 'more liberal than English
Liberals'; it was even suggested by William Digby that he
discard his Parsi headdress for an English hat as it was 'better to
appear altogether like an Englishman'.[41]

Having a fair skin and a western education helped Naoroji to some extent. His long residence in England and his knowledge of Liberal politics were other factors in his favour.[42] He was also strongly in favour of Home Rule for Ireland. He was convinced that 'Irish self-government . . . far from disintegrating the empire' would 'produce a real and lasting union between Great Britain and Ireland in place of the sham, or worse than sham, union which at present exists'.[43] When Holborn first adopted him, his supporters stressed his 'twenty years' residence' in Britain, and his thorough grasp of 'English political questions'.[44] He himself pledged that constituency needs would take precedence over the interests of India.[45] Though no divisions appeared at Holborn, it was not the case that all Liberals were willing to have an Indian candidate. The most important aspect of the Holborn contest was that the interval between Naoroji's adoption and the actual election – a mere nine days – was too short for divisions to emerge and take root. But at Finsbury the Liberals behaved differently. In fact the whole episode from 15 August 1888, when Naoroji was adopted Liberal candidate for Finsbury, to the election in 1892, showed how torn by conflicting loyalties the Liberals were.

Within two days of Naoroji's adoption as the prospective Liberal candidate for Central Finsbury, the ballot was declared invalid and attacks on Naoroji began in the local press.[46] In the face of this, F. Schnadhorst, organizing secretary at Liberal headquarters, pledged Naoroji his support, declaring that he had been 'fairly selected'. He further impressed on Naoroji not to give way at Central Finsbury, for if he did so, no other constituency would accept him in the future, as he would appear to have 'no firmness in maintaining [his] just position'.[47] Schnadhorst had also informed Digby that 'although a Parsi is much handicapped in an English constituency, Naoroji is not only the best man and politician of the two, but is more likely to win'.[48] Naoroji, therefore, believing himself both to have been justly selected, and to have the support of the Party, resolved to stand his ground. But on 3 September 1888, a faction of the local Liberal Party put up Richard Eve as the candidate for Central Finsbury. A motion for arbitration was thrown out but differences among the Liberals in Finsbury persisted. Into this uncertain situation came Lord Salisbury's attack on Naoroji. Liberals of all rank rallied to Naoroji's support. A grand banquet was given in his honour on 21 January 1889, and many speeches were made in his praise. Lord Ripon, the former Viceroy of India, assured the Party that Naoroji would not only make a 'most valuable' MP, but was 'an admirable representative of the Indian people'.[49] After this public support for Naororji, it might be supposed that local differences would have been patched up and the Liberals would not have jettisoned Naoroji.

Locally, however, an Asian was not fully acceptable. A strong caucus in Finsbury remained opposed to Naoroji. Even Schnadhorst, contrary to his earlier pledges of support, now joined in the chorus of demands for 'arbitration'.[50] But Naoroji stood firm. In June 1890, Richard Eve withdrew from the contest as he was offered another seat, leaving Naoroji alone in the field. In January 1891 F.A. Ford was put up by the Finsbury Liberal and Radical Association. Ford claimed that he had been 'selected by a thoroughly representative body of the Party', and that Naoroji did not have the Party's backing.[51] Appeals to Schnadhorst produced no declaration of support from him, although Digby reminded him that if the Asian was now made 'a victim of petty and wholly discreditable intrigue . . . he [would] become the occasion of a great deal of comment' which would harm the Liberal cause.[52] But Schnadhorst would do no more than declare a position of 'neutrality' and regret the 'dual candidature'.[53]

Naoroji felt betrayed. Not wishing to desert his supporters or to allow himself to be 'flung away on the dung pile like a dead cat', he issued a statement in the local press on 28 July 1891 explaining his position.[54] He followed this up, in March 1892, with a pamphlet to all electors in Finsbury outlining his view of the dispute.[55] But Ford stayed put. As late as April 1892, Arnold Morley, Secretary to the London Radical and Liberal Association, was urging Naoroji, in a 'strong letter', to submit himself to arbitration and warning that if he did not do so then 'it would no longer be possible . . . to maintain a neutral position'.[56]

In the end, in the face of Naoroji's determination, Ford withdrew rather than risk an independent Liberal candidature, and the loss of the seat. In 1892, when the election was declared, the Liberal Party rallied round Naoroji. He received much help from Josephine Butler, William Digby and John Burns. Keir Hardie, the Labour leader, supported Naoroji. His supporters were jubilant at Naoroji's victory; the 'cheering' could 'have been heard at St Paul's on one side and Chelsea Hospital on the other'.[57] Parliament welcomed him enthusiastically.

But the country had mixed feelings about his entry into parliament. *The Times* dismissed it as a 'romantic event' which would not be 'frequently repeated'.[58] The *Bristol Times* not only considered it an 'odd choice for an English constituency', but sounded a warning that this was the 'thin end of a wedge', since one fine morning the British would wake up to 'find that English members are in a minority in the Imperial Parliament and that we are legislated for by our own former dependencies'.[59] *St Stephen's Review* was thankful that at least Finsbury had not returned a 'Bengali Baboo' but, all the same, they thought that Central Finsbury 'should be ashamed of itself at having publicly confessed that there was not in the whole of the division an Englishman, a Scotchman, a Welshman or an Irishman as worthy of their votes as the fire-worshipper from Bombay'.[60]

Not all the opinions were so negative or adverse. Some welcomed Naoroji as the 'informal representative of the millions of Her Majesty's subjects'.[61] On the other hand, the *Scottish Leader* was thankful that the electors of Finsbury were 'free from the stupid and illiberal prejudice of colour' and had elected an Asian to parliament.[62] But in all this most of the British people forgot first, the principle of equality behind the famous 1858 Queen's Proclamation, and second, the principle on which the 13 American colonies had fought – 'no taxation without representation'. India now had one lone voice in parliament.

Despite his advanced age of 67, Naoroji proved a hard-working and zealous MP. He involved himself in many constituency issues, supporting organizations like the Friendly and Temperance Societies, working men's clubs and trade unions and causes like municipal reform. He also involved himself in women's organizations such as the Women's Franchise League. As a party man, Naoroji supported the Liberal programme in parliament, attending all the debates and divisions. He voted for the Irish Home Rule Bill of 1893.[63]

Naoroji's hopes for India, however, were not realized. Although he was able to table a resolution in parliament calling for recognition of the principle of simultaneous examination for the Indian civil service, he came up against vested interests. The resolution was passed in the House of Commons in 1895, but the government of India refused to implement it on the ground that the provincial governments were opposed to it. As for Naoroji's crusade against Britain's financial draining of India, a Royal Commission on Finance was appointed in 1895 with Lord Welby as chairman and Sir William Wedderburn, W.S. Caine and Naoroji as members. Naoroji insisted on submitting evidence to the Commission.

Another important achievement in this period was the formation of the Indian Parliamentary Committee. Naoroji, Wedderburn and Caine saw the urgent need for an organization in parliament to act as a pressure group on behalf of India. Wedderburn was the first chairman of this group composed entirely of MPs interested in India, many of whom already belonged to the British Committee of the Indian National Congress. From a membership of about 20 in its early days, it grew into a group of 156. Its members were mostly Liberal MPs, but later on Labour members joined too. The group, which existed until 1915, became the 'Indian Opposition' in parliament.

In and out of parliament, Naoroji also agitated against the opium trade and the degrading status of the Indians in South Africa. In 1904, he persistently questioned the India Office about the high rate of suicides among the indentured labourers in the various colonies. However, the authorities only took notice of the abnormally high rate of suicide statistics when the practice was coming to an end.[64]

Naoroji remained in the House of Commons till 1895.

Though he had no difficulty in securing renomination for Central Finsbury in the 1895 general election, opinion had turned against the Liberals. They were defeated in a massive swing against Gladstone and Home Rule, and Naoroji in Central Finsbury could not stem the anti-Liberal tide.[65] Yet he did not regard this as the end of his parliamentary career. Bad health prevented him from contesting the 1900 election, but he stood at Lambeth North in 1906, though events similar to those in Central Finsbury forced him to contest the seat as an Independent Liberal. In a four-cornered fight (there was also an Independent Tory), Naoroji secured only 733 votes.[66] So ended his parliamentary career. But this was not the end of Asians as Liberal candidates. Manmath Mallik stood as a Liberal for St George's, Hanover Square, in 1906 and in Uxbridge in 1910. He was unsuccessful in both elections.[67]

As a representative of the 250 million Indians, what impact did Naoroji make at Westminster? In India the Congress Nationalists were understandably jubilant.[68] But in Britain *The Times* did not consider that Naoroji had made any 'distinct mark', attributing this to his 'lack of mental adaptation and narrowness of view'.[69] Dusé Mohamed Ali, the pioneering pan-Africanist, dismissed Naoroji's achievement as the first Asian MP as a mere 'feather in the political turban of India'. He concluded that Naoroji did not contribute 'anything of importance in the House' on Indian debates. In fact, according to Dusé Mohamed Ali, Lord Sinha (see p. 195, Chapter 9) did a good deal more for India during 'his month or so' in the House of Lords than Naoroji in the House of Commons.[70]

A harsh judgement indeed. But by the time Lord Sinha entered the House of Lords, the First World War had altered the nature of politics. Naoroji had won his seat in the heyday of Victorian imperialism and against *all* the odds. He paved the way, to some extent, for M.M. Bhownaggree who stood as a Tory at Bethnal Green in 1895. His presence, in parliament and the country, was a constant reminder to the British people of the unjust nature of British imperial rule in India. His success as the first Asian MP showed later generations what could be achieved with determination and clear vision.

Naoroji gave a new impetus to the Indian nationalist movement. It is a fitting tribute that he was three times elected President of the Indian National Congress. Naoroji was critical of British rule but he began as a 'constitutionalist' and 'moderate' nationalist, demanding reforms. His ultimate goal was 'self-government under British paramountcy'. But in the end he lost patience – and faith in the British claim of 'fairness' and 'honour'. Events like the partition of Bengal in 1905 convinced him of the lack of British justice. There is evidence that towards the end of his stay in England, Naoroji held more radical and socialist views.

In 1901 he joined the National Democratic League. The League's radical programme included universal adult suffrage, the paying of MPs and state funding of election expenses. Naoroji also contributed to the fund set up for the maintenance of the Labour leader, Keir Hardie, in parliament. In an undated note, he advocated that 'society is bound in its own interest to take such care of the individual as would render him a healthy and useful member.'[71] He began to see the salvation of the Indian people to lie in the 'hands of the working classes' of Europe and implored them to 'compel their governments to fulfil the promises that have been made to India'.[72] He attended the International Socialist Congress in Amsterdam in 1904.

In India, too, Naoroji introduced a new note. He firmly and clearly advocated self-government as the only remedy to end the plundering of India's resources by a foreign power. At the 1906 session of the Congress, he was the first to use the Indian word *swaraj*, a word that left no doubt in the minds of Indians, of whatever level of education, as to his meaning.[73] He was demanding 'self-government' – as a right.

Naoroji finally left England in 1907 and lived in retirement at Versova, near Bombay. But he still took a lively interest in Indian politics. In 1914, believing Britain to be engaged in a war to protect weak powers, he emerged from his retirement to urge his countrymen to join hands with Britain and fight in the common cause for liberty – an ironic view, which contrasts strongly with that of latter-day nationalists. He died on 30 June 1917 at the age of 92.

Mancherjee M. Bhownaggree

The 1895 swing to the Conservatives unseated Dadabhai Naoroji at Finsbury, but it brought another Asian into parliament. This was Mancherjee Bhownaggree, who in that year won Bethnal Green Northeast for the Conservative Party. Bhownaggree was a man of different political loyalties from Naoroji, and his success as a Tory candidate was looked upon with 'serious apprehension'[74] in Congress circles in India.

The son of a rich Parsi merchant of Bombay, Mancherjee Merwanjee Bhownaggree was born on 15 August 1851. After Elphinstone College and Bombay University, Bhownaggree began his career in Bombay as a sub-editor on a daily paper, the *Statesman*. When his father died, in 1872, he succeeded him to the Bombay agency for the Kathiawar State of Bhavnagar. In 1881, at the age of 30, he came to London to study law at Lincoln's Inn and was called to the bar in 1885. In 1886, the Maharajah of Bhavnagar appointed him Judicial Counsellor. He distinguished himself by introducing administrative reforms – mainly on British lines – in the law courts and the police. For this he attracted violent criticism in the local language press. He sued the paper for libel and won.

Although his background differed from Naoroji's, Bhownaggree also took a deep interest in education and women's rights. In 1885, the Royal Society of Arts awarded him a silver medal for a paper on women's education. He served as a secretary to the Rukhmibai Committee, which upheld the rights of Indian women. Bhownaggree, too, was a writer; but his interests were very different from Naoroji's. He wrote a thesis on *The Constitution of the East India Company* and translated into Gujerati Queen Victoria's *Leaves from the Journal of Our Life in the Highlands*. Bhownaggree was made Companion of the Order of the Indian Empire (CIE) in 1886 and Knight Commander of the Order of the Indian Empire (KCIE) in 1897.[75]

In 1891 Bhownaggree settled permanently in England and soon established himself 'as one of the most prominent and influential' of Indian residents,[76] a position he held for over 40 years. In 1895 he contested Bethnal Green Northeast for the Conservatives. His election victory was a doubly 'remarkable' achievement, as Bethnal Green was not only a constituency with a 'uniformly Radical' tradition, but Bhownaggree was a rich Asian.[77] Even more remarkable was his adoption, within four years of his arrival in England, as a Tory candidate – especially in the light of the views of leading Tories. As we have seen, influential Conservatives like Lord Salisbury and Sir Lepel Griffin believed that candidates of alien race and religion were not a good idea. As a Parsi, Bhownaggree also fell into the same category as Naoroji – an 'alien to the people of India'. So what had led to this turnaround? Why had the Tories put up Bhownaggree to contest Bethnal Green?[78]

The answer lies partly in Tory unease at the growth of the Congress lobby, not only in India but in England too, among Indians and the few radical MPs – the 'Indian Opposition'. Lord Hamilton, Secretary of State for India, writing to Lord Elgin, the Viceroy, in April 1897 voiced this growing concern when he wrote:

I observe that in the debate on the Budget [in India] one of the Native Legislative Members spoke of our government as an alien government. I think that this is the first time that the obnoxious expression has been used at any official gathering. The speech seemed to me to have been a carefully prepared one, and which, not improbably, was written out or drawn up in England.[79]

Bhownaggree was therefore put up by the Tories as a 'counterpoise' to Naoroji the Congress spokesman.[80] Their choice of Bhownaggree was significant: he was a man dear to the Conservative ideal with 'nothing quixotic or crusading' in his temperament.[81] Bhownaggree represented a different Indian voice and was a convenient weapon for the Tories against the Congress and the 'Indian Opposition' in parliament.

Bhownaggree deeply admired the work the British were doing in India, for he believed this work to be in the 'interest of India' – the India as represented by the 'powerful Rajah and contented sepoy, . . . the landholder, the shroff, the merchant and the trader'. When he spoke out, it was to denounce the 'agitators' who tried to 'sow discontent with the British rule'. He dismissed their views as the 'exuberant sentimentality of Youth'.[82] Bhownaggree was against policies like those advocated by Congress, which would bring changes for which India was not 'ripe'.[83] According to him, this was demonstrated daily by the reckless conduct of such Oriental states as Egypt, Turkey and China. He believed that Conservative policy offered the 'best promise of securing the union of India with Great Britain, and the best practical result of that union'. And so he gave the Conservative Party all his support.[84]

Is it any wonder, then, that the Tories were eager to make this 'sound Imperialist'[85] the voice of India? The Conservatives lauded Bhownaggree as a 'mediator', who with his background and education was 'peculiarly suited' to represent India. They felt confident that his views would be successful in the House of Commons as he did not associate himself with those who wished 'to destroy and revolutionize the organic institutions of this country'.[86] Bhownaggree, in short, was an ardent upholder of British rule in India.

Since it suited the party, Bhownaggree received the support of the entire Tory machine – the senior Tory establishment, the Tory ladies and the Tory press all swung behind him.[87] This meant that, unlike Naoroji, Bhownaggree was spared long and lonely battles with the party association; he was spared the indignity of rival candidates and splits at the local level. On the contrary, he was promoted as a politician of 'wide experience', a lawyer and a 'true British citizen'.[88] Bhownaggree had a certain obvious appeal. He was 'an able speaker', had a 'ready wit', and 'in repartee on a platform he always held his own'.[89] His wealth too – he had a generous pension from Bhavnagar – was an asset and his campaigners used it to Bhownaggree's advantage, pointing out that he would be able to give a 'helping hand' to the 'local charities'.[90] Not only did the Tory ladies help to counter criticism of his 'foreignness',[91] but Bhownaggree himself played down his Indian connection, assuring the voters that he would not 'advocate any claims for India, but would take note of matters as they arise'.[92]

And so Bhownaggree was voted in by a working-class electorate, in preference to their long-sitting MP.[93]

Bhownaggree proved to be a popular and a hard-working constituency MP. He tried to secure the status of metropolitan borough for Bethnal Green; he generously supported local charities – even after he had stopped representing Bethnal Green in parliament. In the words of the *Bethnal Green News*, Bhownaggree was 'popular wherever he went, and his short, stout figure and smiling countenance were prominent in any gathering' in the borough.[94]

His popularity in the constituency, together with his staunch support for all official Tory policies, won him readoption as the Tory candidate in the 1900 election. He won the seat easily and increased his majority, securing 53.4 per cent of the vote to his opponent's 46.6 per cent.[95]

Not only were his views on India strongly Conservative, but he helped Lord George Hamilton, Secretary of State for India, to counter the criticisms of Wedderburn and the 'Indian Opposition' in Parliament.[96] In Congress circles, Bhownaggree's attitude was derided as 'Anglo-Indianism run mad', and he earned the nicknames of 'Bow-and-Agree' and 'Bow-the-Knee'.[97]

However, he did on occasion fight a 'hard-hitting battle' for India.[98] He spoke out forcefully against the disabilities and indignities that Indians suffered in South Africa and other parts of the Empire. Together with Dadabhai Naoroji, he questioned the India Office about the high rate of suicides among indentured Indian labourers in the West Indies and South Africa.[99] After the annexation of the Transvaal, when restrictive laws were passed against Indian entry into the Transvaal, Bhownaggree wrote the first 'detailed statement' advocating the case for Indians in the Transvaal.[100]

Bhownaggree stood again at Bethnal Green in the 1905 General Election. But by this time the Conservatives had lost popularity. Bhownaggree, too, faced many personal attacks which damaged his reputation. For instance, the *Morning Leader* attacked him for supporting Curzon's divisive 1905 partition of Bengal – a policy which was bitterly opposed in India. The *Morning Leader* hinted that it was his personal financial interests that caused Bhownaggree to support such an unpopular policy. His support of local charities was also attacked: the paper accused him of buying votes. Moreover, it was implied that the money for this came from India in the form of his pension at the expense of the 'famine-stricken' people of India.[101] Bhownaggree sued the paper and won. But it did not save him: in 1905 he lost to his Liberal opponent, polling only 34 per cent of the vote.[102]

This defeat ended his parliamentary career. But his interest in politics continued and he remained a well-known public figure. Bhownaggree was greatly respected by the India Office establishment for his Conservative views.

In 1916 Bhownaggree again showed his loyalty to the British Raj. Concerned by the defamatory propaganda put out by the Germans about the nature of British rule in India, the War Publications Department in London and the India Office decided to produce a short popular pamphlet 'cracking up'[103] British rule in India. To make it appear more effective, it was decided to get an Indian to write it.[104] Various personalities were suggested but in the end the department selected Bhownaggree[105] as the most 'suitable' person in London, whose word would carry 'weight'.[106] The factual material was provided by the various departments at the India Office and suggestions were made by them as to the format of the pamphlet. The aim, as the India Office saw it, was to project Indian confidence in British rule and emphasize its advantages for India and the Indian 'wish for its continuance'.[107] Bhownaggree excelled himself, producing a 51-page brochure in which he concluded that Indians were 'proud of being British citizens' and that it was 'by right and title of that citizenship' that they could 'revive the ancient glory of their motherland, taking their proper place in the community of Nations side by side with the other children of the Empire'.[108]

The Indian expert at the Foreign Office was very pleased with the result: the Office planned to translate the pamphlet into Urdu and Gurmukhi (the language spoken by the Sikhs, many of whom were in the British Army), for distribution in India.[109] Bhownaggree himself suggested that the pamphlet should be distributed among the Indian soldiers fighting on the Western Front and sent to India for use in schools and among the soldiers in the Native States.[110] The government of India were less enthusiastic: they took 500 copies but dismissed the suggestion that it should be translated and distributed widely in India. They concluded that 'no advantage would be gained' by distribution as 'very little German literary propaganda reaches India, and there appears to be no necessity to take any measures to counteract its influence.' The government did not think that it would be effective 'as a corrective of the Home Rule agitation', which was what concerned them most.[111]

Mancherjee Bhownaggree was influential in his own community. He served as Chairman of the Parsi Association of Europe and in 1927 the Association presented him with a portrait in oils in recognition of his services. He was also active in many other societies, such as the Indian Social Club, the Metropolitan Gardens' Association and the Northbrook Society. It was through the chairmanship of the Northbrook Society that he 'came in helpful contact with the Indian student element' in England,[112] no doubt steering them away from 'undesirable influences'. He donated the Bhownaggree corridor in the eastern wing of the Imperial Institute (later to be the Bhownaggree Gallery at the Commonwealth Institute). Bhownaggree died on 14 November 1933, at the age of 82,[113] Asian links with the Conservative Party have continued to this day.

Syed Ameer Ali

Ameer Ali's brand of nationalism was channelled into safeguarding the interests of his co-religionists, the Muslims of

India, from being 'crushed out of semblance of nationality' by Hindu domination.[114] Syed Ameer Ali was in many respects a conservative, and Islam and the British Empire were the focus of his loyalty. He regarded self-government for India as a 'dream' of the future, believing British rule in India to be a 'vital necessity' for 'many years to come'.[115] In his view, this arose from the fact that, left to themselves, the different races and religious groups of India would 'relapse into anarchy' – a view propounded by the British. British rule also seemed to be in the interest of the Muslims.[116]

Born on 6 April 1849 in Cuttock, Orissa, in eastern India, Ameer Ali came from a distinguished but poor family.[117] He graduated from Hoogli College in 1867 and a year later was the first Muslim to get his MA from Calcutta University. He came to England to study law in January 1869, with a state scholarship, and was called to the Bar at the Inner Temple in 1873. He then returned to India to follow a career in law. He lectured on Islamic law at the Presidency College and, in 1884–5, held the Tagore Law Professorship at Calcutta University. As a lawyer, he served as stipendiary magistrate; in 1879 he was appointed chief Presidency magistrate – an appointment not usually conferred on Indians. In 1890 he was made Judge of the High Court of Calcutta, being the first Muslim to reach this high position, which he held till he retired in 1904. He was then an obvious nominee for political appointments in Bengal. He became a member of the Legislative Council in 1878 and of the Governor General's Council in 1883.[118]

When he retired in 1904, Ameer Ali settled permanently in Britain.[119] In 1909, he was appointed to the Privy Council and its Judicial Committee. He was the first Indian to become a Privy Councillor, and remained the only Indian on the Council until the appointment of Lord Sinha in 1919. Again it was Lord Sinha who followed him on the Judicial Committee in 1926. As a member of the Judicial Committee, Ameer Ali worked with energy: his intimate knowledge of Indian laws and customs contributed much to the final judgements on Indian cases.[120]

The political awakening of the Muslims in India was partly

due to the work of Ameer Ali. The Muslims were not only educationally and economically backward, but also lagged behind the Hindus in political awareness.[121] In 1877, convinced of the 'immense advantage and preponderance the Hindu organizations' gave to the Hindus, Ameer Ali, aged 28, set up the first Muslim political organization in India.[122] This was the National Muhammadan Association, later renamed the Central National Muhammadan Association. Ameer Ali, its secretary for 25 years, travelled all over India to educate and awaken Muslim political consciousness. Within a short time, 55 branches had been set up. Until 1906 the Association remained the political voice of the Muslims, expressing from a 'loyal but independent stand point' their needs and aspirations.[123]

In 1882, on behalf of the Association, Ameer Ali presented a memorial to the government drawing attention to the position of Muslims in Bengal and outlining their grievances and claims. What troubled the Muslims most was the lack of opportunity for them to enter government service; they felt the Muslims were 'jealously blocked by members of a different race'.[124] As a result of the memorial in 1885, Lord Dufferin issued a resolution recognizing these claims and suggesting such measures as special scholarships to help the Muslims.

During his early political career, Ameer Ali saw the welfare of the Muslims to be 'intimately connected with the well-being of the other races of India'.[125] In fact, the Central Muhammadan Association welcomed the Indian National Congress, and some Muslims attended its first session. But by 1886 both Syed Ahmad Khan and Ameer Ali had moved towards a separatist Muslim ideal. Ameer Ali's chief fear of the Congress was that 'tied to the juggernaut of the majority' the Muslim would 'in the end be crushed out of the semblance of nationality'.[126]

After he had retired and was living in England, Ameer Ali still maintained his interest in Muslim politics in India. He helped found the All-India Muslim League in 1906. His concern was that 'concerted action' was necessary to 'prevent further decline' of the Muslims and to 'promote their advancement'.[127] In May 1908, he took the initiative with S.H. Bilgrami and others to launch the London branch of the All-India Muslim League, and became its president. The London League worked side by side with the All-India Muslim League. Many Muslim students joined the London League, gaining their political training in it. From its earliest days it was realized that to be successful the League needed to mobilize public opinion in England, and the London League devoted much time to this.

During its formative years, the London League was not only the most effective branch of the All-India Muslim League, but in some respects its pacesetter. Ameer Ali – through articles in the journals and newspapers and through his correspondence with officialdom – was able to put forward the Muslim point of view and enlighten the British public and parliament about the aspirations of the Muslims in India.[128] The main thrust of his argument was that the Muslims, with their separate identity, needed their 'legitimate share in the political privileges . . . to be extended to the people of India – a share "commensurate" with their number and historical and political importance.'[129]

In Britain it was the London League that was the driving force behind the demand for separate electorates for the Muslims in the planned Morley-Minto reforms in India. Under these, the membership of Indians on the provincial executive councils was to be opened up. Writing to *The Times* in 1908, Ameer Ali reiterated that unless the Muslims were given a 'distinct and separate . . . representation', no reforms would do justice to Muslim aspirations.[130] His demands for separate representation were founded on the argument, presented in a memorial to the Secretary of State, that under the common representation system in force in India the 'Hindus largely predominate in all or almost all the electorates with the result that comparatively few Muslim members have been elected.' Therefore, for Muslim representation to be 'real and not illusory, substantial and not nominal', separate electorates were a necessity.[131]

It was a long and hard struggle in which Ameer Ali, the Aga Khan, the Spiritual Leader of the Ismaili Khojas, Sir Sultan Muhammad Shah and the London League kept up sustained pressure on the government.[132] They used every means to gain support and to convince parliament not only of the justice of the Muslim cause, but also of the importance of Muslim loyalty to the Raj – a very pertinent argument in the face of pan-Islamic movements. Ameer Ali worked hard to obtain the support of MPs; the murder of Sir William Curzon Wyllie, the Political ADC, by a Hindu student in London (p. 108 below), was used to demonstrate to the government the necessity of a loyal Muslim community.

The Government of India Act of 1909 was a victory for the All-India Muslim League. Although it did not satisfy all the Muslim demands, it went a long way to grant the principle of separate electorates.

Whatever the merits or otherwise of a Muslim separatist movement in the struggle for Indian self-government, Ameer Ali, with his energy, and the campaign he organized to win support inside and outside parliament, played an important role in the success of the All-India Muslim League during its formative years. However, he did not lack critics. The Viceroy and the Secretary of State considered him 'a windbag' and the Aga Khan 'an expert on *"cafés chantants"* '.[133]

Ameer Ali's interest in the Muslim community's welfare extended worldwide. He championed the Turkish cause and in 1911–12 set up the British Red Crescent Society, a Muslim version of the Red Cross.[134] Like Naoroji and Bhownaggree, he championed the cause of the Indians in South Africa, especially those in the Transvaal. He warned that the treatment of Indians there would have wide repercussions and eventually lead to disaffection in India itself.[135]

He was also a writer and an eminent authority on Islamic law and history.[136] According to *The Times*, 'his writings give him a permanent place in the English literature as an interpreter of Islamic Code, antiquity and history on the lines of progressive thought.'[137]

For many years Ameer Ali was chairman of the Committee of the Woking Mosque and he took an active part in campaigning for a mosque in central London. He was also a member of the

Reform Club, having been proposed by John Bright, of Anti-Corn Law League fame. Ameer Ali died in England at Pollingford Manor, his house in Sussex, on 3 August 1928. For *The Times*, he represented all that was best in the traditions of the 'east and west'.[138]

The revolutionary student movement in London

The older generation of Indian nationalists represented a class of Indians western in outlook and constitutional in approach. Their objective was to achieve reforms within the continuing framework of British rule in India. The new generation of Indians, students and intellectuals, did not stop at reforms. They wished to go further and rid India of foreign rule. They advocated 'complete non-co-operation with the foreigner in maintaining his domination over India'[139] and proclaimed the doctrine of 'India for the Indians'. To achieve their objective, they were prepared to use force. They took pride in being Indians and derived their inspiration from Indian history, religion and culture.

Certain national and international developments encouraged revolutionary agitation. The teachings of Hindu revivalists like Vivekananda aroused emotional patriotism.[140] Curzon's scornful attitude to nationalist politicians – he thought 'Congress was tottering to its fall' and it was his duty to 'assist it to a peaceful demise' – and his policies in India, and especially the partition of Bengal, lent credence to the revolutionaries' arguments. The victory of Japan – an Asian power – over Russia was seen by the younger generation of nationalists as heralding the start of the march of the East against western domination. Armed with the pistol and the techniques of Russian revolutionary organizations,[141] they used the press and their own literature to spread their ideas. The revolutionary movement originated in western India, with B.G. Tilak as its inspiration,[142] but it extended as far afield as the USA, Japan and Europe.[143]

In Europe the revolutionary movement was based on India House in London, formed by Shyamaji Krishnavarma, and in

Paris by S.R. Rana and Madame Cama.[144] There was constant
movement between Paris, London and India. In 1907, with the
support of Hyndman and the French socialist Jean Jaurès, Rana
and Madame Cama attended the Socialist Congress in Stuttgart
to speak on behalf of the 'dumb millions of Hindustan'. At the
end of her speech, Madame Cama unfurled the Indian national
flag bearing the words *'Bande Mataram'* meaning 'Hail
Motherland'.[145]

Shyamaji Krishnavarma, the founder of India House, born in
1857 in a poor Bania family at Mandvi, Cutch State, was a
Sanskrit and English scholar. Educated at Elphinstone and
Balliol College, Oxford, he was called to the Bar in 1884.[146] After
distinguished service in three Indian states, Krishnavarma
settled permanently in England in 1897; it was later suggested
that he had 'fled' India to escape arrest.[147]

Krishnavarma founded the Indian Home Rule Society on 18
February 1905 and issued the *Indian Sociologist*, a penny
monthly, as its voice. The first copy was published on 1 January
1905. The paper came out regularly till July 1914 and served as a
constant reminder to the British public 'that they can never
succeed in being a nation of freemen and lovers of freedom so
long as they continue to send members of the dominant classes
to exercise despotism in Britain's name upon the various
conquered races that constitute Britain's military power.'[148] An
ardent anti-imperialist, Krishnavarma strongly believed that
only through the use of force could Britain be driven out of
India – as it was not in Britain's self-interest to willingly give up
such a profitable empire. The motto of the *Indian Sociologist*
was: 'Resistance to Aggression is not simply justifiable but
imperative. Non-resistance hurts both altruism and egoism.'
The other motto was borrowed from Krishnavarma's mentor,
Herbert Spencer: 'Every man is free to do that which he wills,
provided he infringes not the equal freedom of any other man.'
The government of India banned the importation of the *Indian
Sociologist* into India in 1907; but copies were smuggled in.

Krishnavarma established a hostel for Indian students at 65
Cromwell Avenue, Highgate. Called India House, it was

officially opened on 1 July 1905 by H.M. Hyndman. At its opening Dadabhai Naoroji and Mrs Despard, who was prominent in the women's suffrage movement, were also present and a telegram of support was read out from Frank Hugh O'Donnell. Krishnavarma also set up various scholarships and fellowships for graduates to come to England to 'equip themselves . . . for the work of spreading . . . knowledge of freedom and unity' in India.[149] India House became a centre for meetings, discussions and the dissemination of revolutionary doctrines. Many idealistic and energetic students were drawn to the House – not only for cheap lodgings and Indian meals, but for what it preached.

Lord Minto's government kept a watchful eye on the activities of India House. Agitation by students in London coincided with the most militant phase of political unrest in India since the Great National Rising of 1857. In the wake of injustices like the Bengal partition, the revolutionary nationalists used a new weapon to attain *swaraj* – the boycott of British manufactures and the use of *swadeshi* ('of one's own country', 'home-made') goods. The student population in London numbered about 50: the most prominent among them were Vinayak Savarkar, V.V.S. Ayer, Barendra Nath Chattopadhaya, Gandurang Mahadev Bapat and Govind Amin. They kept in touch with Paris and from time to time their number was supplemented by the so-called agitators who escaped to London from India.[150]

The 'inflammatory' language of the *Indian Sociologist* and the activities of the India House group did not go unnoticed by the authorities. In 1907 'Mr Rees' suggested to the Secretary of State for India that Krishnavarma should be expelled as an 'undesirable alien' for inspiring the 'loyal subjects of Her Majesty' to rebel.[151] The government did not take any action against Krishnavarma this time, but it suited *The Times* to suggest that he had 'deemed it prudent' to decamp to Paris.[152] However, on 23 July 1909, the government moved against the *Indian Sociologist* and convicted its printer, Arthur Horsley, for publishing 'sedition'. When the anarchist Guy Aldred took over its printing, he was convicted and sentenced to a year's imprisonment. The paper was then printed in Paris. Even after Krishnavarma went to Paris, questions continued to be asked about him in parliament.[153] The British government was convinced that he was the leader of the 'most dangerous seditious movement'[154] whose ideas were responsible for creating anti-British sentiment amongst the young students. The crusade against him continued: in 1909 he was disbarred by the benchers of the Inner Temple, and Oxford University tried to abolish the Herbert Spencer lectureship he had endowed but found that this could not legally be done. Undaunted by all this, Krishnavarma continued to exhort the young to fight for freedom and the *Indian Sociologist* remained an inspiration for them.

At India House, Savarkar became the recognized leader. He had come to England in 1906 to study law on a fellowship offered by Krishnavarma. A middle-class Brahmin, Vinayak Damodar Savarkar was educated at Ferguson College, Poona, and Bombay University. He was a 'youth of great talent'[155] and had already attracted attention to himself by his political activities in India. As a student he had organized the burning of foreign cloth as a protest against the 1905 partition of Bengal. He was also associated with *Mitra Mela*, Friends' Union, a secret society known as the 'beehive of the revolutionaries in western India',[156] and with its successor the *Abhinav Bharat*, New India, founded in 1904. (*Abhinav Bharat* had branches in the USA and other countries.)

Savarkar drew his inspiration from Shivaji's example in India and Mazzini's in Italy. He had already written a translation of Mazzini's autobiography and he couched his revolutionary speeches in Mazzini's language. Long before he came to London, he was a militant nationalist. India House, where he became the guiding spirit, provided him with an outlet for his political views. He founded the Young India Party and inspired his fellow students with his political energy.

The grievances of the India House group were similar to those of other nationalists – they, too, complained about the poverty that British rule inflicted on India[157] – but their demands and their methods were different. They wanted complete freedom from the 'predatory foreign incubus', as Tilak labelled British rule. They organized annual Martyrs' Day celebrations to mark and remember the anniversary of the 1857 Great Indian National Rising.[158] The first such celebration in May 1905 took the form of a dinner for Krishnavarma where patriotic speeches were made.[159] From such small beginnings the annual celebrations had grown into important events; tributes were paid to the memory of the Indian martyrs – Emperor Bahdur Shah, Nana Sahib and Rani Lakshmibai, leaders whom the British labelled 'traitors and rebels'.[160]

The 51st commemorative anniversary of the National Rising lasted for four hours, and over 100 students, including some from Oxford, Cambridge and Edinburgh, attended. Special Martyrs' Day badges[161] were distributed. Hernam Singh, a student at Cirencester Agricultural College, refused to remove the badge on his return to college. He was expelled.[162]

Sunday meetings were held at India House where, in the words of the authorities, 'seditious' speeches were made and tactics for the liberation of the motherland discussed. For instance, at a meeting in June 1908, Dr Desai, a student at London University, gave a talk on how to make bombs; on 23 August Nitisen Dwarkadas suggested infiltrating the Indian Army to win the support of the troops for the freedom movement.[163] Chapters from Savarkar's book, *The War of Independence, 1857*, were read and discussed.

At public gatherings many resolutions were passed. The revolutionary students joined hands with the Young Turks, a nationalist movement in the Ottoman Empire, and showed their sympathy with Irish and Egyptian nationalists. Plans were made to form an Indo-Egyptian Nationalist Association to fight for independence. At a meeting at Caxton Hall to mark Guru Govind Singh Day, a leaflet entitled '*Bande Mataram, Khalsa*' was distributed to awaken the Sikhs – who formed the mainstay of the army in India – to their duty to help overthrow British rule.[164]

The India House group smuggled leaflets into India addressed to specific audiences, such as soldiers and merchants, to win them over to the cause of India's freedom.[165] Cyclostyled copies of a bomb manual obtained from a Russian, together with 20 pistols bought in Paris, were also dispatched to Savarkar's brother, Ganesh. Members of India House themselves took lessons in revolver shooting at a rifle range in Tottenham Court Road.[166]

Although the revolutionary movement was small, its ideology of complete independence and its activities were enough to worry the British authorities and the Indian government. Together with the revolutionary movement in India, it seemed to pose a serious challenge to the British Raj. The proliferation of what the government termed 'seditious leaflets' and the accounts in Indian newspapers of the activities of the India House 'activists' led the government of India to urge the Secretary of State to take action against these revolutionaries. The Viceroy considered it 'intolerable that enemies of British rule in India should any longer be permitted to use the headquarters of the Empire as the centre of a seditous and revolutionary campaign'. What concerned the Viceroy most was the 'evil' result that the 'India House propaganda' would produce on young 'impressionable minds': the students who had come to England to study. The credibility and safety of the Raj were at stake. The government of India was at pains to point out that

Incitement to rebellion and sedition, couched in the most violent language, which fail to do harm in a country where public opinion is accustomed to receive exaggerated political utterances at their true value, may be attended by very dangerous results in their efforts on Indians resident in England, and still more on ill-informed readers in India.[167]

The British government moved against the revolutionaries. Scotland Yard planted informers at India House to learn about the students' plans. Dossiers were compiled on them and their movements watched.[168] Attempts were made to link the radical students of India House and Shyamaji Krishnavarma with every instance of 'seditious' activities. Everything possible was done to ruin their academic careers. For instance, when the government of India learnt that the benchers of Gray's Inn were hesitant about calling Savarkar and Hernam Singh to the Bar, the Viceroy sent 'incriminating evidence' to show the connection between the 'seditious' activities of Ganesh in India and Savarkar in London.[169] The benchers finally decided not to call Savarkar to the Bar.

Madan Lal Dhingra

The student agitation in London reached a climax on the night of 1 July 1909 when Sir William Curzon Wyllie, the Political ADC, was assassinated by a little-known activist 'connected with India House', Madan Lal Dhingra. A Parsi doctor, Kaikhusro Lalcaca, who went to the aid of Wyllie, was also shot and killed.[170]

The assassination gave the authorities the chance to put an end to the 'sedition' emanating from India House. In a series of reports, the authorities tried to 'prove' that the murder had been 'planned by Savarkar in revenge' for the sentencing of his brother Ganesh in India and his own rejection by the benchers of the Bar, and that the 'particular victim' had been chosen 'to satisfy the private grudge of Krishnavarma.[171] Since Krishnavarma approved of the deed and considered Dhingra to be a 'martyr in the cause of Indian independence', his denial in *The Times* of 17 July 1909 that he was implicated was not enough to exonerate him.[172] Even Dhingra's prepared statement found in his pocket on his arrest[173] was attributed to Savarkar since 'the style suggested that it was probably Savarkar's and certainly not Dhingra's composition.'[174]

It was also suggested that on the night of the murder H.H. Koregaonkar had been sent to the Imperial Institute by 'Savarkar, Ayer and Rajan' to 'guide the whole thing', and that he had encouraged Dhingra when Wyllie had arrived.[175] But elsewhere the report contradicted itself: the presence of Koregaonkar was mentioned but the report concluded that he 'was not seen to hold any conversation with Dhingra' and his action afterwards was not such as to 'justify his being cognizant of Dhingra's intention to commit the crime'.[176]

It suited the authorities to incriminate those they believed to be the 'ringleaders' at India House, and so 'net' them in order to put an end to the challenge to the Raj. Dhingra was hanged in Pentonville prison on 17 August 1909. Seven months later, Savarkar was arrested at Victoria Station on his return from Paris and put on board a ship bound for India. When the ship docked at Marseilles, Savarkar escaped by jumping through the porthole of a lavatory. But the French police handed him back to the British and, despite the efforts of the Indian radicals based in Paris and the French socialists, who took the case to the Hague Tribunal, he was handed over to the British.[177] He was tried 'for abetment of murder' and transported for life on 10 December 1910.[178]

India House was closed down. Some of the remaining revolutionaries tried to keep up the activities of the group: on 10 May 1911 the Martyrs' Day celebrations in memory of 1857 were held; attempts were made to set up new societies.[179] But because of the increased repressiveness of the British government, the movement eventually dispersed, and died with the outbreak of the First World War. The agitation of Madame Cama, S.R. Rana and Krishnavarma in Paris came to an end within a few months of the outbreak of the war because the French government put an end to their activities. Krishnavarma went to Switzerland; Madame Cama tried to agitate among the Indian soldiers at Marseilles, but was ordered to leave Marseilles and sent to Bordeaux.

Dhingra's action was condemned by some sections of Indian opinion as a 'national disaster'.[180] However, radical Indian opinion regarded Dhingra as a martyr, and the July number of the *Indian Sociologist* reiterated that 'political assassination is not murder'. H.M. Hyndman, editor of *Justice*, pointed out, in a leading article on 'the Dhingra assassination and its lessons', that he had long warned that if Britain continued its policy of 'despotism and bleeding India', the result would be terrorism.

'That prediction has been fulfilled. Tyranny and torture in India have produced the same results as tyranny and torture in Russia.'[181] In Ireland, owing to Keir Hardie's influence, posters went up in praise of Dhingra's heroism in laying down his life for his country.[182]

But to many Dhingra's motive remained a puzzle. Both the authorities and his family believed that Dhingra had not acted on his own. His family was convinced that the 'outrage was the result of a conspiracy' planned by 'other heads' and that Dhingra had been used as a mere 'tool'.[183] They pointed to his 'eccentric' and withdrawn character,[184] and believed that because of this, he was 'discovered as an excellent tool for the evil purposes of Krishnavarma and his lieutenants'.[185]

Dhingra's family background, too, made his action seem incongruous. He came from a well-educated Punjabi family in Amritsar,[186] a family which was 'deeply loyal to the government' and sincerely believed that the British government's 'mission in India' had been 'in the interests of the people'.[187] The family had made good under the Raj and were prosperous and influential. The young man's association with India House had caused them concern. To 'save' him, they had written to Sir William Curzon Wyllie himself, an old family friend, to 'use his influence . . . to make him desist from such company'.[188]

In India, Dhingra had not been a political person; in London he was not a well-known 'agitator'. According to Scotland Yard's CID, there was no record of Dhingra having taken part in the discussions, or having made speeches at India House. On the other hand, he had certainly attended the Sunday gatherings and on two occasions had lived at India House.[189] He had also taken lessons in revolver shooting at the Tottenham Court Road rifle range.[190] Was Dhingra merely a 'tool' or had he done what he did out of political conviction?

After the assassination, two postcards, both of a political nature, were found at his lodgings. One was a reproduction of the famous scene of the 'Mutiny rebels' being blown out from the cannon; the other was that of Lord Curzon, with 'heathen dog' written across it.[191] In his famous statement, which the authorities insisted was the work of Savarkar, Dhingra pointed out that he had consulted no one but his own 'conscience', and gave the reason for his action as 'a humble protest against the inhuman transportations and hangings of Indian youth'. He regarded the 'slavery' of India as an insult; and India's cause as 'the cause of freedom'. He stated that 'a nation unwillingly held down by foreign bayonets is in a perpetual state of war', and that therefore 'the only lesson required in India is to learn how to die, and the only way to teach it is by dying alone'.[192]

Even more pertinent are his statements at the trial and his behaviour in court. At one point he was reported to have told the judge that he was glad 'to have the honour of dying for [his] country'. When asked if he had anything to say in his defence, he had explained that:

> If it is patriotic in an Englishman to fight against the Germans if they were to occupy this country, it is much more justifiable and patriotic in my case to fight against the English; I hold the English people responsible for the murder of the sons of my countrymen . . . and they are also responsible for taking away £100,000,000 every year from India to this country . . . In case this country is occupied by the Germans and an Englishman not bearing to see the Germans walking with the insolence of conquerors in the streets of London, goes and kills one or two of the Germans, then that Englishman is to be upheld as a patriot of his country, then certainly I am a patriot too, working for the emancipation of my motherland.[193]

This strongly suggests that Dhingra had not acted as a 'tool'. His family background, too, far from making his action a puzzle, not only explains it but also reinforces the reason for it. He was from a western-educated family, loyal to the Raj, a family which had asked Curzon Wyllie to lead Dhingra back to the 'right' path. Under the heady ideology of India House, all this would have appeared to Dhingra in a very different light. A family of collaborators had appealed to Wyllie, the embodiment of the power of the occupier. And so Dhingra had acted – in the name of freedom and patriotism.

The revolutionary student movement in London continued to worry the government. King Edward VII wanted Lord Minto, the Viceroy, to take 'serious steps' to stop these men coming to England as they learnt only 'sedition and treason, which they infuse into the minds of their countrymen both in England and in India'. The King blamed Keir Hardie for 'fomenting sedition against the British mode of government, both in India and in Britain'. He looked with apprehension on the revolutionary group in Paris and wanted the dissemination of their literature banned in India as he considered it 'must have a most injurious effect on the native mind'.[194] In India itself, the government responded with both repression and 'concessions'.[195] And although, after the First World War, Indian politics was dominated by the Gandhian philosophy of non-violence, the radical tradition remained influential.

6. Soldiers of the Empire in Two World Wars

In a telegram dated 11 May 1893, Queen Victoria informed Lord Landsowne, Viceroy of India: 'Anxious to retain Indian escort to George's wedding. Please make arrangements. Would have excellent effect, wedding not long delayed.'[1]

To produce an 'excellent effect' was seen to be one role of Indian soldiers serving the Empire. Not only did these soldiers look exotic with their colourful uniforms and turbans, but – since India formed the most populous and most prized of Imperial possessions – an Indian Army contingent in London, the Empire's capital, highlighted the power, pomp and grandeur of Britain in the eyes of the world. The presence of an 'Indian escort' was therefore a regular feature of all grand occasions like royal weddings, Queen Victoria's Golden Jubilee in 1885, the Diamond Jubilee in 1897 and the coronations of Edward VII in 1902, George V in 1911 and George VI in 1937.

But the Indian Army was not just a decorative emblem of the glory of Empire. It had a much more practical role: to maintain the internal defence of India and to keep peace on the North-West Frontier, and elsewhere in the Empire. Indians saw active service in China, Egypt, the Persian Gulf and in many of the wars of colonial conquest. In fact, the British Empire was built and maintained on 'Indian blood'.[2]

Yet, when it came to confronting a white enemy, the British did not send their Indian troops. This was a matter of policy – white prestige had to be guarded and maintained. During the Boer War of 1899–1902, Indian troops served only as 'bearer corps' with the Indian hospital personnel, and were never used in any fighting capacity. The Boer War was considered to be a 'white man's war'. A European war would be a testing ground of British faith in the Indian Army.

On the eve of the outbreak of the First World War in 1914, the Indian Army was small: its infantry and cavalry divisions consisted of about 155,000 men, of whom 15,000 were British officers.[3] This army was drawn mainly from the 'martial races'. It was commonly believed at the time that people who lived in the hot flat plains of India were flabby and unwarlike, while the ethnic groups from the cold and hilly areas possessed qualities which made them brave soldiers. Furthermore, only certain castes among these hill people were thought to possess soldierly qualities. Recruits for the Indian Army, therefore, came mainly from the Gurkhas, Jats, Dogras, Pathans, Rajputs, Garhwalis and Sikhs. These castes were led to believe that they were privileged to join the army and hence were superior to the other, allegedly non-martial, races of India. As a result they considered the army their special professional preserve and so enlisted with enthusiasm and served the British loyally.[4]

The regiments were organized along caste or ethnic lines and officered entirely by Europeans. The sepoy might distinguish himself – and many did – by training and long service, by heroism and soldierly prowess in battle, but he could only reach the rank of platoon commander. The status of officer was reserved for Europeans alone. Although the Indian sepoys often felt intense loyalty towards their British officers (there often developed a patronizing, 'Ma-Baap' (father figure) kind of relationship between a regiment and the British officers who commanded it), the lack of promotion prospects was resented by Indian troops and civilians. It was considered a blatant example of political hypocrisy that while the Indian soldiers were valued as good warriors they could not be trusted to make good captains.[5] In 1911 Edward VII at the Delhi Durbar decreed Indians eligible for the Victoria Cross. And it was only after the First World War that, in recognition of the services rendered by Indian soldiers, Indians were able to become commissioned officers.[6]

The Indian Army was a highly professional one, and,

although not equipped with modern weapons (its main weapon was the rifle) it was efficient. (Its artillery units had been disbanded after 1857.) Apart from the small Indian Army, Britain could also count on the Imperial Service Troops maintained by the larger princely states in India.[7]

When the First World War broke out in 1914, India rallied to the support of the King-Emperor, offering money, troops and services. It was expected that, true to their tradition of loyalty to the Raj, the princely states would declare for Britain and offer their personal services, troops and resources.[8] More surprisingly letters of support and service poured in from every corner of India, and even the nationalist leaders, like Surendranath Banerjea and Dadabhai Naoroji, made loyal speeches on the Empire's hour of need.

Naoroji urged his fellow citizens to support the 'British fight' against the Germans with their 'life and property' because Britain was engaged, not in a selfish cause of extending her domination over others, but in a 'solemn obligation' in support of 'peace and welfare of minor weak powers'.[9] The Aga Khan, on behalf of the Muslims, assured Britain that he regarded Germany as the 'most dangerous enemy' of the Muslim world and pledged that the Muslims of India would not 'break down the strong wall of their loyalty' to Britain.[10]

After sounding out the opinion of the student and resident Indian community in England, Gandhi offered their services to the government, expressing a desire to 'share the responsibilities of the membership of the Empire'. As a result the Indian Voluntary Aid Contingent was formed to aid the war effort in England.[11]

But amid all these enthusiastic pledges of loyalty, the question remained: would Indian troops be allowed 'the opportunity to prove [themselves] on the battlefields of the west'?[12] The sentiment was aptly summed up by the Lahore *Tribune*, which declared:

We are prepared to make these sacrifices and more at the proper time. And here we would make one suggestion. If any troops are to leave this country for active warfare in Europe, let Indians as well as British soldiers be sent without distinction of race and creed to serve side by side in defence of our united cause. If Indian troops are sent on these terms, there will be unbounded enthusiasm in India. Let there be no question of 'prestige' or the inadvisability of employing brown against white soldiers. Prestige must be based on conduct and on no other consideration.[13]

And so, as part of the British Empire, India was willingly drawn into a war in which she had no direct stake or connection. Her contribution in the First World War in terms of men, materials and money, was vast, especially when put against the state of her economy.

By the end of the war, in November 1918, India had sent 1,302,394 soldiers: these troops formed the largest Empire force after Britain.[14] India also contributed skilled personnel: 1,069 officers of the medical service, 360 officers of the Army Medical Corps, 1,200 nursing sisters, 2,142 assistant and subassistant surgeons served in the war. In addition, India sent 172,815 animals, 3,691,836 tons of supplies and substantial sums of money in the form of war bonds.[15]

By 1918 Indian troops had seen action in all the major theatres of war, in varying climates, terrain and conditions. They had fought in France and Belgium; at Gallipoli and Salonika; in Mesopotamia; in Palestine, Egypt, the Sudan, Aden and the Red Sea; in Somaliland, East Africa and the Cameroons; in Persia, Kurdistan and North China.[16] The Indian people suffered heavy casualties and the war graves in the battlefields of the First World War bear testimony to the Indians who fell.[17] Indian soldiers won renown and military awards for bravery, including 12 who won the Victoria Cross.[18]

Indians on the Western Front

Altogether 138,000 combatants, comprising two infantry divisions, two cavalry divisions and four field artillery brigades served on the Western Front.[19] The first of these divisions left India on 8 August 1914, arriving in Marseilles seven weeks later. The people of Marseilles greeted the Indians with great enthusiasm. Children presented them with flags while 'young girls showered flowers upon them, pinning roses in their tunics and turbans.'[20]

Having been equipped with new rifles, they were dispatched to the front, where the fighting had already reached a critical stage. The British Expeditionary Force in Belgium had almost been wiped out, and although the German advance had been halted at the Battle of the Marne, each side, in a desperate 'race to the sea', was trying to outflank the other, in order to capture and hold as much territory as possible.

The Indian infantry regiments were rushed into this assault. During their stay on the Western Front, the Indian soldiers took active part in the fighting at Ypres, Le Basse, Neuve Chapelle, Festubert and Loos. By the end of 1915, when Kitchener's new armies began to arrive on the Western Front, it was decided to withdraw the Indian infantry divisions from France for use against the Turks in the Middle East. The cavalry brigades, which had already fought as infantry (horses were not suited to trench warfare) remained on the Western Front, and took part in all the later actions, notably on the Somme in 1916, and at Cambrai in 1917.[21]

Trained for frontier warfare, the Indian soldiers had adapted themselves to long marches in heat and cold; to withstand hunger and thirst; and to be alert for ambushes. They had become expert at frontier skirmishes, too. But trench warfare on the Western Front was an entirely different kind of war. For 14 months, the infantry brigades fought in Flanders, standing knee-deep in the muddy trenches. They had to endure endlessly exploding shells, deadly machine-gun fire, and even mustard gas. They suffered heavy casualties. Many were badly frost-bitten, and many died of pneumonia.[22]

We get a unique glimpse of the thoughts and feelings of these Indian soldiers through their letters, many of which have survived thanks to the war censor who was constantly on the

look-out for 'seditious ideas'.[23] The Indian soldiers missed
the sun very much, and the cold and snow made it a trying time
for them. One soldier echoed the thoughts of many when he
wrote: 'May the dear God be merciful to me and release me from
the climate of this country. I have no complaints against
anything else but the climate . . . it is difficult to endure the
trials of winter.'[24] They also met with experiences which were
deeply offensive to their religious practices. Many were
outraged at the way dead bodies were left unburied on the
battlefield.[25]

As for the horrors of trench warfare, a Pathan soldier thought
that

> No-one who has ever seen the war, will forget it to his last
> day. The fighting is going on with great violence. When our
> army attacks 600 guns fire for 35 minutes on the enemy's
> trenches. The very earth shakes. Then our men advance.
> Just like a turnip is cut into pieces, so a man is blown to bits
> by the explosion of a shell. In some places our trenches are
> only 200 yards from the enemy's, in others, 100. Day and
> night there is a rain of shells. No account is taken of the
> dead. There are heaps of them in the trenches. All those
> who came with me have all ceased to exist . . . there is no
> knowing who will win. In taking a hundred yards of trench,
> it is like the destruction of the world.[26]

A Dogra soldier wrote:

> For several days in succession so much rain has fallen and
> such stormy winds have blown that I cannot describe how
> many men have fallen sick and died. All the men who have
> taken part in the war have become mingled with the mud.
> On both sides each man kills his enemy with rifle or gun,
> while the rain and the storm night and day do not cease, so
> that the trenches are filled, and the soldiers suffer much
> trouble from the mud. And all the while machine guns fire
> on them and many men are killed. The whole world is
> defiled with mud so that one cannot describe it. But what
> can one do? Such is the displeasure of the Permeshwar.[27]

Despite the hardships of trench warfare and the harsh weather, the Indians quickly adapted themselves to mechanical warfare,[28] bore their suffering stoically, and came out of the campaign 'creditably, some more than creditably'.[29] E.B. Howell considered that 'never since the days of Hannibal . . . has any body of mercenaries suffered so much and complained so little as some of the regiments of Indian infantry now in France'.[30]

European soldiers, both German and British, were impressed by the Indians' fighting qualities. A German soldier discovered to his cost:

> Today for the first time, we had to fight against the Indians, and the devil knows those brown rascals are not to be underrated. At first we spoke with contempt of the Indians. Today we learned to look at them in a different light . . . With fearful shouting . . . thousands of those brown forms rushed upon us as suddenly as if they were shot out of a fog, so that at first we were completely taken by surprise. At a hundred metres we opened a destructive fire which mowed down hundreds, but in spite of that the others advanced, springing forward like cats and surmounting obstacles with unexampled agility. In no time they were in our trenches, and truly these brown enemies were not to be despised. With butt ends and bayonets, swords and daggers we fought each other, and we had bitter hard work.[31]

An English soldier, referring to the Gurkhas and Garhwalis, declared that 'they are the chaps . . . they fight like tigers'.[32] General Sir James Willcocks who commanded the Indian army corps in France in 1914–15 commented:

> The truth is that the Indians have done well, beyond all expectations; they have stood a long test which indelibly stamps them as worthy of their sovereign's uniform. They have endured more than any easterners were ever called on to endure in Europe.[33]

Lord Birkenhead, unveiling a memorial to the Indians at Neuve Chapelle in 1927, also paid his tribute to the Indians. To

him, the Indians, 'like the Roman legionary' had remained
'faithful unto death', discharging a duty they had accepted.
'Their bodies were often broken . . . but their soul was never
conquered.'[34]

The Indians themselves came out of the experience of the
First World War with a heightened sense of their own soldierly
qualities. This was the first time they had fought in a white
men's war. Their exclusion had seemed to them a stigma of
racial inferiority. But now they had finally proved that they were
equal to any European soldier. For instance, a Hindu student in
England, writing to a friend in France, felt 'proud of the bravery
and courage' with which the Indian soldiers were fighting at the
front. According to him, 'the people in this country have now
realized that India is a part of the Empire, not only a part of the
Empire, but the right arm of the lady and great enthusiasm
prevails throughout.'[35] This feeling was not confined to civilians
or intellectuals. The soldiers at the front shared it too: 'What are
the Germans in the face of Indian troops? They do nothing but
run away in front of us . . . Judged impartially, the Germans are
not equals of the Indian troops.'[36] Many felt proud to be
involved in a white man's war and to have the chance of proving
their courage on an equal footing: 'On both sides are white
troops. It is a place of courage. Men will remember this war all
their lives, and say that so and so died in the German War.'[37]
Not to 'disgrace' the name of India, to add to the reputation of
the regiment or their village and to win individual renown
became incentives to courage.[38] After all, they were chosen to
discharge the trust placed in them as 'the first Indian soldiers of
the King-Emperor' to demonstrate to Europe that the 'sons of
India' had not lost any of their 'ancient martial instincts'.[39]

Coupled with this pride in making a name for India, there
were also, throughout the period of their stay in Europe,
genuine expressions of loyalty to the King-Emperor and to
Britain's cause. Many hopes and prayers for England's victory
were contained in their letters. Many felt that having 'eaten salt'
of the government, this was their chance to 'repay him with . . .
loyalty'.[40]

These sentiments persisted as long as Indian troops remained on the Western Front. However, as the war dragged on, casualties mounted, and the prospect of a return to India seemed remote, a feeling of despondency, despair and fatalism was expressed in many of the letters.[41] Men now began writing poetry, which worried the censor at Boulogne, who interpreted it as an 'ominous sign of mental disquietude'.[42] The feeling of despondency was heightened by trench warfare, the climate and the length of separation from their families. Many felt they were 'trapped' and that India was made to pay a heavier price than Britain for the war. The feeling grew as the wounded were sent back to the trenches after recovery. This became a sore point with many of the soldiers and requests were made – even a petition to the King – to spare the wounded another spell of fighting on the Western Front.[43] Unable to return to India unless crippled, some resorted to requesting friends and relations in India to send them Indian herbs and medicines to 'produce sickness . . . sores on the legs or on the neck or on the chest'.[44]

Indian soldiers were not alone in feeling despondent or in looking for a way out. European soldiers, too, experienced similar emotions and there were instances of malingering and desertions on both sides.[45]

The feeling that Indian troops were being sacrificed to spare British soldiers grew; many began to beg their families and friends in India not to enlist for service on the Western Front. Because of war censorship, an attempt was made to convey this message in code:

The brave English have evolved such a rule as is advantageous to them. The red pepper is little used, while the black pepper is used daily to the extent of at least a thousand maunds.[46]

Or:

Further no black pepper is obtainable in this country. It has all been used up. There is a large quantity of red pepper, but they are still living upon the black, day and night. Owing to the lack of black pepper we are having a hard time.[47]

Reasons were even given as to why Indian troops were preferred:

The black pepper which has come from India has all been used up, and to carry on with I will now send for more, otherwise there would be very little red pepper remaining, because the black is hard and there is plenty of it . . . and this water is not right without black pepper.[48]

The authorities noted this feeling among the sepoys, but typically dismissed it:

Of course in an ordinary campaign their vanity would have been flattered and their loyalty increased, but when they realized it is not the usual kind of frontier campaign, but a long-drawn-out process of exhaustion and attrition, they have evidently begun to calculate the pros and cons . . . and those whose morale or patriotism is not of very high order must consider sacrifice not good enough for them.[49]

Great loyalty to the Raj was demanded! No wonder the Indians implored friends and families not to enlist and rush to Europe. 'Do not send us any more rupees. We will manage with what we have,' was one comment. Another was even more explicit: 'Here is the scene of divine wrath. Do not mention the name of this country ever. We have to endure great hardship and suffering. Do not volunteer as one of the reinforcements . . . they are all lamenting their fate.'[50]

Military and political considerations had brought Indian soldiers to the Western Front. For the first time in their long experience of colonial oppression, they were not only fighting side by side with European soldiers on the battlefields of Europe, but were experiencing, many of them, the first encounter with their Imperial masters on their home ground. It was an encounter shorn of the trappings present at formal state occasions. The Indian sick and wounded were brought to the south coast of England where seven hospitals had been set up.[51] To treat them, personnel from the Indian Medical Service, both British and Indian, were brought over. Indian students and residents in England, who had offered their services to the Indian Voluntary Aid Contingent, were taken on as dressers and assistants in the various Indian hospitals.[52] Indians served in various capacities, both in England and in France: ward orderlies, ward sweepers, water carriers, washermen, tailors, writers, cooks, storekeepers, packers and clerks – all recruited in India, except for some cooks and ward orderlies engaged at the Strangers' Home for Asiatics in Limehouse. All these people created a miniature Indian village in the midst of the English countryside.

The presence of the Indians, and the interaction between Europe and India at this level, had important implications for the future of India's relations with Britain. For the British, the Indian presence raised other issues. Turkey's entry into the war as an ally of Germany caused anxiety about the reactions of Muslim India in the wider context of pan-Islamism. There was also the sensitive issue of nationalist sentiment. And, although both Muslim and nationalist India had made common cause with Britain in the war against Germany, there were sections of Indian opinion, notably the revolutionary movement, which caused anxiety and unease to the British.

The amount of seditious material intercepted by the censor at Boulogne proved to be negligible. Early in the war, an official-looking envelope containing three or four letters was seized. The envelope had been posted in British Columbia, in November 1914. The censor considered the message in the letters to be 'flagrantly seditious', as it exhorted 'breaking the English lock . . . and putting an end to the English . . .'[53] From then on, letters from North America received special attention from the censor. Copies of literature that was officially classified as 'seditious', like *Hamdard*, *Zamindar* and *Ghadr*, were also confiscated.[54]

Because of the 'sensitive' situation in India, one of the British government's main concerns was to secure maximum political mileage out of the presence of Indian troops in England. The

British authorities did not want to give the impression that wounded Indians were treated any differently from other soldiers. Moreover, they sought to emphasize the caring concern of the Raj towards the King-Emperor's Indian troops and so frustrate the 'propaganda' of the 'agitators'. After all, the Indian army was recruited mainly from the peasantry, on whose goodwill the stability of the Raj depended. But that other India, the educated element, 'the noisier classes', in the words of the censor,[55] needed to be 'bought off' and placated, since it had influence over the peasantry. And so for the first time the authorities took an interest in the Indians as 'people'; they could no longer be regarded as merely an 'invisible' mass of humanity, ever ready to serve the pleasure of the Raj.

Elaborate arrangements were made to accommodate religious and caste practices, especially with regard to dietary and other requirements. A special caste committee was formed to supervise hospital arrangements so that 'different classes could live in accordance with their individual customs and as enjoined by their different religions'. For instance, in the Royal Pavilion and Dome Hospital in Brighton, nine separate kitchens were fitted up to cater for different castes – vegetarians, meat-eating Hindus and Muslims who ate meat but abstained from pork. Special arrangements were made for the slaughtering and storing of meat in accordance with religious practices. Separate areas were set aside for the washing up of the utensils used by different castes. Drinking taps, washrooms, recreation rooms, wards – all were arranged according to ethnic group or caste. In short, the 'complicated Indian caste' system 'dominated' all considerations. Multilingual signs (in Hindi, Urdu and Gurmukhi) were used to facilitate the smooth running of the hospital on caste lines. Indian spices, dal (pulses), ghee (clarified butter), flour and Indian sweets were all obtained from abroad to keep the soldiers contented and restore them to health, and to enable those that could to return to the front.[56]

'Native' officers, too, received special attention. For their 'comfort and *"izzat"* ' ('honour') separate suites were set up, comprising private sitting-rooms, Indian-style bathrooms and lavatories. J.N. Macleod, in charge of the Brighton Hospital, requested a signed photograph of the King to be placed in these sitting-rooms as it would be 'an honour these NOs [native officers] would never forget'.[57]

Arrangements were made to enable the Indians to dispose of their dead according to their religious rites. The Muslim dead were taken for burial to the Islamic Mosque at Woking, while a burning ghat, high on the Downs near Patcham, was made available for the cremation of Hindus.[58] Tents were erected in the hospital grounds to serve as places of religious worship.

All other hospitals for Indian soldiers had similar facilities.[59] Each soldier leaving the Pavilion and Dome Hospital was presented with a booklet as a souvenir; it outlined the early history of the Royal Pavilion and its conversion and use as a hospital for Indian soldiers.[60] Special photographs were included which it was thought would 'enhance the value in India' – especially that of a visit by the King and Queen.[61]

An analysis of the censored mails and the souvenir history, taken together with the official correspondence,[62] reveals it to be nothing more than an elaborate propaganda exercise, in much the same vein as the war films shown all over India, and Bhownaggree's *The Verdict of India*.[63] The propaganda effect was achieved not only by what the souvenir history included, but also by what it left out. The photographs, which show the soldiers in their wards, relaxing in the grounds, meeting the King and Queen, and being decorated, all emphasize the grandeur and magnificence of the Pavilion and its grounds, and not only create a dazzling effect but show the value of the Indian soldiers in the eyes of the King-Emperor. To reinforce this idea, emphasis is placed throughout the souvenir history on the initiative of the King in making the Pavilion available as a hospital for the use of Indian soldiers:

At the suggestion of H.M. King George, the Royal Pavilion at Brighton is transformed into a great hospital where Indian soldiers are restored to health ... Thus through the ever watchful thought of two King-Emperors for their soldiers, two Royal Palaces are now being used as Hospitals for those who have been wounded in the Empire's great war in the cause of right, justice and freedom. One is filled with British officers, and the other with the loyal sons of India of every caste and creed.[64]

The fact that since 1837 the Royal Pavilion had ceased to be a royal residence is glossed over, and the role of the mayor (Alderman Otter) and corporation of Brighton in assisting Lord Kitchener by making the buildings available for use as a hospital is considerably played down.[65] The official explanation for this is indeed revealing:

As I wrote the pamphlet solely for its effect *in India* I tried to bring out that the Pavilion was a Royal Palace and that the initiation of all that was done came from the King. To bring the Corporation or Lord Kitchener more prominently into it . . . would confuse things in the eyes of India. It would also spoil the parallel I drew between King Edward's action at Osborne and that of the present King at the Pavilion. The fact of one palace being for British *officers* while the other is for Indian *sepoys* seemed a useful point . . . To give more details of the transfer of the Pavilion might emphasize the fact that the Pavilion is no longer a Royal Palace which would minimize the political impression we want to make in India.[66]

As we have seen, the authorities were also anxious to show that the religious practices of the Indians were sacrosanct and respected by the British. The *Short History* (of the Royal Pavilion) makes great play of this fact, pointing out that 'a visit to these Indian hospitals shows in miniature a great many of the broader facts of Indian life.'[67]

The Muslim soldiers were allowed to observe the fast during the month of Ramadan because 'the political importance of allowing Muhammadans in England to observe the fast overrides the military disadvantage' of postponing the return of a few sepoys to the trenches.[68] Since the overriding consideration was the 'political side of the Indian hospitals in England', the censor of Indian mail watched out for attempts by zealous Christian bodies to gain converts among the Indian wounded in England. He considered such zeal 'ill-timed'. Even the free distribution by the YMCA of envelopes bearing the inscription 'The Army Young Men's Christian Association of India' was described as 'just a little too much' and likely to produce 'lamentable results'.[69] Such headings were cut out as he feared the 'effect in India of what is printed', especially since an 'agitator could make quite a capital out of it'.[70]

Similarly, letters from English soldiers containing racist terms like 'niggers', when referring to the Indian soldiers, were censored.[71]

Visits to the Indian hospitals by royalty, the Secretary of State for India and Lord Kitchener were also given great prominence. The *Short History* dealt with these at great length, as did the press.[72] As the war dragged on, a newsletter called *Akbar i Jang* was printed and circulated in the hospitals. The paper aimed partly to supply the wounded with war news, especially glowing accounts of their regiments, to keep up their spirits,[73] but also to publicize extracts from letters, written by Indians, expressing loyalty to or praise of the hospital's management.[74]

The Indians were impressed by the government's 'bandobast' (arrangements) and by the magnificence of the Pavilion. They were equally gratified by the treatment accorded to them. Their letters home are full of references to their gratitude for the comfort and care of the hospitals. 'My feeding arrangements are perfect. Muhammadan cooks have been brought along with us from Bombay and they cook for the patients . . . Government has made separate kitchens and the meat is previously "Halaled" . . . No fear to his religious requirements,' observed one Muslim soldier.[75] Another thought that the kind of service given to them in hospital was such 'as no-one can get in his own home, not even a noble'.[76] Another, a Sikh, mentioned 'that there is a Sikh church in each hospital . . . and we are very happy in our hospital. Services are held just as in India. Government has

made excellent arrangements for the sick and wounded. There is
no trouble of any kind. We pass our days in joyful ease while
Government showers benefits upon us.'[77]

The censor made special note of all such sentiment. In one
note he commented:

> The excellence of the arrangements made for the comfort
> of the Indian wounded and the kindness of the King and
> Queen on the occasion of their visit to Brighton are all
> mentioned over and over again in terms of the warmest
> admiration. One Sikh goes as far as to apply to Brighton the
> famous Persian couplet inscribed on the walls of the Diwan
> Khas at Delhi, 'If there be paradise on earth, it is this.'[78]

However, although the British took great care to appear
'caring' and especially tolerant of Indian religious practices – all
of which had the desired effect – the Indians were not
completely taken in. Many critical sentiments about the food in
hospitals,[79] as well as other matters, are also expressed in the
letters.

The presence of Indian soldiers in England gave the British a
chance to impress them with Britain's power and might. From
December 1914 onwards, the India Office arranged for small
parties of Indians, about 24 at a time, either all Muslims or all
Hindus, to be taken by car to see the sights of London. A British
officer and someone from Thomas Cook and Sons acted as
guides. The sights included St Paul's Cathedral, the Tower of
London, the Houses of Parliament, Buckingham Palace, Queen
Victoria's statue, the Natural History Museum, Hyde Park, the
Albert Memorial and the Zoo. The sightseers were allowed an
hour's shopping at Selfridges and a ride on London's underground.[80]

The sightseeing list could have been part of any tourist's
itinerary, but it was carefully considered to produce a 'good
effect . . . politically on India', since

> In sympathetic hands the men expand wonderfully, and
> one is able, while giving them a pleasant day, so to direct

their attention and with it their minds that they obtain an impression of England's greatness, wealth and power, which, I feel sure, will not only be lasting, so far as they individually are concerned, but will also through them, react on other Indians of their class, with whom they may come into contact and with whom they may correspond.[81]

To achieve 'good will' all favourable reports connected with the treatment of Indian wounded were widely circulated in India.[82]

Publicity drives apart, the officials were willing to compromise, to some extent, over other issues normally held to be 'sacrosanct' within the ethos of the Empire.[83] This was because they did not wish to appear to be treating the Indian wounded in any way different from their own English soldiers. The admission of English female nurses and visitors to Indian hospitals was one such compromise. After an English nurse in Lady Hardinge Hospital had herself photographed with an Indian V.C. Sir Beauchamp Duff, Commander in Chief, wired from India: 'No nurses for Indians'. Such 'red tape-ism' was deplored by an eminent Bombay Indian, Sir Shapurji Broacha, whose 'good opinion' was valued.[84] So English nurses were allowed, but only in a supervisory capacity. The same preoccupation was echoed in connection with visits of Englishwomen to Indian hospitals. Sir Alfred Keogh at the War Office was opposed to allowing Englishwomen into Indian hospitals on the grounds that it was not part of Indian culture and so the men would 'not understand it'.[85] However, since well-meaning Englishwomen frequently visited the English wounded, it was felt that the Indians might feel slighted and undervalued and would 'soon get to realize the differential treatment' and 'feel that while they have shared the same dangers and hardships as the British soldiers, they are looked upon as suspicious and even dangerous'.[86] Besides, it would have been difficult to justify this exclusion if questions were asked in parliament and the press. Therefore, despite the protective paternalism of the ruling class towards their own women and the Imperial policy of English memsahibs maintaining a haughty distance from the 'natives', in this instance the Indians were allowed the 'privilege' of visits by Englishwomen.

The British had taken great pains not only to appear to be treating Indian soldiers on an equal footing with British soldiers, but also to be seen to be respectful of Indian caste and religious practices. This was in their eyes not only an act of statesmanship befitting an Imperial power, but, more important, one that helped their image in India. However, there was a limit to how far British prestige could be compromised. The sepoys might fight bravely and loyally for Britain, but they could not be allowed 'to conceive a wrong idea of the *"izzat"* of English-women'.[87] To this end, official opinion was not only over-protective about any sexual liaisons between British women and Indians – a theme prevalent throughout Imperial relations[88] – but the authorities were positively obsessed with guarding the reputation and honour of Englishwomen.

All references to 'English morality' were deleted from the Indians' letters by the censor of Indian mails; and sometimes letters were held back. Comments by the censor are revealing. For instance:

> No 81 is indicative of the crude ideas of Orientals about European women; they cannot understand the freedom with which the sexes mingle. Hence when they are allowed unlimited freedom from the hospital etc. to go where they please, they are liable to gain many wrong ideas and impressions which might be difficult afterwards to eliminate.[89]

When a letter referred to the 'easy sexual relations' of the French, the paragraph was cut out on the ground that it was 'calculated to convey a wrong impression and discredit our Allies'.[90]

When the wounded and other Indian personnel first arrived in England, they seem to have been at liberty to move about as they chose. Reports of their enthusiastic welcome in England were published in Indian newspapers, no doubt with maximum benefit to the Raj. For instance, a Parsi serving in the hospital wrote to a woman friend in Bombay that English people

Are greatly impressed by the Indian troops and by the men of India. They show extraordinary affection and even the women and children express unbounded delight. When we first reached England, the people came to the steamer and joyfully mingled with us – When we used to go for walks at Avonmouth the people used to rush out of their houses to 'salaam' to us – we played with the children and kissed them. Many women young and old tried to shake our hands. Whatever has been written in the Indian press in praise of our welcome is quite accurate – There is no difference made in our treatment here.[91]

Such reports of appreciation received special mention in the censor's report,[92] but feelings of unease at this 'joyful mingling' soon became apparent. For instance, when another Parsi, writing from Brighton, mentioned the fact that 'the children and ladies will not let us walk unmolested. They get hold of our hands and want to kiss us, and in other ways make much of us', an unsigned pencilled comment from the India Office was 'I hope only Children'.[93]

The worry here seems not only to be sexual liaisons between black and white and sexually transmitted diseases, but, more pertinently, if Indians were allowed to 'conceive a wrong idea' of Englishwomen's reputation, then it would 'be most detrimental to the prestige and spirit of European rule in India'.[94] The report on the Kitchener Indian Hospital in Brighton was the most revealing about the priorities uppermost in the minds of the British authorities. In this connection it is interesting to note that no British female nurses were allowed to work in the Kitchener Hospital, as 'women as nurses are out of place in an Indian unit'.[95] Furthermore, not a single woman was found on the premises in 'any capacity', and the wives of the doctors had 'a certain say in affairs but never went inside the buildings'.[96] Colonel Bruce Seton, in his report, spelled out that

It was evident from the very first, that drink and sex problem were factors which would have to be reckoned with. A large proportion of the followers, the sweepings of the Bombay city, were found to be habitual drunkards, and the ill-advised conduct of the women of the town, though partly innocent in intention, was bound to result in the gravest of scandals. To deal with these problems it was necessary to draw up absolutely inflexible rules governing the granting of permission of passes outside the precincts.[97]

Under these 'inflexible rules' all Indian personnel were confined to the hospital 'at all times'. However, convalescent Indian officers and the subassistant surgeons were allowed out with passes up to 'named hours' after dusk (8.30, according to J.H. Godbole, a Maratha Brahmin who was a subassistant surgeon at the hospital), while Indian soldiers, in groups of three, accompanied by a 'British officer' were occasionally allowed out for walks. Route marches under escort, for daily exercise, and drives in cars were introduced. To reinforce the system, outside walls were reinforced with barbed wire. Even then, as a further precaution against 'breaking out', a special military police guard was created. The authorities were satisfied with these measures and congratulated themselves that 'there were practically no more cases of breaking out'; of the few that did occur, six of the culprits were flogged, and one, a Parsi storekeeper, was tried by summary court martial and imprisoned in Lewes prison for six weeks.[98]

Godbole worked out the logistics of the system for allowing sepoys, subassistant surgeons and resident men permission to go out. He concluded that many had not left the building for months. He complained bitterly. But the board of inquiry appointed to look into the situation concluded that the hospital had everything the Indians could possibly desire, 'including hockey, football, phonographs and free cinemas, games of all kinds'. Godbole considered all this to be beside the point as it did not provide for 'the liberty of the individual, a right to go about'. To him this was 'ungratefulness' as the sepoys had left their country and come to Europe 'to die for the sake of the Kingdom . . . and yet our Indians are upright and go on their way without giving this matter weight . . . They commit no atrocities.'[99] In the end, unable to bear the 'very great ungratefulness', Godbole decided to do something as a protest against this: he tried to kill Colonel Seton. He was caught, court-martialled, and imprisoned for seven years.[100]

The Kitchener Hospital was not the only hospital to erect walls to keep the Indians within its grounds. A high wooden fence enclosed the Pavilion and Dome grounds and the local population considered it 'worth a penny to take a ride on the trams along the Steyne to get a glimpse of the Indians in the grounds'.[101] Similar precautionary measures were taken in other hospitals too.

Walls, barbed wire and sentries smacked more of prisoner-of-war camps than of hospitals for wounded soldiers.

Godbole was not the only one to complain about the restrictions imposed on the Indians in the hospitals. Many others, both civilians and soldiers, felt the same. A Hindu storekeeper at the convalescent home in New Milton was so disillusioned that he wrote:

> If you ask me the truth, I can say that I have never experienced such hardship in all my life. True, we are well fed, and are given plenty of clothing but the essential thing – freedom – is denied. Convicts in India are sent to Andaman Islands; but we have found our convict station here in England.[102]

Many other letters contain references to 'guards of British soldiers' round the hospital,[103] to the Indians being 'kept as prisoners' or being given 'no more liberty than prisoners'.[104] Some letters were more explicit about the reasons for such treatment. One writer thought it was because of 'the wickedness of this place. The women by force get hold of the wounded who get into trouble and are punished, but the women say nothing.'[105] Another complained that 'if anyone is seen talking to a woman young or old, he is severely punished.'[106]

Although the authorities dismissed many of these complaints as coming from the 'English-speaking storekeepers and writers who have given more trouble',[107] some Englishmen felt that the restrictions were unnecessary. Lieutenant Charles Stiebel of the Indian medical service at the Kitchener Hospital worked towards the relaxation of the restrictions at the hospital; while a writer 'who knows and has a very tender place in his heart for the fighting races of India' wrote to *The Indiaman*:

> The precaution taken to isolate the Indians from the indiscreet attention of silly and ignorant women are all that British prestige could require. It must not be forgotten that soldiers of a victorious army have seldom been chaperoned by sentries set over them.[108]

The censor wrote that 'a certain amount of restriction is of course necessary, but for the men to feel that they are being kept like prisoners is dangerous', and urged steps to be taken to allay this feeling.[109]

In the end, however, Colonel Gentle, the Chief Constable of Brighton, was able to assure the Secretary of State that 'nothing could have been better than the conduct and behaviour of Indian sepoys in Brighton. They have behaved as gentlemen'.[110]

For the majority of the Indian troops and civilian personnel, this was their first encounter with Europe. How did they react to European society? What impressions did they form of the French and English people 'at home'?

From a military point of view, many soldiers, though they deplored the use of gas by the Germans,[111] were much impressed by German military power and technological superiority.[112] One went so far as to suggest that all the 'new inventions' came from Germany, while the English merely 'copy it when they see it'.[113] E.B. Howell, the censor for Indian mail, was not very pleased to see such a favourable impression of German 'power and might'. He had hoped that the 'sooner the war is finished the greater will be the prestige of England'.[114]

But it was France and the French that captured the imagination of many. To one there was 'no country like the country of France',[115] while another felt that whoever had seen France had no need to see England.[116] Not only were many of the soldiers and civilians billeted in French homes, but they saw more of the French people than of the English as there were no petty restrictions like the ones in English hospitals. They got on well with the French and considered them to be 'honourable and kind . . . gentlemen to the backbone'.[117] They were well received and thought highly of by the French people. Muhammad Khan of the 9th Cavalry Brigade reported that 'when once a Hindustani regiment rests in a village the people sing their praises on all sides'.[118] Another felt that they received much more respect in France than they did in England.[119] Some Indians, especially civilians, formed lasting attachments with Frenchwomen, and returned to India with French wives.[120] Indian feelings towards France were summed up by a Muslim who concluded, 'We have been nearly a year and a half in France . . . after we are gone we shall mostly remember France very kindly.'[121]

The Indians' impressions of the English, on the other hand, were not so positive. As we have seen, the British were in many respects able to create the desired effect in the minds of the Indian soldiers. The Indians' treatment in hospitals, the welcome and the kindness of the ordinary English people were appreciated. But many were also shrewd enough to realize the reason behind the respect accorded them. As one Hindu summed it up:

> The public at large . . . are very sympathetic towards India and Indian people as a whole on account of the war and the services – the invaluable services – India is rendering England at present. But I do not know what they will do for India after the war.[122]

Another Hindu considered that the 'English at home' were 'very good people', but it was 'the ruling class that thinks so much of itself and stands in the way of any Indian reforms'.[123]

The progress, technological advance and way of life of the people that the Indians saw in Britain and France not only aroused in them a great admiration but also led them, to some extent, to begin to question traditional Indian values. Many described at great length in their letters mechanical farming methods in France. One thought that the Indians would do well to learn from French farmers and peasants.[124] French women's independence and hard work was noted by many. The way they coped with the work in the absence of their menfolk drew many comments.[125] The honesty of the shopkeepers and especially the absence of bargaining in Europe struck many as admirable.[126]

The standard of living, prosperity and hard work of the people were looked on favourably by many Indians. Many felt that the key to progress lay in education. Over and over again the soldiers noted that in Europe boys and girls went to school from a very early age.[127] Many even resolved to have their own children educated.[128] One was impressed that in England even the working classes read the papers.[129] In fact, many of the soldiers themselves tried to learn to read and write. Many 'primers' and spelling books came in the parcels sent from India.[130]

Indian poverty depressed many. A Hindu subassistant surgeon remarked sadly that Indians only copied the faults of the British. He did not think Indians would advance themselves 'merely by wearing trousers and hats and smoking cigarettes and drinking wine'. It was only by initiative, hard work and education that Indians could make progress, he thought.[131] Others felt that looking to the achievements of their ancestors was not going to take them very far. A Brahmin thought that

> when the English call us uncivilized they are right; our philosophy, our religion, and our morality, what has it done for us? It has merely made us the slaves of others. When the spirit of man is destroyed it cannot be called civilization ... To listen to false doctrine and lazily remain content with the present is no civilization.[132]

A Pathan wrote that although he had not gained any personal advantage by coming to Europe, he had learnt much and had had his eyes opened. The depressed state of India perturbed him, as did some Indian customs. Commenting on an article he had read about Indians quarrelling over separate compartments in railways to segregate 'the higher castes from sweepers and other unclean castes', he wrote:

> I was utterly disgusted to think that Indians can be ashamed of travelling in the same compartment with their fellow countrymen! What progress can you expect in a people like this! God has made all creatures equal, and yet we find some people calling themselves Khans and using higher titles . . . In Europe, sweepers, chamars, bhatiyars, Nawabs, Rajas are all one and sympathize with each other . . . Here labour is not a disgrace, but a glory.[133]

The writer did not recognize the class barriers of European society, but had sensed the sentiment of equality and fraternity.

As the war dragged on, barriers amongst the Indians themselves were, to a certain extent, relaxed. Indians of different tribes and castes mixed together and lived 'like brothers'.[134]

Did the Indians, after their experiences in Europe, question the nature of British rule in India? There is a hint, in some letters, of the awakening of nationalism and a realization of the injustices inherent in the Imperial relationship. Phrases like 'does a man who is another's servant ever live in comfort?' and 'we are the slaves of the English' give some hint of national consciousness.[135] An interesting letter comes from a Hindu storekeeper at the Kitchener Hospital, written to Jacques Devel in France. The writer asks for information about the treatment by the French Republic of its 'Algerian subjects or fellow citizens' serving in the war in France. He asks some very pertinent questions:

> First, how are they kept? Whether they are allowed to go out to the town when off duty without any guard to look after them, which means a sort of generous trust placed in their characters and good conduct . . . Second, what pay they get under the French Republic. Is it what the French soldiers receive? or with some differences and why? What

uniform they are given? I think that in the matter of
uniform there will be some distinction – not of quality but
of distinction as to their nationality, which in my humble
opinion should not be when fighting under the same
French flag.[136]

Injustices like being treated differently and in a very much
inferior manner gave rise to great rancour. Narrating an
incident in which an Indian, accused by an English doctor of
being a 'malingerer', was beaten up by some English ward
orderlies till 'blood ran', the writer continued:

> After that a native officer of India brought the sepoy before
> the colonel commanding [and pointed out] that he had
> been thus unjustly beaten by the ward orderlies. The
> colonel replied, 'Subedar Sahib, I cannot say anything to a
> white man on account of a sepoy'. Now it is time to reflect,
> we took no oath [to serve in] Europe. We have crossed the
> seven seas and left our homes and our dear ones and our
> parents, and for the honour of such an unjust and false-
> promising King. We have sacrificed our lives. And now
> this is the honour that we get in this Council. No doubt
> before them we are regarded as inarticulate animals, but
> who can say that to oppress and dishonour us is good?[137]

A Sikh soldier, commenting on the superior attitude of the
British, had this to say:

> We came to know that the British had no respect for the
> Indians. They regarded us as their servants. The British
> soldiers used to get four times more than our salary. Their
> sepoy did not salute our subedar-major or any NCO.[138]

And a Rajput expressed the thought that 'if we Indians bring
back to India the flag of victory which we shall have helped to
win for our King George, we shall have proved our fitness and
will be entitled to self-government.'[139]

The First World War marked a turning point in the relations
between the Indian people and their British rulers. Indians saw
the brutality with which Europeans fought each other. This

destroyed the myth of Asian barbarity built up by the British. The Indians also proved, once and for all, that they could fight as well as any Europeans. The war released many aspirations and aroused many expectations.

The Second World War and Noor Inayat Khan

India made a vast contribution to the defeat of Fascism and Nazism in the Second World War. When the war began on 3 September 1939, Lord Linlithgrow, Viceroy, declared war on behalf of the government of India without even first consulting the Congress leaders in the government. To Britain's leaders, and especially to Churchill, India was a vast reservoir of manpower and troops; he was little concerned about the feelings of the Indian nationalist politicians in government or the aspirations of the Indian people. India's resources were put at the disposal of Britain and India's industries were turned into one great arsenal in the service of the war effort. As in the First World War, many Indian doctors and students in Britain were called up for service. Indians even served as secret agents in France.

By 1945, India had contributed 2,500,000 troops for service overseas; the Indian navy and air force, too, saw action in the war. At the start, Indian troops were not used against the Germans in Europe. The Second World War was a more global war, and as the Japanese threatened India's back door, the Indian Army was sent to fight them in Malaya and Burma. Indians also fought in the Middle East and in the desert campaign of North Africa.[140]

After the surrender of the Italian army in North Africa in May 1943, it was decided to use Indian troops, who had distinguished themselves in the mountainous terrain of North Africa, for the invasion of southern Italy. Three Indian divisions, the 4th, 8th and 10th, together with the Gurkha Lorried Infantry Brigade, formed part of the Allied army which brought about the fall of Rome on 4 June 1944 and the final surrender of the German armies in Italy on 2 May 1945.[141]

Noor Inayat Khan was a descendent of Tipu Sultan, the Tiger of Mysore.[142] Her father, Inayat Khan, born in July 1882, founded the Sufi religious order in Europe. In September 1910 Inayat Khan married Ora Ray Baker, an American, in New York. They then came to London, where in 1912 she converted to Islam. In 1913 the family went to Moscow, returning to London in the summer of 1914. Inayat Khan then set up the Sufi order in England.

Noor-un-Nisa Inayat Khan was born in Moscow on 1 January 1914; the other children, two boys (Vilayat and Hidayat) and another daughter (Khair-un-Nisa) were born in London. The family had a hard time in England: they were poor and their difficulties were increased by English prejudice against cross-cultural marriages.

In 1920 the family moved to France, where they at length established themselves in a house called Fazal Manzil in a quiet suburb of Paris near Mont Valerian. Inayat Khan established the international headquarters of the Sufi movement in Geneva; he travelled widely in Europe and the USA, visiting the various centres of the Order in the west. His house in Paris became the centre of Sufi teaching in France. In February 1927 he died in Delhi, aged 44, when Noor was only 13 years old. He was a learned man, having written many books, and his children grew up in a world of books, music and religion.

As a child, Noor Inayat Khan was shy and quiet. At school she was interested in music and literature. She took her school-leaving certificate in 1931 and went on to study music at the Ecole Normale de Musique in Paris. She remained there for the next six years. The famous pianist and composer Nadia Boulanger was one of her tutors, and Noor is remembered by her as a 'charming pupil'.[143] In 1932 Noor also enrolled at the Sorbonne for a course in the 'Psycho-Biology of the Child', gaining a degree in 1938. As a student of music, she had various compositions to her credit. She was also the joint author, with Baroness Van Tuyll (who did the illustrations), of *Twenty Jataka Tales*, published in 1939.[144] She contributed stories and articles to the children's page of the *Figaro* newspaper.

After the fall of France in June 1940 the family moved back to Britain. Both Noor Inayat Khan and her brother Vilayat wished to serve in the struggle against Hitler. In November 1940, Noor joined the Women's Auxiliary Air Force, enrolling as 'Nora Inayat Khan'. She was one of the first group of 40 young women in the WAAF to be trained as wireless operators.

In June 1941, with another young woman, Noor was posted to the RAF Bomber Command at Abingdon. She was recommended for intelligence work and, in May 1942, was commissioned for duties as a wireless operator in Wiltshire. Here she was chosen for a specialist course in signal and wireless operation. In fact, Noor was the first WAAF wireless telegraphist to take this specialized training course. She was interviewed at the War Office for an organization known as SOE: Special Operations Executive. This organization, whose largest section was the French section, recruited and trained secret agents who then infiltrated enemy-occupied countries to work with underground resistance movements.

Noor was recruited as a wireless operator for the SOE. The War Office considered her 'almost perfect' for this work; she was 'careful, tidy and painstaking by nature'.[145] She had fluent French and knew France well. At her interview at the War Office she was told the dangerous nature of the work involved and the high risk of capture and interrogation by the Gestapo. She was also made to realize that in the event of capture 'since she would not be in uniform, she would have no protection under the international laws of warfare – that she might not return.'[146]

Despite the dangers involved, Noor agreed to join the resistance movement as a secret agent and at her own request was posted to the Paris area. As Paris was the capital of occupied France, this was the most dangerous section of the French Resistance – and more so for her since, having lived in Paris, she ran the risk of recognition and betrayal. But Noor had wanted to help – in any way – towards the liberation of France. When she and her family had left for England after the fall of France, she had promised herself that she would return. She also had some idea of indirectly helping her other country, India. Although she had been brought up in the west, she took a deep interest in Indian affairs. The 'Quit India' Resolution of 1942, followed by the imprisonment of the Congress leaders, including both Gandhi and Nehru, had made a strong impression on her. She was a firm believer in Indian self-government and hoped that India's contribution to the war effort would help the Indian cause of freedom:

> I wish some Indians would win high military distinctions in this war. If one or two could do something in the Allied service which was very brave and which everybody admired it would help to make a bridge between the English people and the Indians.[147]

In February 1943 Noor was posted to the Air Ministry Directorate of Intelligence, seconded to FANY (Women's Transport Service First Aid Nursing Yeomanry), and sent for further training. Her training included the use of explosives, hand grenades and small arms. In addition she was given training in 'field security', involving lessons in avoiding detection and capture in enemy-occupied territory and in shaking off a pursuer. The training ended with a 'mock Gestapo interrogation'.

In the underground movement, teams worked in groups of three, consisting of an organizer, a wireless operator and a courier. Hitherto, women had been recruited only as couriers. Because of the nature of the work, wireless operators ran the greatest risk of detection and capture.

Noor Inayat Khan was to be the first woman wireless operator infiltrated into occupied France. She was given the code name 'Madeleine'. Equipped with a cover story (she was ostensibly working as a children's nanny), a false name (Jeanne-Marie Regnier), a false identity card, a ration book and a kit of pills, she was secretly flown into Paris on 16 June 1943. She was given four different types of pills: pills for the enemy that induced six hours of sleep; stimulants to keep her awake and working; pills to produce stomach disorders and finally one pill with which to end her life. So began her work as wireless operator, transmitting coded messages between London and the Paris Resistance.

Within a few weeks of her arrival in Paris, the Gestapo raided the Paris organization and mass arrests followed. Nevertheless, Noor continued with her mission. In July 1943, with her comrades, she fell into an SS ambush: they shot their way out. Noor was offered the chance of returning to Britain, but refused; she decided to stay at her post. Being the only wireless operator still in the Paris region, she did not wish to abandon her French comrades and leave them without any means of communication. She also hoped that by staying she would be able to rebuild the group. For the next three and a half months she carried on in the most dangerous circumstances, the only British officer in Paris.[148] She was finally arrested in October 1943 and was imprisoned at the Paris headquarters of the Gestapo in the Avenue Foch. During the next few weeks she faced constant interrogation, but refused to answer any questions. Twice she tried to escape, and refused to sign a declaration giving an undertaking that she would not try to do so again.

Finally, in November 1943, she was sent to Germany for 'safe custody'.[149] She was the first agent to be transferred to Germany. She was imprisoned in the main prison in Pforzheim, a small town on the borders of the Black Forest. The Germans considered her to be 'a particularly dangerous and uncooperative prisoner'.[150] She remained in prison, handcuffed in her cell, for ten months. On 12 September 1944, in the company of three other prisoners, she was taken to Dachau camp and executed.

Noor Inayat Khan was posthumously awarded the *Croix de Guerre* with Gold Star (1946), the George Cross (1949) and gained a mention in despatches for her excellent work.[151]

7. Radical Voices

Between the wars, Indian nationalism entered a new phase: increasingly, and with greater and greater clarity, nationalists saw their goal to be complete independence from British control. In India, the National Congress, inspired by Gandhi and Nehru, stepped up the struggle for freedom. In Britain, the cause of Indian freedom found two radical voices: Shapurji Saklatvala and Vengalil Krishnan Krishna Menon.

Shapurji Saklatvala

Saklatvala carried the struggle for Indian freedom into parliament, and became the third Asian to sit in the House of Commons. Like Dadabhai Naoroji and Mancherjee Bhownaggree, he was a Parsi. But his political loyalties were different from theirs. Saklatvala was the first Asian MP to sit in the Commons as a representative of the British Labour Party.

Saklatvala was born in Bombay on 28 March 1874, the son of a Parsi merchant of Bombay (later of Manchester). His mother, Jerbai, was the sister of the pioneering industrialist J.N. Tata. He was educated at St Xavier's School and at college in Bombay. He then joined the family firm of J.N. Tata, spending three years in the forests of Bihar and Orissa prospecting for iron, coal and limestone.

Although he came from a wealthy background, Saklatvala's concern for India's poor began in the 1890s when he did welfare work in the plague hospitals and slums of Bombay. This was the beginning of his social awakening and his interest in Indian labour problems.

In 1905, at the age of 31, Saklatvala came to England as a representative of the Tata firm, joining the family business in Manchester.[1] In 1907 he married Sarah Marsh, who came from a poor working-class background.

When first in Britain he joined the National Liberal Club, but his rapid disenchantment with the Liberals led him to the left wing of British politics. An ardent anti-imperialist, Saklatvala believed that the Left in Britain was the only movement committed to anti-colonialism. He saw the struggle for emancipation in a wider context: not only were the masses in India, Africa and China to be set free from colonialism; the working class suffered capitalist exploitation in Britain and elsewhere. Saklatvala threw himself into working-class politics, devoting his life to the cause of Indian freedom and the struggle for socialism in Britain. In 1909, while still at Manchester, he joined the Independent Labour Party (ILP).[2] The ILP, which had been formed in 1893, had helped in the birth of the Labour Party in 1900 and was affiliated to it. So began Saklatvala's association with the British Labour movement.

Even during his early years in Britain, Saklatvala did not escape the notice of the Criminal Intelligence Office. The dossier compiled on him in 1911 noted that he kept in touch with Madame Cama and B.C. Pal, and showed 'considerable interest in the extremist movement'. He was named as 'one of the most violent anti-British agitators in England', but the report added that he had not 'hitherto shown his hand openly as such'.[3]

Besides the ILP, Saklatvala also joined the Workers' Union, the National Union of Clerks and the Co-operative movement. By 1915 he had become active in the National Union of Clerks. He later joined the British Socialist Party which had been formed in 1911 and, after the 1917 Bolshevik Revolution in Russia, was one of the leading figures in the newly established People's Russian Information Bureau. The aim of the Bureau was to counter rightwing propaganda about Russia. The Russian Revolution stirred Saklatvala's imagination; he saw it as the dawn of a new beginning for the working class and, with

people like Rajani Palme Dutt, Emile Burns, J.T. Walton
Newbold and Helen Crawfurd, he became active in the Marxist
wing of the ILP. When the Communist International was
formed in 1919, Saklatvala argued that the ILP should affiliate.
But the resolution was defeated by 521 votes to 97 at the 1921
ILP Conference, and Saklatvala, with some 200 others, left the
ILP and joined the newly founded Communist Party of Great
Britain.[4]

Saklatvala was one of the founder members of the Workers'
Welfare League of India (formed in 1916), being its secretary,
with K.S. Bhat as its president. The League worked among
Indian seamen and its aim was to equalize the pay and working
conditions of European and Asian seamen. However, it soon
widened its scope to cover all Indian workers in Britain and in
1921 it became recognized as the agent of the All-India Trades
Union Congress. In February 1923, the Indian Seamen's
Association was set up, with Saklatvala as its president, and two
lascar lodging-house keepers as assistant secretaries. British
Intelligence considered it to be 'practically a branch of the Red
International Labour Union' (its correct title was the Red
International of Labour Unions), disseminating its literature,
translated into several Indian languages, among the seamen.[5]
Another prominent name associated with the Seamen's Association, and in whom Saklatvala took an interest, was Nathalal
Jagjiwan Upadhyaya (known as 'Paddy'). He was active among
the lascar population in the East End of London. The authorities suspected Upadhyaya of distributing among the lascars,
'at the instigation of the CPGB', communist literature translated into Indian languages, and of encouraging them to form
unions.

After the founding of the All-India Trades Union Congress
in 1920, Saklatvala was elected as a delegate and he attended
various trades union congresses in England as its representative.[6]
As an active trade unionist, Saklatvala addressed meetings all
over Britain and came face to face with the poverty and misery of
the working classes. He was shocked to find that in Britain
where medical science and an industrial economy produced

'articles to improve the health and comfort of the people', the same society condemned '90% of the population' to live in unsanitary and overcrowded, decrepit homes.[7] Labour conditions in Britain made him aware that poverty was a problem throughout the world.

In 1922, Saklatvala stood for parliament at Battersea North. The choice of constituency was significant. Battersea, a predominantly working-class borough with a large Irish population, was the home of a fiercely radical and independent tradition. John Burns had been its local working-class MP for many years. It had elected Roman Catholics to its council and in 1913, John Archer, the Liverpool-born pan-Africanist, had become mayor, the first black mayor in Britain. Battersea was also the borough which had declared itself against the jingoism of the Boer War, naming some streets after the Boer generals.[8]

Thus, for someone like Saklatvala, with a long record in the Labour movement, to be accepted by the people of Battersea had not proved too difficult a task. John Archer, who had introduced him at the London Session of the Second Pan-African Congress in 1921, was not only instrumental in introducing him to Battersea Labour politics, but played a leading role in negotiating Saklatvala's candidature for Labour in Battersea. Archer also resigned his seat on the council to become Saklatvala's election agent.[9] With the Battersea Trades Council as his sponsoring body, and the support of John Archer and William Sanders, Saklatvala stood in the 1922 general election as a Labour candidate, pledging to support the Labour programme if elected to parliament.[10] He won the election with a majority of 2,000. He stood again in 1923, but narrowly lost to his Liberal opponent.[11] In 1924, however, contesting the constituency as a Communist with Labour support (although the Labour Party had recently outlawed Communists from Party membership), and on a record turnout of 73.1 per cent, Saklatvala defeated his 'Constitutionalist' opponent by a majority of 542.[12] Saklatvala thus became the first and only Asian MP to sit as a Communist. (Saklatvala was the second Communist MP in the Commons, Walton Newbold being the first.) How did he manage this feat? Part of the explanation lies in Saklatvala's tremendous personal popularity. Many could not even pronounce his name correctly,[13] and yet his passionate concern for social justice and his eloquent oratory, which cast 'an almost magnetic spell' on his audience, encouraged them to vote for him.[14] A reporter from the *Daily Graphic*, after a visit to Battersea on the eve of the 1924 election, pointed out:

> Leaders and leader-writers can preach evolution against revolution, national against class interest, and any other appeals to abstract principles, but it is still the man who counts most . . . The Parsee might be a Svengali or an Indian Fakir with a knowledge of black magic. He wields a magnetic influence over his audience that verges on hypnotism. I met a Battersea charwoman yesterday who was almost in tears because she lived on the wrong side of her street and could not vote for Saklatvala. And I saw excited women waving his handbills and actually kissing his portrait pinned on them.[15]

A voter told another reporter that 'it was the women of Nine Elms [a solidly working-class district] that put Saklatvala in!'[16] The *Daily Graphic* pointed out:

> Nor is it only hysterical women that he captures, but solid British working men. A burly taxi driver stood for twenty minutes at his door arguing, politely but stubbornly, with Colonel H.V. Combs, who had come up from the country to help his friend Hogbin. One of the taxi man's arguments was that he had fought side by side with Indian regiments, and that their soldiers were as brave as any white soldiers. That the Oriental firm of which Saklatvala is a departmental manager pays very capitalist dividends didn't matter to him – nor apparently to the rest of his supporters.

In despair, the *Daily Graphic* reporter concluded that 'it's not a question of logic.'[17]

But what the reporter did not appreciate was that the main reason for Saklatvala's success lay in the unswerving support he

William Palmer with his Indian wife, the Bibi Faiz Baksh, Calcutta, 1786. Painting by Francesco Renaldi. *(India Office)*

The ayahs outside the Ayahs' Home in Hackney, London. (*Hackney Archives*)

The ayahs in the Ayahs' Home in Hackney, London. (*British Library*)

Lascars in London, from a painting by H.H. Flère. *(British Library)*

The East in the West: Oriental sailors in the London Docks (1896). *(British Library)*

Doctor Bokanky, the street herbalist. *(British Library)*

A Hindoo tract-seller with his son. *(British Library)*

Sake Deen Mahomed, Shampooing Surgeon to George IV. *(Brighton Library)*

Pandit Shyamji Krishnavarma

Savarkar in London

Madanlal Dhingra

Madame Cama

Indian Radicals. *(India Office)*

Mahomed's Baths in Brighton. *(Brighton Library)*

The Duke and Duchess of Kent receiving the Indian contingent in London in 1883, painted by S.P. Hall. (*National Portrait Gallery*)

Indian stretcher-bearers bringing in an Indian wounded officer, near Ginchy, September 1914. (*Imperial War Museum*)

Indian soldiers during the Battle of the Somme, July 1916. (*Imperial War Museum*)

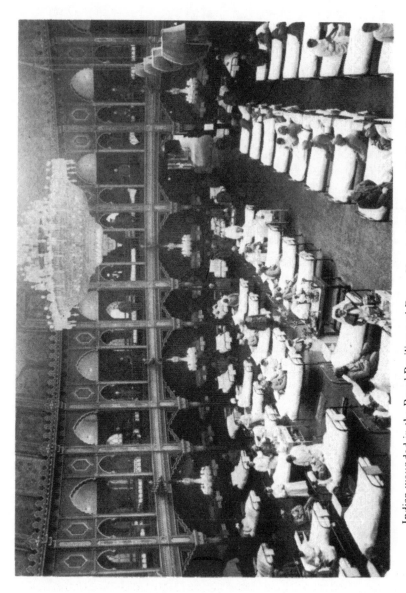

Indian wounded in the Royal Pavilion and Dome Hospital, Brighton. (*India Office*)

Cornelia Sorabji

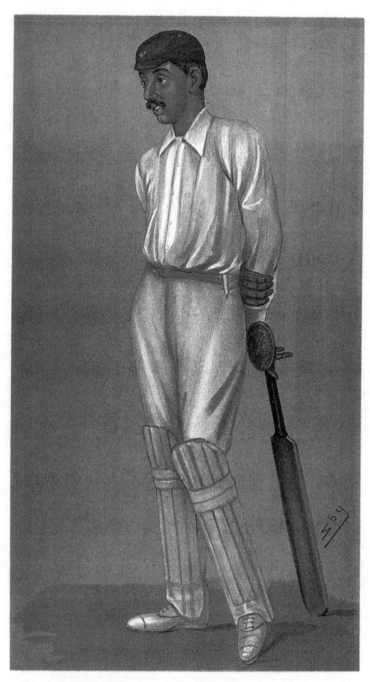

Ranjitsinhji by Spy. *(Mary Evans Picture Library)*

received from the Battersea Labour Party. So long as he retained its wholehearted backing, neither the attacks in the Conservative press, nor his Communist sympathies, nor the colour of his skin dissuaded the electors of Battersea North from voting for him. The *British Weekly* reporter, Malcolm M. Thomson, sent to investigate Battersea after it had returned a Communist to parliament in 1924, did not find any 'serious alarm' at the 'Communist label of their champion' among the supporters of Saklatvala. What mattered was that 'he had declared himself willing to accept the Labour whip'. The Battersea Labour Party, too, although torn by conflicting loyalties after the ban their party had in 1924 imposed on Communist Party candidates, had decided to stand by Saklatvala. As the party agent explained to the *British Weekly* reporter, Saklatvala had 'spent a lot of money in the district. He had worked hard; we liked him; and more, we felt it would be mean to throw him over at such short notice.' And so, in the end, they had decided by a clear majority of 114 votes to 14 to adopt him, in defiance of Labour Party headquarters. Although he stood as a Communist, Saklatvala fought the election on a *Labour* platform; and he received the full support of the local Labour Party machine. To his supporters his victory 'was largely a moral enthusiasm, passionate for reform, for equal justice, for the uplifting of the "underdog".'[18]

Saklatvala himself ascribed his success in Battersea to the loyalty of 'all sections of the Labour movement' in the constituency. And although his opponents had tried to sow discord,

> this plank never even once balanced itself on two firm ends. More loudly, more emphatically, and more repeatedly did the candidate himself declare and fully explain his Communism than the adversaries had the ability to do. What assisted the Labour Candidate most was the very genuineness of his Communist principles; as, in a truly proletarian spirit, he got by his side members of all sections of the Labour Movement in Battersea to stand as solid as a

rock. The comrades of the ILP, the comrades of the Battersea Labour League (a creation of John Burns), the comrades of Trades Unions and Labour Party Wards, and the Irish Rebels stood solid as a rock without one woman or one man in the active Labour ranks making an exception.[19]

By the election of 1929 things had changed. Not only had the Battersea Labour Party fallen in line with the Labour Party headquarters' resolution of 1924 which no longer permitted dual membership, and adopted an 'orthodox Labour candidate',[20] but local party activists had 'tired' of their Communist MP.[21] Saklatvala's attacks on the Labour Party (the 'new line' imposed by the Comintern) had alienated many of his supporters, while his increasingly flamboyant Communist rhetoric appeared out of touch with local issues. And so the Battersea Labour Party chose the veteran socialist, William S. Sanders, a product of Battersea's pioneering Labour days. Faced with a Labour opponent with such credentials, Saklatvala did not have a chance with the mainstream of Labour voters in North Battersea. As Sanders himself pointed out:

> Mr Saklatvala's supporters have dwindled to a mere handful. His perpetual attacks on local, as well as national, Labour leaders, have wearied Battersea workers, and his avowed object of smashing the Labour Party is only too obvious. If he has any support, it will only come from a few disgruntled elements. Practically every one of the local trade union branches has promised me its support. I can see no more danger to Labour in the candidature of Mr Saklatvala than I can in those of the capitalist candidates.[22]

Saklatvala lost the 1929 election, polling only 18 per cent of the vote, and coming third behind Sanders and the Conservative candidate. In 1930, he contested Glasgow, Shettleston, but did not succeed there either. And although he contested Battersea North in 1931, he did not regain his seat.[23]

If Battersea accepted Saklatvala – at least, so long as he had local Labour Party support – how did the nation and his Liberal and Tory opponents, in particular, view his candidature? The right wing tried to whip up the British people's deep-seated prejudice against 'men of colour'. The leading Communist, Palme Dutt, whose parents lived in Battersea, remembered the 'Constitutionalist' candidate telling his mother, a Swede married to an Indian, 'of course you will not want to vote for the black man.'[24] Captain Godfrey, on the other hand, representing Hogbin, the Liberal candidate, was said to have 'an instinctive preference for an Englishman', and derided what he termed Saklatvala's 'Eastern mentality'.[25]

But in Battersea, confronted with an Asian candidate, the Conservatives did not overplay the race card. This was because, in their eyes, they had a much stronger card to play – that of the Communist bogey. That being the case, race was not made much of as an issue. Saklatvala was referred to as the 'Parsi candidate' or the 'Indian Communist',[26] the emphasis being on the word *communist*. Slogans like 'Red Battersea' and 'avowed apostle of Bolshevism' made many a banner headline.[27] The voters of Battersea were implored, in many a newspaper leader, to choose between 'constitutional progress and frank and flagrant Communism'.[28] The *Daily Telegraph*, in a scaremongering article, informed Battersea North that the 'battle' was between 'Constitutionalism on the one side and Communism, with chaos and ruin in its train, on the other'.[29] Hogbin was held up as the candidate of 'law and order',[30] and so the appeal went out in search of that proverbial 'moderate-thinking British worker . . . the real, good, honest labour man' who was informed that Saklatvala represented 'all that [was] inimical to the best interest of the labour man'.[31] Labour was accused of deliberately causing 'rowdyism', and the press even went so far as to insinuate that 'the motley statesmen of international Socialist headquarters' would hardly dare condemn rowdy behaviour.[32] But what the rightwing papers forgot was that rowdy scenes were a common feature of any election campaign in those days, and had occurred before the Labour Party had even existed.

Saklatvala's radical political ideology proved to be the main weapon with which the authorities and the press tried to hound him. Because in private life he was a departmental manager of Tata Ltd, a subsidiary of the Tata Power Company Limited of Bombay, with an authorized capital of £4,000,000, the press used this to accuse him of 'hypocrisy'.[33] In 1925 Saklatvala resigned as a matter of principle from the family firm.[34] In an interview with the *Sunday Worker*, he exposed the efforts to embarrass him. His opponents, he said, had been at work 'for the last dozen years' to induce his employers and his relatives to 'throw [him] overboard and make an example of [him]'. Saklatvala did not 'regret the step' he had taken – although in the end it meant great personal hardship – on the grounds that, freed of the responsibilities of the post, he would be able to devote more time to the 'cause of the struggling workers' who were fighting to overthrow a 'callous system of society'.[35]

In 1925, he had to pay the price once again for his ideology. An Inter-Parliamentary Union delegation of some 41 MPs was to visit the USA, and Saklatvala was to be part of that delegation. But his inclusion created a furore. Three MPs withdrew from the delegation in protest at the prospect of sharing the platform with the 'Parsee Communist . . . whose watchword is "Let us abolish the Union Jack".'[36] In the end, the delegation sailed without him as the US government stepped in to rescind Saklatvala's visa. Frank Kellog, the American Secretary of State, gave Saklatvala's 'subversive . . . propaganda contrary to [American] institutions' as the reason for taking this action. Kellog added that he did not wish to make America 'the stamping ground for every revolutionary agitator from other countries'.[37] Although in the US anti-red hysteria was plentiful, there is reason to believe that the British government had a hand in the ban.[38] Predictably, Conservative MPs were jubilant at the turn of events. Sir Robert Horne, leader of the delegation, went so far as to express the wish that the electors of Battersea North would do the same:

> I hope, indeed, that this will be an object lesson to our people, and that this incident, which has been embarrassing many of us in the last few weeks, may produce a beneficent

result. It will do so if it brings home to the minds of the
electors in North Battersea what a disgrace they bring upon
themselves and upon the whole of their fellow subjects by
electing as their representative in the House of Commons
such a notorious person as Mr Saklatvala.[39]

The *Birmingham Mail*, in a long leader condemning Saklatvala's views, considered it entirely legitimate to ban such
people, who 'preach revolution and the overthrow of the
Empire'.[40]

Amid all this condemnation of Saklatvala, the governments of
Britain and the USA forgot two important things. One was
pointed out to them by the *Daily Herald*, which reminded its
readers that Saklatvala's views were 'the result of his country,
India, being under the domination of Britain, a domination of
which the mass of the American people strongly disapprove'.[41]
The second was that both Britain and the USA were democra-
cies, and that Saklatvala was an elected Member of Parliament.

In the USA itself the ban did not go unchallenged. The *New
York Times* considered that, in this instance, Washington had
displayed 'too much zeal'.[42] A 'monster protest meeting' to greet
the Inter-Parliamentary Union delegation was organized by the
Civil Liberties Union; and Senator Borah, chairman of the
Senate's Foreign Relations Committee, made a strong protest,
as did the Workers' Party of America.[43]

This was not the only time the British government thwarted
Saklatvala's freedom of movement. His house had been searched,
and his movements watched in 1921. In 1927 it delayed issuing
him with a passport when he was planning a tour of India. It
attributed the delay to the need for consultation with the
government of India. This was of course a pretext: Saklatvala
was after all a British subject *and* an Indian. Saklatvala had to
write a strong letter of protest to Stanley Baldwin, the Prime
Minister, to ask him to stop interfering with the 'legitimate
functions and duties' of a Member of Parliament, who happened
to belong to a party which 'your party may even hate or dread'.
Saklatvala pointed out that since he had contested three

elections as a Communist, his membership of the Communist Party was neither new nor secret.[44]

Although he got his passport, the 1927 tour of India was to be Saklatvala's last trip there. All subsequent endorsements for a visit to India were refused; and in 1929, a Labour Secretary of State refused to lift the ban imposed by a Tory government.[45] In 1927, Saklatvala had also been refused a visa for a visit to Egypt where he wished to spend some time on his way back from India.[46] And in 1929 the Belgian police arrested him and sent him back to England when he was on his way to an anti-imperialist meeting.

Despite harassment,[47] Saklatvala remained loyal to his principles and continued to be a staunch critic of British imperialism and a champion of the working class. During the 1926 general strike, he was arrested when giving a speech in Hyde Park on May Day in which he urged the 'Army boys' to refuse to 'fire on' the workers. He was charged with sedition and sentenced to two months in Wormwood Scrubs, having refused to find sureties for his good behaviour. He told the court that 'in the circumstances such as those existing today, I shall refuse to be silenced except by *force majeure*'.[48]

Harassment apart, the work of nationalists like Saklatvala was made doubly difficult by the prevailing climate in Britain and internationally. The 1920s and 1930s were a time of economic troubles. The collapse of the currency, rising unemployment, hunger marches and the retrenchment policies practised by successive governments meant that the conditions of the workers had become gradually more depressed. With the Wall Street crash of 1929 and the onset of the Great Depression, unemployment reached record levels. If conditions for the workers in Britain were grim, life was far worse for Indians living under colonialism. As the upsurge of Indian nationalism began, the British government in India retaliated with the most vicious repression. In the 1919 massacre of unarmed Indians at Amritsar the death toll had been 379 dead and 1,200 wounded. When Indians protested against injustices like the Salt Tax, the government clapped the protesters into jail. Massive non-violent civil disobedience demonstrations were organized all over India by the Congress: the government responded with the lathi (a bamboo stick with metal hoops on either end), charges, violent beatings and more imprisonments. It was common practice to flog and chain political prisoners in jails.[49] Thousands suffered and the prisons were heavily overcrowded. Sir Samuel Hoare, answering a question in April 1932, naturally denied this: 'I would deny altogether the charge that because there are 26,000 men and women imprisoned in India, that means that India is suffering under the iron heel of a Russian tyranny.'[50]

The overwhelming majority of the British people were not only apathetic but ignorant of the true nature of British imperialism. They still entertained a romantic notion of Britain's civilizing colonial role. And the British government's propaganda machine both fed on and helped to sustain this image of colonialism. The Indian national struggle for independence was largely unknown and unrecognized in Britain. The Indian National Congress was made out to be a bunch of discontented troublemakers – a mere 'microscopic movement' in Lord Dufferin's words. Government propaganda was on a massive scale and it gave most Britons a totally false picture of India.

In the face of such opposition, Saklatvala chipped away relentlessly but steadily both outside and on the floor of the House, spotlighting the true state of affairs in India. In one notable speech in parliament in which he exposed British hypocrisy, he said:

We are talking of the Indian Empire just in the same strain of common agreement, with that very placid attitude of mind and phraseology of speech as if we are discussing some matters relating to the renewal of furniture in the library . . . We are debating here as if the Bengal Ordinances were never promulgated, as if the shooting of Bombay operatives during the cotton strike had never taken place, as if a great strike of thousands of railway workers is not even now going on in the Punjab, with men starving . . . Is there a single man or woman today, is there a

person in any country in Europe, in any of the backward
countries, in the Balkan states, in any of the small nations
which are not yet so fully developed as Great Britain, who
would tolerate for one day a power so despotic and arbitrary
as the Crown, under the Imperial system, is insisting upon
enjoying in India?[51]

Saklatvala found farcical the idea of Britain sending a
commission – the Simons Commission – to test the 'fitness' of
Indians to govern themselves. He denounced the whole nature
of British imperialism for what it was: 'getting hold of citizens
and keeping them in prison without trial and without charge,
holding them in bondage, ruling people in the name of
civilization, and exploiting them industrially on miserable
wages.'[52]

It was not only British rule in India that concerned him. In
his very first speech in the Commons, speaking on behalf of *all*
the colonized peoples, he said:

No Britisher would for a moment tolerate a constitution for
Great Britain if it were written outside of Great Britain by
people who are not British. In a similar way the constitutions
for Ireland, and India and Egypt and Mesopotamia should
be constitutions written by the men of those countries, in
those countries, without interference from outside.[53]

Not surprisingly, Saklatvala was highly critical of the 1922 Irish
Bill which proposed the setting up of the Irish Free State.

For his constant denunciation of British imperialism, he
earned the title of the 'enemy of the Union Jack'. His speeches
on behalf of India in the House of Commons provoked Sir
Philip Sassoon to argue in the House that 'we English are no
more intruders in India than you Parsees.'[54] Saklatvala wrote
articles on India[55] and spoke at meetings to popularize India's
cause and to try to gain support for Indian independence among
the British working class. For instance, the 1925 Trades Union
Congress in Scarborough adopted a resolution by 3,083,000
votes to 79,000 condemning 'domination of non-British peoples'

by Britain as a 'form of capitalist exploitation'. It also declared
its 'complete opposition to imperialism', resolving to

> support the workers in all parts of the British Empire in
> organizing trade unions and political parties in order to
> further their interest, and to support the right of all peoples
> in the British Empire to self-determination, including the
> right to choose complete separation from the Empire.[56]

He kept in touch with developments in India. In 1927, he
went on a three-month tour of India, addressing large gatherings
and communicating to them his vision for India. He was
enthusiastically received as a loyal and tireless worker for Indian
freedom. While in India he urged the formation of an all-India
workers' and peasants' party, which should be affiliated to the
National Congress in order to make it a 'truly national and really
powerful' movement for freedom. Saklatvala denounced
capitalist exploitation of the workers. He urged the workers to
organize themselves and form trade unions to better their
conditions of work. His message was everywhere the same: 'that
imperialism was running down human life . . . and that freedom
was a human asset', and as such he stood for the freedom of not
only India, 'but that of Egypt, Arabia, Africa, China and
Japan'.[57] He pleaded for unity between Muslims and Hindus,
and among the workers. He asked Indians not to be content with
Dominion Status, since India was not a dominion in the sense of
Canada or Australia, and without control of the army and
foreign relations, freedom was incomplete.[58]

During his successful tour, critical voices were raised.
Saklatvala's radical ideology caused some 'mental reservations'
about his message;[59] the Bombay Corporation resolved by a
majority not to present him with an address.[60] Saklatvala had
great doubts about Gandhi's economic ideas of the 'charka and
khaddar' (the spinning wheel and 'khadi' or homespun cloth) in
an age of machinery and large-scale production. These views
were not well received.[61] To nationalists, his assertion that the
boycott of English cloth hurt the poor workers of Lancashire
appeared contradictory.[62] But to a man of Saklatvala's inter-

national outlook, the interests of the workers in different countries were interdependent. He viewed the Indian struggle for freedom on a par with the struggle carried on by the mass of the working class in England.[63]

In 1927, after his return from India, Saklatvala had his five children – two daughters and three sons – initiated into the Parsi faith in a Navjot ceremony. This earned him the censure of the Communist Party of Great Britain.[64] Despite his membership of the Communist Party, Saklatvala maintained his links with the Parsi community in London.[65] In 1934 he travelled to the Soviet Union, visiting factories and collective farms. He was impressed with Russian educational and industrial development.

Saklatvala's tireless work in the cause of workers' freedom earned him the respect of many in Britain and his selfless devotion to duty was greatly appreciated. Harry Pollitt wrote in the *Daily Worker*:

> Night after night, year after year, in all parts of Britain he carried out his task of working-class agitation, education and organization ... No comrade ever did more of his work so uncomplainingly as Comrade Saklatvala. No call was ever made upon him to which he did not respond. Be the meeting large or small, it was always the same. Be it near or far, it was always the same.[66]

And he carried on his crusade on behalf of India and the workers to the last. When he died in January 1936, tributes poured in from India, the USSR and Labour circles in Britain. He was considered to have done more than any other man to 'bring the sufferings of the Indian toilers before the attention of the British Labour movement'.[67] And Nehru, in his tribute to Saklatvala, described him as 'a brave and intrepid soldier of freedom'.[68] Although *The Times* in its obituary of 17 January 1936 did not think that Saklatvala made 'much of an impression' in parliament because of his mildness in expressing the 'extreme character of his views',[69] he was considered to be a formidable man at question time and a great parliamentary debater.[70]

Vengalil Krishnan Krishna Menon

Krishna Menon came from a prosperous family in Malabar, South India. His father had a successful legal practice and his mother was an accomplished musician and Sanskrit scholar. Menon was born on 3 May 1896 and educated at the Municipal School, Tellicherry, and the Native High School, Calicut. He graduated from the Presidency College, Madras, in 1918 and went to the Madras Law College. But within a few months he had given up the law college for social and political work, becoming a volunteer worker in Annie Besant's Home Rule movement. He spent nearly five years at Adyar College, founded by Mrs Besant, teaching history and working on *New India*, a weekly.

It was at the Presidency College in Madras that Menon had first come in contact with Annie Besant's Theosophical Society and the Home Rule League. The home rulers considered self-government to be every nation's birthright, and worked to achieve that goal for India. While at the Presidency College, Menon, fired by the home rule ideal, had risked expulsion by planting the red and green flag of the Home Rule League on the college roof-top.

In 1924, at the age of 28, he came to London to study for a teaching diploma, intending to stay for only six months. But he stayed on till 1947, the year India regained her independence. He made a living by teaching history for a year at St Christopher's School, Letchworth, Hertfordshire. In 1925, he obtained his teaching diploma and then enrolled at the London School of Economics, under Harold Laski, obtaining a first-class honours degree in 1927. He joined University College, London, gaining an MA in 1930, then an MSc from the LSE in 1934. In the same year he was called to the Bar by the Middle Temple. Since Menon regarded his work for India's freedom as his life's main mission, most of his studying was done in his spare time.[71]

During most of his time in Britain, Menon lived frugally in two rooms in Camden Town, London. He supported himself partly by practising as a lawyer – but he did not have much success, partly because he took up cases of lascars who had fallen foul of the law. Professionally, this advocacy lacked status; financially, it was unrewarding, since lascars were themselves mainly destitute, receiving wages far below the rate for white sailors. But the main reason for Menon's lack of success as a lawyer was racism in the legal profession.[72]

Menon also worked as London correspondent for several Indian newspapers and periodicals. The authorities in London viewed Menon's journalistic work with suspicion, considering it to be of a 'sensational and "disclosure" type', designed to attribute 'sinisterly imperialistic' motives to the West.[73] It was as editor and publisher that Menon met with the most success. For three years, starting in 1932, he worked for Bodley Head. He edited the Twentieth Century Library, a series of books of social and topical interest.[74] He also edited a topical books list for another publishing firm, Selwyn and Blount.[75] But his greatest publishing contribution was to the Pelican series of books. In 1935, Allen Lane brought out the first Penguins. Then in 1936 the Lane brothers were introduced by Krishna Menon to W.E. Williams, secretary of the British Institute of Adult Education, and H.L. Beals of the LSE. The meeting led to the birth of Pelican Books, a sister series to the Penguins. The Pelicans were more serious in content and had an educational bias. Krishna Menon became the general editor of this venture, while Allen Lane looked after Penguin fiction. The first title in the Pelican series, which came out in May 1937, was George Bernard Shaw's *The Intelligent Woman's Guide to Socialism, Capitalism, Sovietism and Fascism.*[76] Shaw wrote the section on Fascism specially for this edition. In the words of *The Times* in 1974, 'there is still an intellectual thrill in going down the list of his first twenty magnificent authors.'[77]

During his 20 years in Britain, Menon devoted his life to two things above all else: Indian independence and the borough of St Pancras. Like Saklatvala, Menon was an internationalist who saw freedom as a universal human right. The toiling masses of India, the oppressed of South Africa or China and the poor in

London's slums all deserved justice.

When he first came to England in 1924, it was natural for Menon to gravitate towards the Commonwealth of India League, an organization working for 'Dominion Status' for India. The League had been set up by Annie Besant in 1912 as the Home Rule for India British Auxiliary and, in 1923, was renamed the Commonwealth of India League. Its membership included Indian students and sympathizers of the Indian National Congress; but it was, by now, little more than a debating club. In 1928 Menon was elected the league's joint secretary. Soon he not only gave it a new direction, but also made it a real political force.

As a staunch nationalist, Menon, like Jawaharlal Nehru and other Congress radicals, considered the goal of 'Dominion Status' insufficient. He wrote:

> We think that greater good both in world affairs and in the domestic concerns of both nations will result from free and equal partnership within the Commonwealth. But we acknowledge the right to separate and we seek to make that acknowledgement explicit.[78]

The radicals wanted to substitute 'freedom and self-determination' for Dominion Status. By 1930, Menon and the radicals in the league had won their argument against 'Dominion Status'. The league in its old form was wound up and the conservative old guard resigned.

The league, as the India League, began the fight for '*purna swaraj*' ('complete self-rule') for India. During the 17 years to independence, Krishna Menon and his supporters succeeded in building up the league's influence in the British labour movement, enlisting the support of influential MPs and making it the voice of Congress in Britain and on the continent. How did they manage to do this?

On one level, they aimed to counter government propaganda with an equally relentless information campaign by the league; on another, they tried to enlist support for India by raising public consciousness. They bombarded the British public with facts.

Menon addressed meetings everywhere, including Speakers' Corner in Hyde Park. He travelled all over Britain. He spoke to gatherings of students, factory workers and miners, to women's groups and church groups – to anyone who was prepared to listen to him. No gathering was considered too small or trivial. His grasp of facts, his ability to communicate them with eloquence and conviction, his passion and intensity about the justice of India's cause, stirred many a heart. One man who heard him speak recalled that 'you could almost hear the pounding of his heart'.[79] Always, his appeal was to his hearers' intellect and their heart. Reginald Sorensen was won over to the 'moral significance of India's cause' when Menon travelled miles to address a small gathering of Unitarians in an obscure church in Walthamstow.[80]

Menon regularly contributed articles to newspapers and periodicals, both in Britain and abroad;[81] he wrote pamphlets on issues involving India, putting forward India's point of view.[82] He answered every letter sent to him, regardless of whether the motive of the writer was a genuine desire for information or merely to ridicule. For instance, to a writer who had sent him a press cutting about Mahatma Gandhi's style of dress, Menon replied:

> Englishmen in India wear the clothes to which they are accustomed in their own country, irrespective of the climate. Surely it cannot be wrong for an Indian leader to dress like his following. In any case, it is not Gandhi's clothes but his ideas and what he has done for his people that worries his critics. If they were worried about the unclad condition of millions of their fellow subjects in India, Britain's rule of that country would have directed its main energies to the improvement of the economic standards of its masses.[83]

Indian nationalist leaders visiting England spoke from the league's platform at public meetings. It organized film shows, concerts, dance displays and other cultural events, as well as readings from the works of the Bengali poet Rabindranath

Tagore. All this activity was designed not only to keep India in the public eye but also to break down the wall of ignorance surrounding the British public's image of India.

To give the league status, and to gain support in parliament, Menon tried to enlist members of the British public and MPs. Bertrand Russell became the league's chairman, while Harold Laski, Sir Stafford Cripps, Palme Dutt, Reginald Sorensen, Monica Whately, Ellen Wilkinson and J.B.S. Haldane were among its notable speakers. Others associated with the league included Fenner Brockway, H.N. Brailsford, George Hicks, A.A. Purcell, and J.F. Horrabin. Through the league's parliamentary committee, which at one time included about 100 MPs, it acquired a forceful voice in parliament.

Menon's complete and selfless dedication to India attracted much notice. Branch units of the league sprang up all over Britain, especially among student bodies. Many voluntary workers came to Menon's aid – women, Quakers, Communists and Labour party supporters. The league became an official voice of the Congress Party. But, in the process, Menon's health was ruined. He not only gave his time and energy to the league, but often what little money he made went into the league's coffers, while he lived on tea, potatoes and buns.

In 1932, the India League organized a fact-finding mission to India. Ellen Wilkinson, Monica Whately and Leonard Matters (all Labour MPs), spent 83 days in India with Menon accompanying them as secretary. What they saw and heard shocked and sickened them. They visited villages, factories, prisons; they talked with Indians of every class, religion and political opinion and with members of the English resident population; they interviewed government officials, both European and Indian; they met managers, trade unionists and workers. Their report, *Condition of India* forms a searing indictment of the Raj in India.[84] The atrocities and brutalities it revealed stunned many in Britain. Typical of the cruelties was the story of the heroic prisoner Mohan Kaul, aged 19. His 'crime' was to refuse to salaam at the call of '*Sarkar Salaam*' (salute the government) – a compulsory disciplinary measure in all prisons. For this 'crime'

He was put in standing handcuffs and given other punishments. Each time he was brought before the superintendent he declined to make the required obeisance. Altogether, he suffered five and a half months of solitary confinement. After the first three months, when he was still adamant about his refusal to salaam, he was put into a cage with his hands fettered behind his back. The cage was 7 by 5 feet. In this cage Mohan Kaul spent all hours of the day and night; he was obliged to take his food and answer the calls of nature in it.[85]

Another incident the MPs witnessed took place at Madura in August:

Fifteen persons were gathered to salute the Congress flag, as is the custom on the last Sunday of each month. It was at an open public space. They were set upon by the police who encircled them and beat the boys and men, until they fell on the ground. When the police left volunteers attended to the victims, whose ages ranged from 15 to 20.[86]

The government of India proscribed the book; Whitehall tried to discredit its findings.

During the Second World War, Menon again tried to publicize India's viewpoint in *India, Britain and Freedom*. He revealed Britain's failure to consult the central legislature, thus breaking its word to India. Britain had promised that no Indian troops would leave India without prior consultation with Indian leaders. But this promise had not been kept.

Menon also tried to enlist public opinion in Europe in favour of Indian independence. After the signing of the Atlantic Charter in 1942, he tried to enlist American support.

Menon was the life blood of the India League. But in some circles in Britain he was regarded as 'just a dark-skinned St Pancras intellectual'.[87] The British government were eager to condemn him by emphasizing his leftwing sympathies and to discredit him for his 'extreme political views' and 'anti-British mentality', and as such 'a *persona non grata*'.[88]

Menon had been drawn to the Labour Party while still at the LSE. He became a committed party worker and, during the grim days of the hunger marches, an active campaigner with Ellen Wilkinson.[89] In November 1934 he was elected Labour councillor for Ward 4 in St Pancras, London. He promised to fight for a better deal for the borough. Initially elected for three years, Menon proved to be such a popular and dynamic politician that at each subsequent election he was returned with an increased majority.[90] He resigned from the council when he became High Commissioner for India in 1947.

Menon served on all the major committees of the council – highways, sewers and public works, baths and cemeteries, general purposes, and education and public libraries. He was the prime mover in the formation of the St Pancras Arts and Civic Council, becoming its first chairman in 1946. As the chairman, he played an important role in starting the St Pancras Annual Arts Festival. This was the beginning of today's Camden Festival of Arts.[91]

It was as chairman of the library committee that Menon is best remembered. During the two years that he chaired its meetings, he became primarily responsible for the development of the public library service in St Pancras, introducing many innovations. He set up a mobile library service and made sure that everyone living in the borough was within easy reach of a branch library.[92]

During the Second World War when, to help the war effort, the council reduced the number of councillors, Menon remained as part of the three-man team on the borough council. He served on the food control committee and was active in civil defence. He was also an air-raid warden in St Pancras and, through his membership of the council, he succeeded in persuading the authorities to improve the safety standards and conditions of the air-raid shelters. There are many stories of his personal courage in the dark days of the blitz in London.

In 1939, Menon was adopted as Labour parliamentary candidate for Dundee. The choice was significant. Dundee was a town that lived on one of India's major products: jute.

However, in 1941 he clashed with the party over its lack of commitment to Indian independence and the national executive withdrew support from his candidature on the ground that his views were at variance with those of the rest of the party. While 'his bona fides as a socialist' were undeniable, it was considered 'questionable whether a person having double loyalty' was suitable as a Labour parliamentary candidate.[93] Menon resigned from the party and sat as an Independent on St Pancras borough council.

It has been suggested that Menon was dropped as a candidate for speaking at a Communist meeting in 1941.[94] But although Menon used any platform available to plead for India's independence, he remained a firm believer in constitutional advance.

In 1945, the Labour Party accepted the principle of self-government for India and Menon rejoined the party. He organized a meeting in St Pancras town hall to mark Nehru's birthday. In an impassioned speech, Harold Laski asked:

> When are we going to realize our sense of responsibility towards the Indian people? . . . Indian freedom is inevitable, and inescapable, and what we have to decide is whether that freedom shall come gracefully by British co-operation or, instead, by British hostility. We have to decide whether we are capable as a Labour Party and a Labour movement of moving swiftly to the proud day when we can claim that we have assisted in the emancipation of a great civilization . . . A Labour Party which is unwilling to play its full part in the emancipation of India will, sooner or later, be unwilling to play its full part in the emancipation of the British working class.[95]

This marked a victory for India, Menon and the India League. The Labour Party had finally committed itself to Indian independence.

In the months leading up to independence, Krishna Menon played quite an influential role as an intermediary between the Congress leaders and the Viceroy. Earl Mountbatten considered

Menon 'invaluable as a "go-between" ', and believed that 'history will show that you have helped the future of India very much by the advice that you gave me'.[96]

Krishna Menon served as a special representative of the government of India at the UN General Assembly between 1946 and 1947. He is warmly remembered by many in New York.[97]

Menon's career entered a new phase in 1947. He became India's High Commissioner in London during 1947-52. There was some opposition to his appointment to this post. But Nehru, a close friend of Krishna Menon's, insisted that Menon's intimate knowledge of both India and England would be of great help to India. As High Commissioner, he served India loyally. He continued to lead an austere life in one room at India House, living on tea and biscuits - as he had done during his India League days. After a spell as a leader of India's delegation to the United Nations, he served as adviser to the Prime Minister, Nehru, in defence matters, playing a leading part in the 1956 Suez negotiations. From 1957 to 1962, he held the defence ministry. Responsibility for India's humiliating defeat in the Indo-Chinese War of 1962 was laid at his door, and Menon lost much popularity in India. He resigned from the government and lived in virtual retirement. He died in October 1974.

All his life, Menon had worked untiringly for India and for Camden (St Pancras as it then was). Reminders of his zeal and devotion to the people of the borough still stand - the travelling library and the Camden Festival. In 1955, the borough conferred on him its highest honour, not only in recognition of his outstanding services to local government, but also for his achievements as politician and diplomat. This honour was the honorary freedom of the borough. Camden has bestowed this honour only twice: both times on 'adopted sons of the borough' - George Bernard Shaw and Vengalil Krishnan Krishna Menon.[98]

In 1974, Camden paid tribute to Menon's memory once again by putting the council's own special 'brown plaque' outside his old home, 57 Camden Square. They had hoped that the GLC would put up a blue plaque. But they discovered that this was not done 'until the notable had been dead for about 10 years'. The council therefore decided to issue their own special plaque. Menon was the first person in Camden to receive this distinction.[99] In 1977, Camden Council contributed a plinth for the statue of Menon erected by the India League in Fitzroy Square.[100]

8. Princes, Students and Travellers

From the middle of the nineteenth century a growing number of Asians arrived in Britain. Businessmen, diplomats, literary figures, princes and students were all represented. None stirred people's imagination so much as the Indian princes. Many column inches were devoted to them in the court circulars and in society magazines. In fact, to many people in Britain, India *was* the land of the maharajahs. But it was the students who formed the largest group. They came to Britain to obtain vital qualifications without which they could never hope to enter most professions and the civil service. Some of these visitors have left us records of their stay in Britain. These records help us understand Imperial Britain, the Indians who wrote them and their interaction with British society.[1]

The first recorded official visit to Britain was that of Rajah Rammohun Roy, a high-caste Hindu, who landed in Liverpool on 8 April 1831, accompanied by his adopted son and by a Brahmin cook, a servant and two cows. A man of many interests and accomplishments, Rammohun Roy came to England as an ambassador of the Mughal Emperor Akbar Shah II to plead the Emperor's case against the East India Company which had possessed his lands and owed him money.[2] While in England, Roy appealed to the Privy Council against the reintroduction of sati. (The pro-sati lobby refused to accept the 1829 law banning self-immolation by a widow on her husband's funeral pyre.) He also presented the Indian viewpoint, in the form of a written statement, to parliament in the debate on the renewal of the East India Company's Charter.

Rammohun Roy's visit created a great impression on the

British public. In church circles and in high society he was much in demand. Many were surprised to hear 'a native of India' speaking English, while his knowledge of the Christian religion, British politics and world affairs caused surprise.[3] His quiet dignity and cultured bearing gave the lie to the stereotyped Anglo-Indian image of an 'uncivilized native of the east'. This is how Lucy Aikin of Hampstead described him:

> Scarcely any description can do justice to his admirable qualities, and the charm of his society, his extended knowledge, his comprehension of mind, his universal philanthropy, his tender humanity, his genuine dignity mixed with perfect courtesy, and the most touching humility. His memory I shall cherish with affectionate reverence on many accounts, but the character in which I best love to contemplate him is that of the friend and champion of women.[4]

Rammohun Roy was presented to William IV and, seated among other foreign ambassadors, attended his coronation in Westminster Abbey. He met many important British figures including Jeremy Bentham and Robert Owen. Even the East India Company, which had treated him with disdain in India, gave a dinner in his honour.

Rammohun Roy made an equally strong impression on the poorer classes. During a visit to a Manchester factory, he was mobbed:

> Men, women and children rushed in crowds to see 'the King of Ingee'! Many of the great unwashed insisted upon shaking hands with him; some of the ladies who had not stayed to make their toilets very carefully wished to embrace him, and he with great difficulty escaped . . . The aid of the police was required to make way for him to the manufactories, and when he entered, it was necessary to close and bolt the gate to keep out the mob . . . After shaking hands with hundreds of them he turned round and addressed them, hoping they would all support the King

and his Ministers in obtaining Reform; so happily had he caught the spirit of the people. He was answered with loud shouts, 'The King and Reform for ever!'[5]

But a discordant note was sounded by the Anglo-Indian community. At a fashionable party, an Anglo-Indian officer was overheard to remark angrily, 'What is that *black fellow* doing here?'[6]

Rammohun Roy also visited Liverpool, London and Bristol. He went to France in 1832, lamenting the use of passports and visas for international travel. Roy considered this a necessity only in time of war, not in peace. He wrote a long letter on this subject to Prince Talleyrand, the French Foreign Minister.[7]

Rammohun Roy died in Bristol on 27 September 1833 after a short illness. In deference to his own wishes, he was buried in 'silence and without ceremony' in the grounds of Beech House (now Purdown Hospital, Bristol), where he had stayed.[8] Ten years later, in 1843, Dwarkanath Tagore, the grandfather of the poet Rabindranath Tagore, had his remains reinterred in the Arno's Vale cemetery in Bath Road, Bristol, with a *chatri* ('shrine') made out of local stone over it. Another visible memorial to Rammohun Roy's visit to Bristol is a plaque on the wall of the Lewin's Mead Unitarian chapel, where he spoke to 'an overflowing congregation'.[9]

Dwarkanath Tagore followed in Rammohun Roy's footsteps, visiting England and France in 1842 and again in 1845-6. He died in London on 1 August 1846 and is buried in Kensal Green cemetery.

A succession of visitors, especially Bengalis, visited Bristol after Rammohun Roy's death. The visit of Keshub Chunder Sen, a religious and social reformer and a member of the Brahmo Samaj, in 1870, is commemorated by a plaque on the wall of Lewin's Mead chapel. In 1871, another young Bengali reformer and educationist, Sisipada Banerjee, visited Bristol together with his wife. He travelled to Birmingham, Walsall, Manchester, Bolton and Liverpool, addressing meetings. On 18 October 1871 at Red Lodge House, Mary Carpenter's residence in Bristol, Banerjee's wife gave birth to a son. In the words of the *Journal of the National Indian Association*, 'as this is the first Brahmin subject of Her Majesty Queen Victoria born on British ground, he bears the name of Albion in commemoration of the event.'[10]

The princes

The India of the princely states – there were about 600 of them – covered about two-fifths of the Indian subcontinent. The states were ruled by hereditary princes who owed allegiance to the British Crown. Every year rulers of some of these 'Native states' came to Britain – to pay their respects to the sovereign, or simply for pleasure, or on invitation to attend a formal state occasion, since no royal state function was complete without these elegant maharajahs and rajahs.[11] Many acquired a taste for foreign travel; some sent their children to be educated in Britain.[12]

The Rajah of Kolhapoor, a youth of 20 called Rajaram Maharaj Churuputte, was the first representative of the princely states to visit Britain, in June 1870. He made quite an impression in high society. At the Queen's Ball, where he appeared dressed 'in gorgeous apparel . . . in his cloth-of-gold tissues, necklaces and strings of jewels, he looked like the prince in a fairy tale'.[13] He died in Florence on his way back to India and was cremated, according to Hindu rites, on the banks of the River Arno. The Rajah kept a diary of his visit to Britain which was posthumously published in this country.

A succession of maharajahs and rajahs came after him to Britain.[14] For their formal reception in Britain, a Political Aide-de-Camp was appointed in 1872. His task was to make arrangements for their presentation at court, their attendance at naval and military reviews and other public spectacles, and their inspection of Britain's arsenals and dockyards and centres of industry – all illustrating Britain's Imperial power and wealth.[15] The princes mingled with the upper classes in Britain, played polo and cricket with them, and went to shooting parties. They attended state balls and dances, went to the races, and gave extravagant presents and parties. Their wealth and splendour dazzled and many of them became indispensable in Edwardian England – like 'orchids and champagne'.[16]

One prince who drew the crowds was Ranjitsinhji, later to become Maharajah the Jam Saheb of Nawanagar, the living legend of cricket. He was not the first Indian to play cricket on British soil: a Parsi team from India had toured Britain in 1886 when Ranji was only 14.[17] But Ranji was the first Indian to play for England, and his game made him the favourite of every cricket lover in England. Songs were written and music composed in his praise, and in capturing space on the music albums of the day he was second only to W.G. Grace.[18]

Ranji had come to Britain in 1888 at the age of 16, and attended Trinity College, Cambridge from 1889 to 1893. He was admitted to Cambridge without taking the entrance examination and left without graduating. He was known as 'Smith' at Cambridge, and made his mark both socially and in cricket. He won his cricket blue in 1893. In 1895 he began to play for Sussex County Club and in 1896 and 1900 he was the champion batsman for the All England team. In the 1897-8 season he went to Australia as part of Stoddart's All England Eleven.

Cricketing hero, author of books on cricket, and later owner of 30,000 acres in Connemara, Ranji was worshipped by cricket fans.[19] In a match against Australia in 1899, when the rest of the England team had let the side down by playing badly, the 'popular' newspapers in England greeted him with the headline: 'Ranji saves England'.

Ranji seems to have been a brilliant cricketer. He was considered to be

> graceful as a panther in action, with lean but steely muscles under his smooth brown skin; wrists supple and tough as a creeper of the Indian jungle, and dark eyes which see every turn and twist of the bounding ball, he has adopted cricket and turned it into an Oriental poem of action.[20]

A tribute – but one which is not innocent of stereotyped image!

Ranji's nephew Dheleepsinhji followed the family tradition; he played for England in the 1930s, while the Nawab of Pataudi, another Indian prince, became well known for cricket in the 1940s. In fact Ranji was the first in the long line of Indian cricketers to play for England.

Cricket was not the only sporting encounter between the Indian upper classes and the British. Polo and racing had their stars too. Sir Pratab Singh of Jodhpur (he introduced jodhpur riding breeches to London in 1899) brought the first Indian polo team to England during Queen Victoria's Diamond Jubilee. The young Maharajah of Jaipur, Man Singh, known as 'Jai', was only 22 when he brought his polo team to England in 1933. His team won every match that season. The Aga Khan, Sir Sultan Muhammad Shah, KCIE, GCIE and GCSI, spiritual leader of the Ismaili Khoja, was well known for his rich stud horses and Derby winners. The 1935 Derby, won by the Aga Khan's horse Bahram, was hailed as an Indian victory.

Some universities conferred honorary degrees on the princes. For instance, the Maharajah Sir Madho Rao Scindia of Gwalior received the law degree of LLD of Cambridge University in 1903; Edinburgh University honoured the Maharajah of Jaipur Sir Sawai Madho Singh similarly.

Queen Victoria had a soft spot for the maharajahs and the rajahs; the Prince of Wales, later Edward VII, considered himself above prejudice. During his tour of India in 1875, he is known to have declared that 'because a man has a black face and a different religion from our own, there is no reason why he should be treated as a brute'.[21] The upper classes in Britain not only socialized with them, but lauded and honoured them. Many an ordinary Briton regarded them with awe and wonderment. But all this did not pass without a ripple in some government circles. Referring to the treatment accorded to the Rajah of Kapurthala in England, Lord Curzon, Viceroy of India from 1899 to 1905, wrote in disgust in July 1900:

Here is a third-class chief, of fifth-rate character and morals, who when he comes to Simla we look upon as one of our black sheep, who goes to Paris in order to have intercourse with French women, whose general character and proceedings are of the shadiest description, whom in India I discourage in every possible way, but who goes home to Europe, is treated like a Royal Prince, has an interview with the President of the French Republic, shares the Presidential lodge at the races at Longchamps, then goes to England, figures at a State Ball (I saw him dancing the Jubilee Ball at Buckingham Palace in 1897 with the daughter of the Duchess of Roxburgh), and for all I know, has the honour of an audience with the Queen . . . Where everyone who calls himself a prince is regarded as a royalty, where a man who wears a turban with bad pearls in it is regarded as a lineal descendant of Nebuchadnezzar or Tamerlane.[22]

In another letter to Lord Hamilton, the Secretary of State for India, Curzon reiterated his complaint that 'at home every man with a turban, a sufficient number of jewels and a black skin, is mistaken for a miniature Akbar, and becomes the darling of drawing rooms, the honoured guest of municipalities and the hero of newspapers'.[23] Curzon in fact did not have a very high opinion of the princes of these 'Native States' of India. He looked upon them as a bunch of 'unruly and ignorant and rather undisciplined schoolboys', who needed to be guided by a 'grandmotherly interference' in their affairs and subjected to the sort of discipline found in an English public school. He considered their foreign trips as a 'dereliction of public duty'. Curzon strongly believed that the first duty of a 'native prince', like that of the Viceroy, lay to his own people. In his opinion, the only justification for retaining indirect rule through the 'native princes' in India was the confidence of the people in their own rulers. This being the case, princes should not be allowed to become a 'horde of frivolous absentees'. An occasional trip to Europe, to pay homage to the sovereign or in pursuit of knowledge of good government, was acceptable. But frequent pleasure trips only encouraged western tastes and habits of extravagance in the 'Oriental mind', and filled their palaces with 'expensive gew-gaws'.[24] To discourage such pleasure trips abroad, Curzon instituted an elaborate system of 'leave circulars' whereby the rulers had to give detailed notice in advance of the reason for their travel.[25]

But behind this concern for the welfare of the princely states' subjects lay other, deeper, reasons for discouraging their rulers from coming to Europe – reasons which are a recurring theme in the administration of the British Empire – and the maintenance of the superiority of rulers over the ruled. In an important minute on the 'Native States', Curzon commented:

> Already I have heard cases in which Indian princes have been addressed as 'sir' by ignorant but highly placed persons in England, and the Maharajah of Idar told me with disgust that at Buckingham Palace he had seen English ladies of the highest rank curtseying to the Maharani of Kuch Behar.[26]

To treat Indian princes as sovereigns or 'royalties' was going too far. In another note, Lord Hamilton, Secretary of State, told Curzon that the only thing against the Rajah of Puddukotta 'is that he wants to marry a white woman'.[27] In a similar vein, when considering the question of Indian 'orderlies' requested to attend King Edward VII's court during the coronation, Curzon voiced his concern:

> The 'woman' aspect of the question is rather a difficulty, since, strange as it may seem, Englishwomen of the house-maid class, and even higher, do offer themselves to these Indian soldiers, attracted by their uniform, enamoured by their physique, and with a sort of idea that the warrior is also an Oriental prince.[28]

It was in wars that the maharajahs made their greatest Imperial contribution, placing their troops and their wealth at the disposal of the British government. The armies of the 'Native States', as we have seen, fought on the Western Front, and in Palestine, Egypt, Mesopotamia and East Africa during the First World War. In the Second World War they fought in Burma, the Middle East, Eritrea and Italy. Some of the princes donated field ambulances and hospital ships for the care of wounded soldiers; others accompanied their troops into battle. The Maharajah of Bikaner, Ganga Singh, took his famous Camel Corps to China during the Boxer Rising of 1900 when the Chinese attempted to rid their country of Europeans, and again in 1903 in Somaliland during an uprising against British domination led by the so-called 'Mad Mullah'. The Camel Corps were again present during the First World War. Despite his age, Maharajah Pratab Singh at 70 insisted on accompanying his Jodhpur Lancers to the Western Front in 1914.

As diplomats and statesmen some of the princes attended international conferences. The Maharajah of Bikaner was one of the British representatives at the Imperial War Conference in 1917 and again at Versailles in 1919. The Maharajah of Patiala, Sir Bupender Singh, attended the Imperial War Conference, and in 1925 the Assembly of the League of Nations in Geneva. The Aga Khan, who was active in Muslim politics in India, was present at the 1931 Round Table Conference in London.

Students

Lord Macaulay's 1835 Education Minute introduced western scientific and literary education into India. However, entry into the Indian civil service could be gained only by a competitive examination in England; the Bar in Calcutta and Bombay was confined to barristers trained in England; the engineering staff was recruited from those trained at Coopers Hill. The police, medical, public works and forestry appointments were all obtained by qualifications gained in Britain. So, at great cost and despite many hardships, parents began to send their sons and sometimes their daughters for study in Britain. A few came at government expense but most were private students. Some ambitious parents even sent their children first to public schools in Britain and then to British universities.

Many famous names form part of this roll call of an Indian

elite educated in Britain. One of the founders of the Indian
National Congress, Surendranath Banerjea, came to Britain to
take the Indian civil service examination in 1869. Although he
passed the examination, he risked disqualification on the
grounds of age.[29] Both Gandhi and Muhammad Ali Jinnah were
law students in London, while Jawaharlal Nehru spent seven
years in Britain, first at Harrow, then at Cambridge and finally
at the Inner Temple, where he qualified as a barrister. His
daughter, Indira Gandhi, studied at Somerville College, Oxford.
Hundreds of other, lesser known, students came to Britain.
Some have left records of their impressions of life in British
universities; many more, however, are merely names in the
registers of the places where they studied, and sometimes in
official records.[30]

The first four students from India arrived in England in 1845.
By 1880 about 100 students were studying in Britain. The
largest number were Bengalis, followed by students from
Bombay. Though there was a steady rise in the number of
Indian students at British universities – in 1885 for instance the
number had risen to 160 – the total in the early years remained
small and was largely confined to London, Oxford and
Cambridge.[31] By 1910 there were more than 700 students in the
United Kingdom. By the 1920s Indian students, both male and
female, were coming in greater numbers, and could be found
not only at the universities of London, Oxford, Cambridge and
Edinburgh, but also at Manchester, Birmingham, Bristol,
Leeds, Liverpool, Sheffield and Aberystwyth. The largest
number, however, remained in London.[32] By 1930 the largest
group of overseas students in British universities was from India.
By 1931, the number of all foreign students in Britain stood at
5,408. Of these India sent 1,800 compared with 532 from South
Africa and Rhodesia, 212 from Canada and Newfoundland, 190
from Australia and 134 from New Zealand. The number of
Indian female students too was going up; in 1934 there were 100
women students, studying mainly medicine and education.[33]

Concern began to be voiced at the turn of the century about
the 'large number of raw youths' beginning to arrive in Britian

from India who were considered in 'no way fitted to encounter the temptations to which they will be exposed and to which many of them succumb'.[34] A large number of law students lived in private lodgings in London. There were between 150 and 200 of these in 1902, and no control could be exercised over them. Some thought that the life led by many of these young Indian students had become a 'scandal', as they lacked all 'self-control'.[35] They were said to find the 'attractions of a London brothel and intercourse with white women almost irresistible'.[36] It was also pointed out that in India white women 'hate and despise the ordinary Bengali Baboos', but in England white women 'rush at them' and were 'only too willing to become their victims'.[37] The steward of Gray's Inn knew of the case of one student in the past ten years who had killed himself with drink and fast living; and another, a promising young man, it was said, having ruined his parents with his extravagance, had been prosecuted for obtaining money under false pretences and had ended up by marrying a prostitute.[38]

And so, to exercise control and supervision over these 'raw youths', the idea of setting up a hostel for Indian students in London was born. But opinion soon became divided, not only on the real extent of the 'ruination' of Indian students, but on whether such a scheme would alienate educated Indian opinion and so become counterproductive. Sir Henry Cotton and others considered the reports of Indian students going astray highly exaggerated; and all those consulted thought a government-sponsored hostel would only create suspicion in India about the motive of the government in controlling Indians in London.[39] Only a private and unofficial institution could succeed. Lord Curzon foresaw another danger in boarding students in one establishment:

It is the fact that even now they are got hold of (and would be still more in a hostel) by political agitators, who at once make them members of Radical associations and indoctrinate them with unwise political theories. Most of the so-called friends of India at home are Radical politicians.

Their influence in this direction is already strong. We
should be careful about any steps that would tend to give it
further organization and strength. Of course if any such
association were formed, . . . the way in which to avoid the
above danger would be by inducing prominent Conservatives, such as Sir M. Bhownaggree, to belong to it and to
insist that it did not acquire an exclusive political
complexion.[40]

In the end, the idea of a government-sponsored hostel was
ruled out. But the idea of a private and unofficial institution
remained under consideration. And in 1910 such a hostel was
opened at 21 Cromwell Road, West London, to serve as a 'centre
for Indian students and for English societies and persons
interested in India and Indian students'. There were beds for
newly arrived students who had yet to find suitable lodgings. A
management committee controlled the running of the hostel
and a warden remained in charge. The Education Advisory
Office, the Bureau of Information, the National Indian
Association and the Northbrook Society were housed at the
hostel, which remained in existence till May 1936.[41]
    To help and guide the students various associations sprang
up: some were inspired by well-meaning Anglo-Indians or
Britons; others were organized and run by Indian students
themselves. The first association was the National Indian
Association (NIA), set up in 1870 by Mary Carpenter, editor of
The Last Days in England of the Rajah Rammohun Roy.[42] The
NIA aimed to bring Indians and Britons together socially and
break down 'old-fashioned barriers and prejudice'.[43] The
association published a journal, issued a *Handbook of Information*,
arranged social gatherings and helped students find their feet
when they first arrived in London.[44] The brain behind the
Northbrook Society and Club was the Political ADC, Sir
Gerald Fitzgerald. Its primary function was social and its aim
was to spread 'good influence' among the students from India.[45]
Bhownaggree was a prominent member. In 1916 the Indian
Gymkhana was set up to promote sporting and social relations

with English clubs and public schools. Tennis and cricket were the favourite sports. In February 1920, under the auspices of the Indian National Council of the YMCA, an Indian Students' Union and Hostel opened at Keppel Street in London; later it moved to nearby Gower Street. In 1920 a women's hostel was established in Highbury by well-known Indian women, and an Indian Women's Education Association provided scholarships for Indian women to be educated in Britain.[46]

Indian students at various universities set up their own associations. The Edinburgh Indian Association was founded in 1883 to meet the social and cultural needs of the Indian students at the university. At the time of its founding, there were only six students, but by the turn of the century the number had risen to 200.[47] An Indian hostel was opened at 5 Grosvenor Crescent, Edinburgh, providing accommodation for 38 students.[48]

Many students formed political associations to work for Indian independence. As we have seen, the London Indian Society and the revolutionary student movement attracted many students. In the thirties, many students joined the India League. During the Second World War many graduate students were called up; other students had to find employment – mostly unskilled factory work – as their families were unable to send them money.[49]

The Indian students were separated by thousands of miles from family and friends, and many lived on insufficient funds. They led a hard life. Not only was 'everything strange – the people, their ways and even their dwellings', as Gandhi put it[50] – but the students' difficulties were compounded by religious, cultural and dietary practices. So many students felt lonely and isolated. Though Indians had been coming to Britain long before the students started arriving, the latter looked strange to British eyes in their Indian clothes, especially in the early years. Two Parsis who came to London in 1838 to learn shipbuilding noted with great amusement the large crowds they attracted around them because of the 'peculiarity of our dress', and they were looked upon 'quite as curiosities'.[51] Attempts were often made to convert these 'heathens' from the East. D.F. Karaka, another Parsi, who was to become first Indian president of the Oxford Union, arrived in England in 1930 at the age of 19. His first greeting in Oxford was a letter which read: 'I understand you come from India. Have you a copy of the Bible? If not, can I send you one?'[52] Cornelia Sorabji, a law student at Somerville in 1889, found 'dear old ladies' were always trying to convert her. Cornelia Sorabji was a Christian convert, but dressed in her sari she was considered to '*look* so very heathen'.[53]

With so many 'benevolent' associations to guide and help Indian students, and with so many well-meaning and sympathetic families willing to befriend overseas visitors, many students found that they were treated with friendliness and invited into British homes.[54] Many made lasting friends not only among British students, but also with liberal-minded British people of the older generation. Such treatment led one student at Cambridge in the 1890s to remark that the 'English in India and the English at home are two entirely different people'. This student felt that when the English left their homes they lost their genuineness and that it was only at their firesides that their kindness and consideration, their unaffectedness and their liberality of mind was met with. The writer was not blind to the fact that

> there is an innate sense of superiority in the Englishman, which makes him look upon himself as belonging to a race the first in all the world. To his eyes even his immediate neighbours, the French and the Germans, are his inferiors; and he becomes more alive to this superiority when he leaves his island home to mix with foreigners. He makes up his mind to stand on the dignity of his race and to assume an unbendable stiffness, so as to show others what he readily is and how far he is above them. But *at home*, he is himself – natural and genuine.[55]

Whether the Indian students were tolerated or grudgingly accommodated, whether they were received with apathy or condescending patronage or genuine acceptance, racial prejudice confronted them all. Being looked down upon as a 'black man',[56] or otherwise insulted and abused, was a common experience. One student who was in Britain during 1839–41 believed that it was the 'lower orders' who were 'very rude in their manners and behaviour towards strangers', whom they did not like to see in their country.[57] The 'colour bar' – blatant or subtle – existed in lodgings, hotels and other public places. Many students found that they were discriminated against when they applied for practical and professional training. Universities were not immune from racism.[58] When D.F. Karaka was elected president of the Oxford Union, he found one London newspaper suggesting 'somewhat ungraciously, that now that an Indian had been made President of the Union, the office was no longer what it was'. Because of his experiences in Britain, Karaka made the 'colour bar' the theme of his farewell speech to the union.[59]

Commenting on the war effort of Indians in the First World War, the official report optimistically remarked that 'the magnificent response of Indians during the war had had an excellent effect in England, and that as a consequence any racial prejudice that might have existed seems very much on the decline.'[60] It was a vain hope.

Indian students were not alone in experiencing racial prejudice. The leftwing *Negro Worker* put it bluntly in 1932:

Despite the fact that it is otherwise, British imperialist agents in the colonies, especially the Church of England missionaries try to create the impression among native peoples that no matter what injustices they suffer in the colonies, in England a warm welcome awaits them! These apologists of British imperialism try their best to paint England as the most democratic country in the world, where all peoples, irrespective of colour or race, are treated as equals. However, every Negro, Indian, Arab or other coloured person who has ever lived in England knows from actual experience that all this missionary twaddle is nothing but a lie.[61]

Imperial attitudes led many in Britain to consider themselves superior to all others. D.H. Lawrence's vicious attack on

Rabindranath Tagore, who had won the Nobel Prize for literature in 1913, is a case in point. Writing to Lady Ottoline Morrell in 1916, Lawrence observed:

> I become more and more suprised to see how far higher, in reality, our European civilization stands than the East, India or Persia ever dreamed of. And one is glad to *realize* how these Hindus are horribly decadent and reverting to all forms of barbarism in all sorts of ugly ways. We feel surer on our feet, then. But this fraud of looking up to them – this wretched worship-of-Tagore attitude – is disgusting. 'Better fifty years of Europe' even as she is. Buddha worship is completely decadent and foul nowadays: and it *was* always only half-civilized.[62]

What other impressions did these visitors from India form of Imperial Britain? Most of them were impressed, even bewildered, by the traffic in London; by the hustle and bustle of commercial activity; by the pace of life; by people's energy and enterprise. The beauty of London's parks was another feature that many remarked on.[63] The pollution of industrial cities was disliked. For instance, the Rajah of Kolhapor who visited Britain in 1870 thought Manchester was spoilt by its factories, while Thakore Saheb of Gondal who was in this country in 1883 remarked that London 'though the metropolis of the Empire, is very smoky and sooty'.[64]

To the visitor from India the freedom women in the west enjoyed, compared with their sisters in the east, was another talking point. One visitor in the 1890s, B.M. Malabari, a journalist and social reformer, advocated that women should have the right to vote and should be given equal wages when the quality of work done was the same. He was pained to see not 'a single bust' in the Abbey or the cathedrals that honoured the memory of women. He concluded that this omission was not accidental.[65]

The contrasts in British society, the glaring inequality between the rich and the poor, came as a great shock to many. Commenting on the streets in the vicinity of the Thames

Tunnel, Thakore Saheb of Gondal observed:

All the streets in its vicinity are very narrow, dirty and unpleasant, and present a great contrast to the West End of London, where we live. I was labouring under the impression that of all the cities of the world London, the metropolis of the vast English empire, must not only be a charming place to live in, but that its lanes and by-lanes must be entirely free of filth. The results of my personal observation, however, have been disappointing.[66]

On the other hand, B.M. Malabari was thankful that, however poor India was, it did not experience the kind of poverty he had seen in parts of London (the East End), Glasgow and other congested cities, where

men and women living in a chronic state of emaciation, till they can hardly be recognized as human, picking up, as food, what even animals will turn away from; sleeping 50, 60, 80, of them together, of all ages, of both sexes, in a hole that could not hold ten with decency; swearing, fighting, trampling on one another; filling the room with foul confusion and fouler air. This is not a picture of occasional misery, in some places it represents the everyday life of the victims of misfortune . . . Thousands of men and women, disabled by accident, or thrown out of work, trudge aimlessly about . . . Thousands drag out a miserable existence, embittered by disease from which death, too long delayed, is the only relief . . . And side by side with such heart-rending scenes of misery, one sees gorgeously dressed luxury flaunting in the streets.[67]

The same writer blamed the 'grasping monopoly of capital' and its exploitation of labour for this sad state of affairs.[68]

For colonial subjects, the relationship between the rulers and ruled was a matter of utmost concern. B.M. Malabari considered that the English asserted their Imperial instincts and attitudes more in the matter of language than in any other way. This was shown by the way the English scorned learning foreign languages, and insisted that others spoke to them in English. The English may poke fun at 'Babu English', but how many of them could speak Bengali half as well as the Bengalis spoke English?[69] A student writing in the 1890s noted the sterility of higher education in India: the only remedy the government of India adopted was to encourage students to study in England. For him, the cause of 'the sterility and barrenness of the Indian intellectual field' was due mainly to the education policy of Lord Macaulay and the loss of vernacular languages from the education available in India. If only the indigenous cultures had been encouraged and developed, if Indians had been allowed to retain the study of their languages and literature in the high schools and universities, Indian intellectual development would have flourished. Because of the emphasis on English, Indians had suffered a great loss:

> loss of energy, loss of creative power, loss of originality. Our acquisitive faculties have been taxed to the utmost; no wonder that our creative faculties have suffered in consequence.[70]

B.M. Malabari found the indifference of MPs to Indian affairs in parliament chilling.[71] Most of these Indian visitors, like the nationalists, wanted equal justice and believed that Indians should be given more share in the running of their country. Thakore Saheb of Gondal was of the opinion that all higher posts in the government and the military should be, as in the times of the Mughals, open to the 'deserving children of the soil'. As many Indians had acquired a western-style education, he did not see any justification in the denial of this right. He also thought that the time was ripe for Indians to be represented in the British parliament, or be given their own parliament in India.[72] The burden of taxation on the Indians was another grievance many visitors wished to see remedied. B.M. Malabari commented that he did not ask for Britain's 'superfluous wealth'. But 'we do want her to manage our resources in India as carefully as she manages her own'.[73]

Many, like Rabindranath Tagore, found painful 'the arrogant

spirit of contempt and callousness about India', and concluded that India's salvation lay in her own hands.[74]

Cornelia Sorabji

Social reformer and barrister, Cornelia Sorabji was the first-ever woman law student at a British university. Born at Nasik on 15 November 1866, she was the fifth child in a family of seven girls and one boy. Her father, the Reverend Sorabji Karsedji, was a Christian convert, and his children were 'brought up English', but were taught also to retain and respect their Indian culture.[75]

Cornelia came to England to study law, a career not open to women at that time. Her motive for this choice was to help the '*purdah nasheen*', women who lived secluded lives because of religious customs.[76] These women – widows and orphans – suffered many injustices. In their seclusion, they were not able to fight for their legal rights.

To realize her ambition, Cornelia Sorabji had to overcome many hurdles, and her university career illustrates the battles women – and not Indian women alone – have had to fight to win educational and academic equality. She was the first woman to be admitted to the Deccan College in Poona. She lived at home and travelled to lectures. Having gained a first-class degree, she was eligible for the government of India scholarship to study at a university in Britain. But as a woman she was barred from this award. Undaunted, she accepted a temporary post teaching English Literature at Gujerat College, Ahmedabad. Thus, at the age of 18, she became the first woman professor in an all-male college. Finally, using her savings and with the help of friends in England who launched a 'substitute scholarship' fund, she was able to come to Somerville Hall, Oxford, in 1889.[77] And so she became the first woman to enrol for the Bachelorship of Civil Law (BCL).

At Oxford the Master of Balliol, Benjamin Jowett, became her tutor and friend. Through her influential friends Cornelia Sorabji also met many literary and political personalities. She

met Florence Nightingale, who had been one of the contributors
to her 'substitute scholarship' fund. She was presented at court
and Queen Victoria sent a 'gracious message' allowing her to
appear there in a coloured sari.[78]

Being the first and only woman law student at Oxford,
Cornelia Sorabji found the male dons patronizing. She wrote of
one of them: 'I wish he would treat me like a man and not make
gallant speeches about my "intellect" and "quickness of perception" . . . He is frightfully apologetic, too, and wonders if he is
not wasting my time when he is coaching me.' She put up with
his 'eccentricities in consideration of his mental value'.[79]

She was not allowed to sit the BCL examinations with the
men. It was proposed that she should take the BCL papers
alone, at her own college, supervised by the warden. Cornelia
Sorabji was most indignant at this discriminatory treatment.
She considered that 'some day when women are allowed to take
degrees mine might be withheld because I had not sat in the
schools with the men'.[80] In the end, because of the fuss she
made, her tutor appealed to the Vice Chancellor on her behalf
and a special dispensation was granted. She informed her
family:

> The difficulty about my schools was favourably settled the
> evening before I went in and settled far beyond my hopes –
> for I had a special decree and I could write in the schools; so
> that though the schools are not public, my exam was
> official.[81]

She was awarded a degree but was not admitted to the legal
profession. It was not until 1919 that women could become
barristers. After leaving Oxford, she joined Lee and Pemberton,
a firm of solicitors at Lincoln's Inn, to obtain professional
training. Old ladies regarded Cornelia Sorabji's presence in
chambers with awe and dubbed her 'a new Woman'.[82] Because
of her sex, she was prevented from taking the solicitor's
examination. In 1922, after the Bar was finally thrown open to
women, she became a member of Lincoln's Inn; she was called
to the Bar in the following year.

As 'legal adviser', the lowly status accorded to her, she had in the meantime carried on successful legal and welfare work in India for almost 30 years. After returning to India in 1894 she had laboured, against all odds, on behalf of hundreds of widows, wives and orphans. In 1909 she was awarded the Kaiser-i-Hind gold medal in recognition of this work. Cornelia Sorabji was also the author of five books. In 1929, she retired from active work and settled in Britain, where she died in July 1954, aged 88.

9. Into the Twentieth Century: Indian Influences in Britain

As we have seen, Indians have long been in Britain as part of the legacy of the British control of India. The community in the period before 1947 was, as now, not a homogenous body: different castes, religions and classes were represented.

In 1961 there were 182,172 Asians in the United Kingdom, of whom 151,435 came from India and 30,737 from Pakistan. No official statistics are available for the period before 1947, the year in which India regained independence from Britain. This is because before the 1960s census data did not record the population by ethnic origins. However, in 1932, the Indian National Congress survey of 'all Indians outside India' estimated that there were 7,128 Indians in the United Kingdom.[1]

The earliest Indian settlers lived in the seaport cities of Glasgow, Newcastle, Liverpool, Southampton and London. These were the lascars, employed by British merchant lines like the P. & O. for their cheapness. In 1917, lascar wages had declined even further when the newly established National Maritime Board put up British sailors' rates of pay. During the two world wars, more lascars were employed in the growing fleet of merchant ships required to help the war effort, and took the places of European crews required for the navy. Over the years, despite stringent rules, lascars had deserted to escape the rough treatment meted out to them on board the liners and had settled in the seaports. In common with other black sailors, they faced discrimination. Many worked at unskilled jobs in the dock areas; others set up as small street traders. Many married local women. During the Second World War, some sailors moved inland to work in Midlands foundries and factories where demand for labour was high. Attracted by high wages, many more sailors jumped ship; and because of the great need for labour, no attempts were made to trace the lascars who had deserted.[2] In 1939 the Indian population in Birmingham was about 100, which included some 20 doctors and students. By 1945, it had grown to 1,000.[3]

The only authoritative inquiry into the lascar workforce was undertaken in 1949; no such study was made during the Imperial period. According to the 1949 report, based on the information given by the Indian Ministry of Commerce, there was a strict religious demarcation in the work done – Muslims tended to work in the engine-rooms, Hindus on the decks, and Christians in the saloons. From the West, Sylhet, in what is now Bangladesh, supplied the engine-room staff, while the deck-hands came from Noakhali. Bombay recruited deck workers from the Malabar Coast, Ahmedabad and Surat; the stewards and catering staff came from Goa and the Cochin area, while the engine-room workforce was made up of Punjabis and Pathans.[4] The seafaring community in Britain reflected these regional and religious groupings.

At the other end of the scale was the professional class, whose largest group was members of the medical profession. It is estimated that before 1947 about 1,000 Indian doctors practised throughout Britain, 200 of them in London alone.[5] The tradition of Indian doctors working in Britain goes back a long way to Fram Gotla and K.M. Pardhy – and before that to the Shampooing Surgeon, Sake Deen Mahomed and his grandson Akbar Mahomed, who worked at Guy's Hospital. During the 1930s and 1940s many Indian medical students stayed in Britain to practise as doctors. In the days before the National Health Service, doctors had to set up their own private practices and build up a clientèle – no easy task. But many Indian doctors succeeded. Some also worked as panel doctors. The Indian doctors were well liked and respected. Many became very popular with their patients. The Indian Doctors' Association and the Overseas Doctors' Association were founded in this period.[6]

Other professions were represented too; the case of R.B. Jillani provides an interesting example. Having qualified as a civil engineer in 1935, he secured an appointment in Britain with the help of his professor. During the Second World War he was called up, as were many doctors and graduate students.[7]

The 1920s and 1930s also saw the arrival of Sikhs from the Punjab, many of whom took up door-to-door selling of hosiery, knitwear and woollens. They were a familiar sight in the Midlands, Glasgow, Peterborough and London. Some displayed their wares in Oxford Street and Hyde Park, while living in the East End of London. One Sikh hawker, who had become fluent in Gaelic, settled in the Hebrides.[8]

In 1938, the first Indian Workers' Association was set up in Coventry, its membership consisting mainly of factory workers from Coventry and hawkers from the Midlands. Soon after, another association was founded in London. The aim of these early Indian workers' associations, like that of the India League, was to fight for India's independence and to promote social and cultural activities among the Indian residents in Britain. After 1947 these early IWAs declined, but flourished again in the early 1950s.[9]

Such was the rich variety of the Indian community in Britain. When comparison is made with the settlers who came from India to Britain after 1947, several differences emerge. Before 1947 the community was not only much smaller, but it was to a greater extent made up of skilled personnel, many having obtained their qualifications in British universities. There was no set pattern of migration: some had been brought over; some were involved in the campaign for India's freedom; others had settled for professional reasons, having first come either as students or as businessmen; others, again, were trained in Britain, had successful careers in India and then returned to Britain to retire. The migration of Asians to Britain after 1947 follows a different pattern. It coincided with two economic developments: one in Britain and the other on the Indian subcontinent. Britain, like other European countries, experienced a severe labour shortage as a result of the postwar economic boom, and naturally looked to the 'Empire' for a cheap source of labour. Partition (the division into India and Pakistan) had created social and economic problems. Pressure on the land encouraged many to seek new opportunities, so they took advantage of the British economic boom and came to work in the industrial towns of Britain.

The experiences of Asians in Britain in the period before 1947 were similar to those of these later arrivals and of the black community in general. As subject peoples from colonial India, they faced patronizing 'concern' and apathy, and had to endure the racist stereotyped perceptions of the British. They suffered from racial prejudice and racial hatred from some sections of the population. In this respect, the experiences of Asians in Britain today have a long history.

The Indian connection with Britain has had a great economic, social and cultural impact on Britain. In India, Britain came into contact with a rich ancient civilization which captured the imagination of many British people. Witness the Oriental fantasy of the Royal Pavilion in Brighton, built for King George IV when he was Prince of Wales, or the country mansion of Sezincote House in Gloucestershire, built for the nabob Charles Cockerell. Indian miniature paintings, tapestries, carpets and china in Britain's museums, like the Victoria and Albert, are examples of treasures taken from India to Britain. Tastes in furniture, food and decorations have all been influenced by the Indian connection.

It is often forgotten also that the English language, that vehicle of cultural imperialism, has absorbed many words of Indian origin into its vocabulary; words like bungalow, verandah, khaki, pyjamas, jodhpurs, dungarees, puttee, loot, thug, yoga, punch (the drink), chutney, and pariah. Indian experience has also enriched English speech with new words created out of corruptions of Indian words: juggernaut (*Jaganath*), blighty (*bilayati*), and Hobson-Jobson (*Ya Hasan! Ya Hosain!*).[10] And the term 'civil service', without which no government can function, originated with the East India Company in India.

The Indian Empire, that most prized jewel, contributed

much to Britain's prosperity and power. Not only did India provide employment for the thousands of British men and women who went there, but many received their pensions from India. The cost of all this was borne by the Indian taxpayer. The British 'developed' India's economy to suit their industrial needs and to benefit British trade and manufactures. Indians were used as a cheap source of labour to transport this wealth to Britain, and to create and exploit resources for the British economy in other parts of the Empire (e.g. South Africa, the West Indies, Sri Lanka).

The Indians who came to Britain have made a significant contribution to the development of the British Isles – a contribution largely ignored. They have enriched the British way of life, economically, politically and in the social field. Not surprisingly, a few individuals stand out. But the lascars need a mention, and so do those hundreds of women, the ayahs, who left their families and children and grandchildren to the care of others as they accompanied the memsahibs to these shores and nursed and mothered their children.

During the colonial period, the preoccupation of many Indians who came to Britain was to work for their country's freedom. But on the way many played an important role in the politics of this country. Three Asians were elected to the House of Commons between 1893 and 1929. Local government was another field in which Asians participated. The contribution made by Krishna Menon in St Pancras is well known. But there were others. Chuni Lal Katial became the first Asian mayor, elected in 1938-9 in Finsbury, the constituency which had returned Dadabhai Naoroji to parliament. Katial, a physician, spent 23 years in public service. He was an alderman and councillor of the borough of Finsbury from 1934, and a member of the London County Council. In 1948 he was given the freedom of Finsbury in recognition of his services to the borough, particularly in the field of public health, housing and social welfare, and to the medical profession.[11] He retired in 1948. Other Indians, too, have worked in local government. Another doctor, D.R. Prem, was elected Labour councillor in

Birmingham soon after the Second World War.[12]

One Asian, Satyendra Prasanno, had the distinction of being elevated to the House of Lords, as Baron Sinha of Raipur, in 1919. Lord Sinha was given the task of piloting the 1919 Government of India Act through the House of Lords. Born in March 1863, Lord Sinha had first come to Britain in 1881 as a law student at Lincoln's Inn. He was called to the Bar in 1886, returning to India to follow a career in law and politics. A 'moderate', he joined the Indian National Congress in 1896, and was active in the Congress, becoming its president for the 1915 Bombay Session. He left the Congress, together with other moderates in 1919. Lord Sinha had returned to England again in 1917 as the Indian representative at the Imperial War Conference. He was given the freedom of the City of London in 1919, and in the same year he joined Ameer Ali as a privy councillor. In 1926 he was appointed to the Judicial Committee of the Privy Council and was also made a bencher of Lincoln's Inn. Lord Sinha died in 1928.[13]

It was not only the political and medical fields that attracted Indians. Many have been connected with education too. Mention has been made of Dadabhai Naoroji, who combined his political work with being Professor of Gujerati at London University, and Syed Abdoollah, Professor of Hindustani at University College, London. Another Asian, Ganendra Mohan Tagore, was Professor of Hindu Law and Bengali Language at London University in the 1860s. Indians helped to promote educational research by setting up scholarship funds and endowments to the universities. Sir Ratan Tata, a Parsi, founded the Department of Social Science and Administration at the London School of Economics, and in 1912 he set up a fund (the Ratan Tata Fund) to promote the 'study and further knowledge of the principles and methods of preventing and relieving destitution and poverty'.[14] Another Parsi, Dr Nanabhai Navroji Katrak, inaugurated a series of lectures at Oxford. There is also a tradition of Indian writing in English. Sake Deen Mahomed's *Travels* were published in Ireland in 1794. Naoroji as an economist and Ameer Ali as a lawyer wrote important works in their respective fields. And Rabindranath Tagore, Nobel Prize winner for literature in 1913, is well known in the west.

In the field of religion, too, Indians have made important contributions. The Reverend Shapurji Edalji, a Parsi convert to Christianity, became the vicar of Great Wyrley, Staffordshire, in the 1870s. The Reverend James Kerriman Mahomed, another grandson of Sake Deen Mahomed, was vicar of Hove, Sussex. He died in 1935 at the age of 81.[15] A Singhalese, Pastor Kamal Chunchie, a Muslim convert to Christianity, was appointed to the Queen Victoria Seamen's Rest in Poplar, an arm of the Methodist church. He worked among the seafaring community in Canning Town. His reports on his 'work among the coloured brethren', written in the annual reports of the Queen Victoria Seamen's Rest, give a clear picture of the difficulties and discrimination suffered by black sailors in the East End. Pastor Chunchie was also the founder of the Coloured Men's Institute in Tidal Basin Road, Canning Town.[16]

Though not kith and kin, Indian soldiers fought in both the world wars. To this day, the Gurkhas provide a full brigade of troops to the British Army.

Finally, the women's contribution must not be ignored. Mrs Bhikaji Cama, active in radical student politics in London and Paris, Noor Inayat Khan, secret agent in France during the Second World War, and social reformers like Cornelia Sorabji, have worked for both India and Britain.

And so the process continues. Asians, like other settlers who come to Britain, bring with them their rich and varied cultures, elements of which, in the course of time, they bestow upon their adopted country for its development and enrichment.

Appendix I

Tryal sloop: Articles with lascar crew 23 October 1746

Articles of Agreement Indentured made concluded and agreed
upon this Twenty-third of October in the Year of our Lord One
thousand Seven hundred and Forty-six between John Forster
Esq President and Governor of Fort William in the Kingdom of
Bengal in the East India Council on behalf of the Honble United
Company of Merchants of England trading to the East Indies on
the one part and Vessenti De Cruz Syrang Joseph de Cruz
Carpenter John Cornel Tindal Domingo Dodiego Domingo
Gabriel Domingo Soles Augustin Suriano Gasper Santiago
Bernaldo De Cruz Joseph Demont Culds De Dosa Thomas
Deaquino John Pasqual Bitorino Tesera Luis De Santo Michal
Fernandes Panchico De Cruz Christobal Barnaldo Pedro de
Rosario John Anico and Manuel Duarte Lascars inhabitants of
Calcutta in the Kingdom of Bengal in the East Indies aforesaid
on the other part and first We in behalf of the said Honble
United East India Company do covenant promise and agree to
and with the said Syrang Carpenter Tindal and Lascars and
every of them by these presents in manner and form following
(that is to say) that we in behalf of the said Honble United
Company for and in consideration of the service and labour of
the said Syrang Carpenter Tindal and Lascars and after their
working in their several stations on board the Tryal Snow
whereof is master Richard Thelwall from the Port of Calcutta
aforesaid of the Port of London in the Kingdom of England do
hereby promise and agree to allow and pay or cause to be paid to
the said Vessenti De Cruz Syrang and Joseph De Cruz

Carpenter the sum of twenty Rupees Arcot each per month or stirling money of Great Britain two pounds and ten shillings to the said John Cornel Tindal seventeen Arcot Rupees per month or stirling money of Great Britain two pounds two shillings and six pence and to the said Domingo Dodiego Domingo Gabriel Domingo Soles Augustin Suriano Gasper Santiago Bernaldo De Cruz Joseph Demont Culas De Sosa Thomas Deaquino John Pasqual Bitorino Tesera Luis de Santo Michal Fernandez Panchico De Cruz Christobal Barnaldo Pedro De Resario John Anico and Manuel Duarte Lascars each of them fifteen Arcot Rupees per month or sterling money of Great Britain one pound seventeen shillings and six pence for and during so long time as the Snow Tryal shall be on her passage or voyage from Calcutta aforesaid to the said Port of London and from end immediately after the arrival of the said Snow Tryal in the Port of London aforesaid We the said John Forster Esq etc Council do hereby promise and agree to pay or cause to be paid to the said Vessenti De Cruz Syrang and Joseph De Cruz Carpenter eight shillings and nine pence each per week to the said John Cornel Tindal eight shillings and two pence per week and to the said Lascars seven shillings per week each man during and for so long a time as necessary provisions can be made for their voyage and return to Calcutta aforesaid and in further consideration of their good behaviour and the time that they may be out of business that they do receive two months pay as bounty money besides the allowance of diet money And the said John Forster Esq etc Council in behalf of the said Honble United Company do covenant and agree to and with the said Syrang Carpenter Tindal and Lascars that the said Honble United Company shall so soon after the arrival of the said Snow Tryal at the said Port of London as they conveniently can obtain and provide a passage for the said Syrang Carpenter Tindal and Lascars and all necessary provision for such their passage from the said Port of London to Calcutta aforesaid in consideration whereof and of the said several articles and agreements herein before stipulated to be paid done and performed by the said Honble United East India Company the said Syrang Carpenter Tindal and Lascars

do all and every of them hereby covenant and promise and agree
to and with the said John Forster Esq etc Council to go on board
the said Snow Tryal and to perform and do their several and
respective duties or offices as shall be required of them
according to their several and respective capacities and knowledge from the said Port of Calcutta to the Port of London
aforesaid and on or after the arrival of the said Snow Tryal at the
said Port of London the said Syrang Carpenter and Lascars do
hereby promise and agree to do and perform all such work and
duty as shall be required of each and every of them to be done by
the said Honble United East India Company during and until
such time as the said Honble United company shall obtain and
provide a passage for their returning from the said Port of
London to Calcutta aforesaid And lastly the said Syrang
Carpenter Tindal and Lascars all and each of them do hereby
also agree to and promise not to stay or inhabit in England after
such Passage is obtained for their return to Bengal as aforesaid
without the licence and approbation of the said Honble United
East India Company anything herein contained to the contrary
thereof notwithstanding. In witness whereof the said parties to
these presents have hereunto set their hand and seals the day
and year first above mentioned.
Sealed and Delivered in the presence of us

Richard Thelwall   The Mark of Lascars (marks)

We the undersigned Syrang Carpenter Tindal and Lascars of
the Honble United Company's Tryal Snow do acknowledge to
have received of Captain Richard Thelwall commander of the
said vessel six months Impress [?] advanced from the 1st
November 1746 as specified in the body of the bond.
Witness our hands in Fort William this 8th Day of November
1746.

The Mark

IOR: L/MAR/B/580B(2)

Appendix II

Society for the Protection of Asiatic Sailors,
The Times, Friday 9 December, 1814. No. 9387

Asiatic sailors [advertisement]

A memorial concerning the Asiatic Sailors who assist in navigating ships from the East Indies to this country, drawn up at instance of a Society formed for their Protection, founded on documents in their possession, and respectfully presented to Lord Sidmouth, his Majesty's principal Secretary of State for the Home Department; to the Right Honourable Nicholas Vansittart, Chancellor of the Exchequer; to the Honourable the Board of Control for the Affairs of India; and the Honourable the Board of Directors of the East India Company:

That many Lascars are forcibly taken from the street and put on ship in India, by Peons employed for that purpose, and brought away against their consent, who had previously never seen a ship; and others are kidnapped both by their countrymen and Europeans, to facilitate which a number of crimpting houses are established in every principal sea port in the East Indies.

That, in such cases, the bounty money and wages usually paid Lascars in advance, are received by other persons, and not by the Lascars themselves.

That, the bounty money and wages usually paid in advance, and received by Lascars, of four months a coasting voyage, and six months a voyage to this country, do all pass through the hands of the Ghat Serangs, who deduct eight rupees therefrom from each man they engage for the voyage of the former, and fourteen rupees for each man engaged for a voyage of the latter description. The Ghat Serang next deduct twenty rupees as their commission for every thousand rupees which pass through their hands to the ship Serang for Lascars, and nine rupees for the use of the room wherein they meet to be engaged for the voyage. And the Sircars deduct one anna from each rupee which passes through hands from Captain to Ghat Serang, all which, together with the profit obtained in different ways by the ship Serangs, reduces the amount received by each Lascar to a mere pittance, while the navy agent in this country, who has sometimes been necessarily employed by them to obtain the remainder of their wages of Captains and owners of several sums amounting to £1,517 received £262. 10s. And as every Lascar who comes to this country pays one shilling per month at the Merchants' Shipping-office, the amount received by the Lascars is reduced still lower. See Schedule A.

That notwithstanding the very ample provision of clothing, medicines, medical assistant, good and sufficient quantity of provisions, intended to be secured by deed of covenant which is entered into with the Honourable East India Company, and signed by the Captain of each country ship for himself and owners before he sails from the port of India, there appears to be a very material and almost universal deficiency in these particulars. It being usual for the Lascars on first going on board ship to be supplied with animal food, until they set sail, after which from Bengal to England, and also from England to Bengal rice and ghee, and in some instances rice only, and that of the worst quality.

That whatever may be the stock of medicines laid in, it appears that a medical attendant is seldom to be found on board country ships during the voyage.

That the Lascars have not always obtained suitable clothing on arrival at certain latitude, south and north, to the extent provided by the beforementioned deed, and even whether such clothing be obtained or not, notwithstanding the prices for such articles are fixed in the charter party, they are generally charged enormous sums for them.

That Lascars have not always brought with them, nor obtained suitable clothing for the season of the year wherein they have arrived, nor during their stay in this country; nor have the necessary medical assistance always been afforded nor so much as permitted gratuitously to be afforded them, in this country, not even in the last stages of the sickness.

That the custom of boarding and lodging the healthy in the same apartment with the sick, the dying and the dead, of making no difference between the diet of the sick and the healthy, of their being, whether well or ill, alike necessitated to lie on bare and damp floors in this country, without covering, and even during the winter season, when six, eight, and ten, night after night, have been found dead, together with the consequence of their promiscuous intercourse with the most abandoned females, to which that situation of their residence affords them many facilities, is most pernicious to their health, and eventually is more fatal among them than any other calamity under which they labour.

That the too general practice with the superintendent and his assistant of capriciously beating the Lascars, and of withholding the whole or part of their food from them; of the Lascars themselves combining against, and inflicting inhuman and excessive punishment on each other, even on their own Serangs, by the mode of tying their hands together, extending their arms over their heads by a rope thrown across a beam in their lodging room, their toes just touching the ground, and of tying six, eight, ten of them at a time to the pump which stands in the yard, and beating them with a cane for a considerable time on their bare bodies out of the view of the public, is not in unison with the wise and humane laws of England, nor calculated to support good discipline and subordination among them, and in justification of such cruel practices none of them advance any argument derived from their religious opinions.

That during the present year, measures, little short of compulsory, have been necessarily resorted to, to induce the Captains and owners of the ships to pay wages due to the Lascars, amounting to £1,457 which, there is ground to fear, they had not intended to pay them.

That it is to be apprehended many of the Asiatic seamen get

materially injured in their health, and even lose their lives, from want of food, clothing, and lodging, while in this country; seeing that during the present year a very considerable number of them, who had been several days and nights without food, and lodging, have been relieved by orders obtained at the India House, for their admittance into the Company's barracks, from which they had been provisionally driven; their chest, containing their clothes, turned out of doors, exposed to all kinds of weather; while some, who obtained notes from India House, and flattered themselves they contained orders to the same effect, have had the mortification of seeing them torn to pieces immediately on being presented, have been ordered off the premises without any reason being assigned, and turned adrift in a country whither they had never come before; and a great proportion of those who have succeeded and received orders for relief, have first been vexatiously sent backward and forward from the barracks to their Captains, from Captains to owners, and from owners back again to barracks, have been necessitated to sell or pledge most or all of their wearing apparel, have been reduced to the necessity of taking up their abode with bad characters, to want the common means of subsistence, and have been seen in a state bordering on absolute nudity, and often times have been relieved when the cases appeared so flagrant as to excite public execration; and recently upwards of a month sixteen, and for a fortnight nineteen of these people, who had previously been refused lodging and provision at the Company's barracks, have been kept from perishing by obtaining the most frugal and plainest fare, at the expense of the Society formed for their protection, while a considerable number, from the want of funds to enable the Society to provide them also with the like, have been left to wander about the streets in the utmost distress and misery and even exposed to death, as in the recent instances of a West Indian or African who was one morning found dead in one of the streets at Poplar, and on whose body the Coroner's inquest sat on Friday, the 12th inst, at the sign of the Arrow, when part of the verdict given, was that the man died through the inclemency of the weather; and also in the instance of John

Dennis, who on first coming on shore from the East India ship
Minerva, Captain Anderson Master, was directed to apply to
the India-house for an order to be lodged and victualled at the
Company's barracks, when he presented the note which he
there received, it was instantly torn to pieces, and the man
ordered off the premises, together with John De Cruz and
William Davison, who came in the same ship with Dennis
(while John Baptist, another of the crew, was taken into and
remained in the barracks); after wandering about for weeks,
sometimes stealing into the barracks to lodge at night, and
gladly accepting the smallest quantity of provisions, which some
of his countrymen reserved for him from their own allowance
during the day, (but when detected in this way of keeping
himself alive, was repeatedly driven from the premises), at last
dropped and lay speechless outside the barracks, until carried
inside by two men belonging to the premises, where he was seen
four days afterwards, during which time he received no
sustenance, lying in his own filth on the bare floor without bed
or hammock, wrapped up in a blanket with his feet and legs bare
and cold as though dead, and who eventually fell a sacrifice to
hunger and nakedness; the Coroner's Inquest sat on this body at
the Sign of Grave Maurice, Whitechapel-road, on the 3rd of
November, 1814, returned the verdict, 'died through the inclemency of the weather, and for want of care and nourishment.'

Finally, that the custom of sending upwards of three
thousand Lascars annually back to India as passengers, some of
whom have families, who are previously pennyless, appears a
grievous evil; and when their ship gets out of sight of land, after
having paid for their passage, either to compel them by coercive
measures to work her during the voyage without any wages; or
to induce them to do so because of their necessity, by promising
them an indefinite present, or on very low specific terms, is a
mode of proceeding which must be reprobated by every humane
and liberal mind.

Committee of the aforesaid Society: John William Adam, Esq.
Mile-end Road; William Allen, Plough-court; Mr Samuel

Schedule A

[Wages of] One hundred men for seven months

Serang	25 Rupees, or	£3	2	6	per month	£21	7	6
First Tyndal	20 Rupees or	2	10	0	,,	17	10	0
Second Tyndal	16 Rupees or	2	0	0	,,	14	0	0
Third Tyndal	14 Rupees or	1	15	0	,,	12	5	0
96 Lascars	12 Rupees or	1	10	0	,,	1008	0	0

1073. 12. 6

Deductions

Ghat Serang 14 Repees or £1 15 0 for hiring each man	175	0	0
Ghat Serang 20 Repees for every 1,000 paid ships Serang in advance	18	7	11½
Ghat Serang 9 Rupees for use of room	1	2	6
Sircar one anna every Rupee	57	10	3½
Ships Serang, profit in various ways, at least 11 each man	99	0	0
Navy agent in England	105	0	0
Fees at Merchant's Shipping office, 1s. each man per month	35	0	0

£582. 11. 8¼

[BALANCE] 491. 0. 9¼

Allen, St Catherine's; Rev Henry Atley, Stepney-square; Andrew Burt, Esq. King David's-lande; William Cardale, Esq. Islington; Rev J Clayton, jun. Hackney; Rev George Ford, Mile-end; Thos. S. Forster Esq. St Helen's-place; George Hammond, Esq. Whitechapel; John Harris, Broad-street; Mr John Hebditch, Limehouse; Henry Knight, Glasshouse-fields; Peter Lindeman, Esq. Whitechapel; Mr Luke Matthews, Fenchurch-street; Mr Thos Monds, Commercial-road; Mr Thos Robinson, Wapping; Mr John Tindall, Cockhill; Rev Thos Williams, New-road; Rev David Wilson, Chapel-street, Bedford-row; Mr Thos Wontner, Minories ; Edward Forster, Esq. Mansionhouse-street; George Knight, Glasshouse-yard; by whom donations and subscriptions to enable them to prosecute the object of their designations will be gladly received and acknowledged.

Appendix III

Statistics Showing Lascar Employment (Sailors) 1891-1914

(*Source*: British Parliamentary Papers Annual Statement of Trade and Navigation)

Year	Total	British	Foreign	Lascars	Lascars (per cent)
1891	240,480	186,176	30,267	24,037	10
1892	241,735	185,437	30,899	25,399	10.5
1893	240,974	186,628	29,549	24,797	10
1894	240,458	183,233	31,050	26,175	11
1895	240,486	180,074	32,235	28,077	12
1896	242,039	178,994	33,046	29,999	12.5
1897	240,931	175,549	33,898	31,484	13
1898	242,553	174,980	35,308	32,265	13.5
1899	244,135	174,266	36,064	33,805	14
1900	247,448	174,532	36,893	36,023	14.5
1901	247,973	172,912	37,630	37,431	15
1902	253,540	174,538	39,825	39,177	15.5
1903	257,937	176,520	40,396	41,021	16
1904	259,489	176,975	39,832	42,682	16.5
1905	263,686	180,492	39,711	43,483	16.5
1906	270,791	183,340	38,084	44,367	16.5
1907	277,146	194,848	37,694	44,604	16
1908	275,721	196,834	34,735	44,152	16
1909	274,307	198,474	31,873	43,960	16
1910	276,306	201,910	30,462	43,934	16
1911	281,300	205,065	30,783	45,452	16
1912	286,806	208,635	30,960	47,211	16.5
1913	292.057	212,570	32,639	46,848	16
1914	295,652	212,640	31,396	51,616	17.5

Appendix IV

D. *Naoroji* – Address to his Fellow Electors in Central
Finsbury, July 1895

Central Finsbury Parliamentary Election, 1895

Gentlemen and Fellow Electors,

In my address to you at the last Parliamentary Election in
July, 1892, when you did me the honour of electing me as your
Representative in the House of Commons, I promised that –

'Should you do me the honour to return me, I will devote all
my time to Parliamentary duties, and your local wants and
interests shall have my especial attention.'

Both of these promises I have faithfully fulfilled to the very
letter, as will be seen by the following record:

In 1892 there was only one division in Parliament, and I voted
in it.

In 1893–4 the Session was divided into two parts. In the first
part there were 310 divisions, and I voted in 304 of them.

During the second part of the Session I visited India, carrying
with me your generous and kind message given through the
Council of the Central Finsbury United Liberal and Radical
Association. This journey necessitated a short absence.

In 1894 there were 246 divisions, and of these I voted in 231.

In 1895 there were 139 divisions, and of these I voted in 118.

It was only when my attendance was required at some
function in Clerkenwell, or when engaged in advancing the
Liberal cause in some other way, that I was absent from any
division. But as even in my few personal absences from the
Division Lobby I was always paired, not a single vote was ever
lost by the constituency.

In my Committee work also, I have been as closely attentive.

With regard to my second promise – the local wants and interests of Clerkenwell have always had my prompt, earnest, and careful attention.

I have thus fulfilled my pledges, and for which, I gratefully acknowledge, you several times generously expressed your entire satisfaction. I cannot, therefore, but hope that you will return me again with a large majority.

Within the limits of this address, it would be impossible to do adequate justice to the great and good work accomplished by the Liberal and Radical Party during the last three years, but I may be permitted to point out, that despite all the continuous obstructive opposition of its opponents, the Government has to their credit, as having passed 73 Public Acts and 229 Local and Private Acts in 1893-4; 68 Public Acts and 216 Local and Private Acts were passed in 1894, while up to 21st June in 1895, 17 Public Acts passed, and 16 Bills passed in the House of Commons; and 8 Local and Private Acts have been passed; and 39 Bills passed in the House of Commons.

In 1892 the Liberal Party was returned with a majority to carry out the Reforms included in what is known as the Newcastle Program, and the way this party has fulfilled its mandate has been described by the Right Hon. Joseph Chamberlain in the following words:

'I do not think that in the history of our legislation for the last 20 years, you can find any Parliament in which more has been done as to the importance of the Bills which have been passed.' (18th July, 1894.)

The next day The Times said in its leader: 'Few Governments have passed a greater body of important legislation in a single Session.'

The Home Rule Bill, the Budget of 1894, the Parish Councils' Act, the Employers' Liability Bill, the Factory and Workshops' Bill (expected to pass), may well evoke such testimony, and will remain monuments of beneficial Liberal Statesmanship.

We are generally apt to fix our attention on the great Acts, but we have also to remember much useful legislation which affects our everyday life and comfort. I append a list of some of the Acts passed, from which it will be seen that the tendency and spirit of all this legislation has been the promotion of the welfare of the masses of the people, and of labour particularly, which is the backbone or foundation of all National wealth and greatness. Over and above actual legislation, much reform has been effected departmentally and by resolutions.

Though thus, a good deal of beneficent, progressive, and important legislation has been done, much of the great Newcastle Programme still remains to be carried. It follows that all Liberal and Radical Electors should exercise their sovereign power, and send back the Liberal Party to carry through successfully the great work which was entrusted to them in 1892. I shall state a few of the items of progressive and important work which is still before us.

For the Irish Home Rule, the Liberal Party are bound by every duty of honour, and even by self-interest. It will be one of those glorious land-marks of civilization in British history with which it is replete during the present century. The Welsh Disestablishment; Home Rule for London in all its various important requirements; the restriction of the Veto of the House of Lords, if not its Abolition; Taxation of Land Values for National and Municipal Purposes (a Bill for the latter purpose has been twice introduced by me); Division of Rates between Owners and Occupiers; Payment of Members; Perfect and Easy Registration of Electors by Responsible Public Registration Officers; One Man One Vote; Residential Adult Suffrage; Eight Hours; Direct Popular Veto of the Liquor Traffic, and many other important Liberal Measures.

It is the Liberal Party who has mainly done, or forced the Conservatives to do, progressive legislation; and it is from the Liberal or Progressive Party alone that we can expect such legislation in the future.

India
Lastly, I address a few words about India. The Electors of Central Finsbury have inaugurated a great and brilliant chapter in the already great history of the British people, by holding out

their generous and kind hand of common fellowship to their Indian fellow-subjects, and I trust the Electors will renew that noble and generous act in the present election by returning me again.

When I visited India in 1893-4 the people of India, of all classes and creeds, gave me a reception the like of which has not been, it is said, witnessed in living memory, in its vast extent, spontaneity and enthusiasm, with an expression of gratitude, deep and sincere, towards the Electors of Central Finsbury – a name which is a household word throughout India.

I content myself with appending the expressions of sentiments that have taken place both in Central Finsbury and in India towards each other. The sentiments of gratitude to the Electors in all parts of India which I visited, were similar to and reflected in the resolution of the Indian National Congress.

During the three years I have been your Representative in the House of Commons, I have experienced at your hands uniform courtesy and kindness, and I take this opportunity of making my sincere acknowledgments for the same.

Trusting that you will continue your generous confidence in me, and return me again as your Member to the House of Commons,
I have the honour to be, Yours faithfully,

D. NAOROJI.
8, Percival Street, Clerkenwell, E.C.
and
National Liberal Club, Whitehall, S.W.   5th July, 1895

Appendix referred to in my foregoing Address.–D.N.

A Message from India
Being a Resolution passed at the Meeting of the Great Indian National Congress at Nagpur, December 30th, 1891:

'That this Congress hereby puts formally on record its high estimate and deep appreciation of the great services which Mr. Dadabhai Naoroji has rendered, during more than a quarter of a century, to the cause of India, that it expresses its unshaken confidence in him, and its earnest hope that he may prove successful at the coming elections in his candidature for Central Finsbury; and at the same time tenders, on behalf of the vast population it represents, India's most cordial acknowledgements to all in England, whether in Central Finsbury or elsewhere, who have aided or may aid him to win a seat in the House of Commons.'

India's Thanks in 1892
Eighth Indian National Congress, held at Allahabad on 28th, 29th, and 30th December, 1892:

Resolved, that this Congress most respectfully and cordially tenders, on behalf of the vast population it represents, India's most heartfelt thanks to the electors of Central Finsbury for electing Mr. D. Naoroji their Member in the House of Commons. And it again puts on record its high estimate and deep appreciation of the services which that gentleman has rendered to this country, reiterates its unshaken confidence in him, and looks upon him as India's representative in the House of Commons.

The Central Finsbury United Liberal and Radical Association, send a Greeting to the forthcoming Indian National Congress, 1893.

The Central Finsbury United Liberal and Radical Association, in view of Mr. Naoroji's visit to India at the end of November next, have passed the following Resolution:

'1. That the General Council of the Central Finsbury United Liberal and Radical Association desire to record their high appreciation of the admirable and most exemplary manner in which Mr. Dadabhai Naoroji has performed his duties as representative of this constituency in the House of Commons, and, learning that he is, in the course of a few months, to visit India to preside over the Ninth Session of the Indian National Congress, request him to communicate to that body an expression of their full sympathy alike with all the efforts of that Congress for the welfare of India, and with the Resolution which has been recently passed by the House of Commons (in the adoption of which Mr. Dadabhai Naoroji has been so largely instrumental) in favour of holding Simultaneous Examinations in India and in Britain of candidates for all the Indian Civil Services; and further express the earnest hope that full effect will, as speedily as possible, be given by the Government to this measure of justice which has been already too long delayed.

'2. That a copy of this resolution be forwarded to Mr. Dadabhai Naoroji.

'(Signed) Joseph Walton,
'Chairman of Meeting.'

India's Thanks
Resolved, – That this Congress tender its best thanks to the Electors of Central Finsbury, both for their kindly sympathy in its objects, and for having so generously accorded to it the valuable services of their honoured member Mr. Naoroji, who is destined, the Congress hopes, long to represent both Central Finsbury and India in the British House of Parliament.

Some Acts relating to the United Kingdom passed in 1893
Trade Union Provident Funds, Police Disabilities Removal, Municipal Corporations, Weights and Measures, Public Works Loans Railway Regulation, Friendly Societies, Prevention of use of Barbed Wire in Road Fences, Conveyance of Mails, Industrial and Provident Societies, Public Works Loans, Education of Deaf and Blind Children, Public Health Act (London, 1891) Amendment, Elementary Education School Attendances, Statue Law Revision, Metropolis Management (Plumstead and Hackney), Company's Winding up, Married Women's Property, Shop Hours Regulation, Hospital Isolation, Savings Banks, Parish Councils Acts, Day Industrial Schools (Scotland), Local Authorities' Loans (Scotland), Reformatory Schools (Scotland), Burgh Police (Scotland), Improvement of Land (Scotland), Burghs Gas Supply (Scotland), Cholera Hospitals (Ireland), Congested District Boards (Ireland), Law of Distress and Small Debts (Ireland), Irish Education, County Surveyors (Ireland), and Light Railways (Ireland).

Some Public Acts in 1894
Industrial and Provident Societies, Trustee Act (1893) Amendment, Public Works' Loans, Merchandise Marks' Prosecutions, Commissioners of Works, Wild Birds' Protection, Outdoor Relief Friendly Societies, Prevention of Cruelty to Children (Amending Clauses), Registration of Electors' Acceleration, Industrial Schools' Act Amendments, Charitable Trusts, Prize Courts, Regulation of Quarries, Building Societies Amendments Act, Coal Mines' Check Weighers, London Equalization of Rates, Railway and Canal Traffic, Housing of the Working Classes, Merchant Shipping.

The above are only some of the Acts passed.

Appendix V

Address by Shapurji Saklatvala,
Parliamentary Election, 1923, North Battersea
Division. Polling day – Thursday, December 6th,
8 a.m. to 9 p.m.

Central Committee Rooms,
455, Battersea Park Road, S.W.11.

Electors of North Battersea,
I take this opportunity of conveying my thanks to comrades
who have once again nominated me as their Standard Bearer at
this wanton election thrust upon us.

Members of the Conservative Party
May I ask you a simple question? Have you political principles
or Party honour? Your union with the Liberals in 1918 has led
this country into a moral and economic disaster. It is now
suggested that this course should be repeated locally. To do this
would be using Parliamentary democracy not for national ends
but for political conspiracy. I have sufficient faith in my fellow-
men that such a course will hardly be agreed to by ALL of you.

Members of the Liberal Party
You admit that this Election is unnecessary, and that you are
driven only to oppose any scheme of tariff duties. You are fully
aware that Labour is opposed to all forms of indirect taxation.
You may not be aware that the *Daily Telegraph*, *Evening
Standard*, and *Daily Express* of November 19th have suggested
that the choice of North Battersea Liberals will be such as to be
acceptable to Protectionist Conservative voters. Yet you get

angry at the suggestion that Liberals and Conservatives are as one.

Members of the Labour Party, and all Workers by Hand and Brain
I enclose herewith the Labour Party's Official Manifesto, which I pledge to support, with the only criticism that that is the least that one can demand under the present conditions of life all over the world, while our moral instincts, which transcend political conveniences, require us to go further. If re-elected, I shall, as usual, submit myself to you at least once every month to receive your instructions and give attention to your wishes. I would here warn you against the attempt to misrepresent my position in the Labour world, by identifying me with others of a like name connected with Finance in India and America.

Electors of North Battersea, the Real Issue is Unemployment
The need of the hour is immediate relief, and the true purpose of politics is to seek a permanent cure of Unemployment, which has existed and grown to unmanageable dimensions during three long years of Lloyd George's rule, and which the Conservatives found impossible to remedy.

The diplomacy of Liberal Rule, 1906 to 1914, of Asquith, Grey, Lloyd George, Churchill and others, with its underlying motive of trade monopoly in the East, gave us the horrible War.

The Liberals and Conservatives, combined under Lloyd George from 1918 to 1922, shattered the markets of Europe, brought the Workers to serfdom on low wages, created and made permanent Unemployment on a large scale in Great Britain.

Here we now have our UNEMPLOYED, our UNDEREMPLOYED, our UNDERPAID WORKERS, our EX-SERVICEMEN, shattered in limb and vitality, and sent to starvation, AND 600,000 BOYS AND GIRLS prematurely thrown out every year from the Schools to face a dismal life of no maintenance and no employment or education.

Underpaid German and Continental labour is now added to the large mass of Asiatic and African labour – purposely created by Conservative and Liberal Financiers, more largely by Liberal Financiers – with the object of gaining profits, and breaking the backs of British Trade Union standards. Liberal and Conservative Financiers are busy to-day helping to start new industries in the East, where coolie labour is employed on literally 7/- a month, as in Assam Tea Plantations, to about 15/- a week in TEXTILE, IRON AND STEEL, OIL, COAL MINING, and other industries. The Conservative Financier says: 'I will exploit human beings in other parts of the world, using for my purpose the Union Jack and Armaments,' but he says, 'I will now put on a Tariff duty at home, make everthing costly for the worker and the consumer, sweat them at wages and prices different from wages abroad, and thus earn dividends at home also!' The Liberal says: 'I will exploit the Negro, the Chinaman, the Indian in the same manner, but I will keep my door open, and when my own goods, produced by cheap labour, flood the markets of the world, I will propose to the British Worker to accept a reduction in wages'. The Liberal pretends to be opposed to food taxes, but during his long period of office from 1906 we had to pay taxes on tea, sugar, cocoa, coffee, dried fruit, tobacco, beer, and even theatre tickets. Lloyd George was the origin of the enmity with Russia. Churchill, without the consent of Parliament, handed over £95,000,000 worth of munitions to the enemies of Russia, to reduce her to the conditions which prevail now in Germany, and they now pledge themselves to enter into relations with Russia. Recently visiting Russia, I know how completely we would be discredited did we ever reinstate Lloyd George or Churchill with that responsibility. Liberals now promise to remove from old age pensions, unequal franchise rights for women, inadequate provision for children's education, all those shameful obstacles which they themselves created.

LIBERALS BOAST THAT FREE TRADE FINANCED THE LAST WAR. This is untrue. The war was not carried on from accumulated profit made in the past. Instead, to finance the War, the workers of this country are called upon to pay £1,000,000 per day indefinitely.

Did you read the Liberal Party's Manifesto? They say the Labour Party will drive Capital out of this country! How many Liberal and Conservative Investors are every day using British wealth originally produced by British Workers in countries abroad, where they can find human beings to work at cheaper rates and in more docile manner? WITH BRITISH MONEY AND WITH BRITISH FOREMEN THAT THEY TOOK ABROAD WHY DID THEY NOT TAKE BRITISH STANDARDS OF WAGES ALSO? Cotton, Wool, Jute, Silk, Raw Hides, Oil Seeds, Rubber, Mica, a variety of Metals, and many other articles required for British factories, now come in exchange for dividend warrants instead of in exchange for British manufactured goods.

Thus, regardless of the fiscal system, the Conservatives and the Liberals create a double shrinkage in British industrial employment, and create no new market amongst the Oriental serf labour, and when on top of that they put a penalty of a million pounds a day upon the Workers' existence, and give back as interest to the rich more than the Income Tax and Death duties received from the rich, no wonder they are starving all social services, as Education, Pensions, Housing, &c.

Let us, therefore, talk of the Capital Levy in a sane mood
The National Debt is not a genuine investment of already acquired wealth. Seven thousand million pounds have not been withdrawn from British Industries and used for war, Seven thousand million pounds were not existing in the pockets of the rich, doing nothing, which they invested. All the rich individuals and corporations had their wealth expressed in terms of materials or documents. On strength of this wealth they were accommodated with credit by the Banks, from time to time. The financiers, their puppet Government, and their Banks, all agreed that on the credit of this wealth, with the addition of large book entries for unjustifiable war profits, they would allow the rich financiers to acquire War Loans, and on these War Loans they would continue to get the same accommodation which they used to get before. THUS ON ONE FORM OF WEALTH THE RICH MEN SUDDENLY BUILT UP TWO CREDITS. One was the

original existing credit, in the eyes of the Bankers, who, without the War Loans, used to give them accommodation for industrial and social purposes. The second credit was built up against the Nation, and the Nation is asked to pay one million pounds every day; after generations the Nation will have paid up against this second artificial credit. The effect of the Labour Party's policy would be to take off the backs of the Nation this second untold burden, and this in no way should destroy the original credit of the one substantive wealth which the Nation required for its normal economic activity and life, but would make available for social needs the millions that are swallowed up by Interest. They have created the bogey that the poor would be deprived of their savings. The total Interest on the poor people's Loans of £240,000,000 is one million pounds a month, and in order to obtain this payment one day in the month they have to contribute out of their toil payment during 29 days for others.

THE FACT IS THAT INDIVIDUAL OWNERSHIP AND CONTROL OF INDUSTRIAL WEALTH IS UNNATURAL, IS INHUMAN AND HAS BEEN GROSSLY ABUSED. All the religious founders and teachers of the East and West have warned the Nations against the worship of gold by individuals. We see the disastrous results to-day. Almost all crime against morality emanates from unequal economic conditions: poverty and degradation on the one hand, and over-abundance and allurement on the other hand. Every known law of science for fresh air, good food, sanitation, medical assistance, mental education., mental recreation, is violated – in spite of our knowledge of it – because of dividends and interest. We do not want to rob, but we desire to stop the people being robbed. There can be no peace, no effective disarmament, no full life, and no permanent security of maintenance for all individuals in Society until everything created by the Community is owned by the Community and is co-ordinated with International Communal and Social considerations. When Nationalised industries are controlled and administered by the direct voice of the Trade Unions of all the Workers by hand and brain in that industry, and in the Allied industries, there will be no bureaucratic coercion to interfere with the rights of Society, as in the case of bureaucratic nationalisation.

Before I close, I must ask your permission to say a word about my undoubted membership of the Communist Party, as for the last twelve months our opponents have been assiduously working a stunt under the vague term 'Bolshevism'. Last week Edwin Percival Power, age 20, cabinet maker, of Chester Street, Bethnal Green, through depression from continued unemployment, took poison and died in Epping Forest, faithfully clutching his young sweetheart's photograph. A letter found on the body by the police read: 'I have come out in the open to die – out in the glorious air away from the paltry deceit and strife of the world. It will be a merciful release to die to ease the aching of my heart. May the Lord have mercy on my soul and receive me into the kingdom of Heaven'. Liebknecht, Rosa Luxemburg, Eisner, Vorovsky were assassinated by Fascist hands, but Edwin Power and his like are daily driven to despair and death by masters who shut their factories, and where Society has no right to take charge of them and work them.

The King of Spain has just met the King of Italy, and said, 'THIS IS MY MUSSOLINI'. This in a word sums up the position of Europe, from the Balkans to the Western Shores of Spain. In Russia, where the Communists, the Trade Unionists, the Asiatic and European Agriculturalists, and the Socialists, in spite of their internal differences, have all clung together, no Georges, no Poincarés, no Churchills, no Baldwins, no Mussolinis, no Ludendorfs have been able to remove the Trade Unionists and the Agriculturalists from their secure position of possessing and administering all lands and all industries. In the rest of Europe the condition of life is one of immense distress – the workers are reduced to serfdom and beggary. Our opponents are closing their ranks, and are keeping their Mussolinis ready everywhere, and advise us to split amongst ourselves.

The new I.L.P. and Labour Party International, as well as the Moscow International, are described as anti-British alien influences. When militarist jingoes of all nations work together it is called 'COUNCIL OF WAR,' when intriguing politicians of all nations conspire together, they are called 'COUNCIL OF AMBASSADORS'; when armed financiers meet together to rob unarmed nations they are called the 'LEAGUE OF NATIONS'; when workers of all nations meet and work together they are called 'ALIEN BOLSHEVIKS'. We MUST HAVE UNIFORM STANDARDS FOR THE WORKERS all over Europe and Asia, and we can neither leave the Communists or the right wing Trade Unionists or the Social Democrats to fight their own battles singly. Before the final and universal success we shall all have to get a united plan of action.

We want a solid, unbroken, united front at home, backing our Labour Party, as far as we are ALL prepared to go, and then planning our further onward march, till we bring ourselves into an international unity with our brethren in other countries of the world, through a joint organisation that operates on our behalf every day, and thus to secure what is the minimum as well as the maximum, namely,

All Power to the Workers by Hand and Brain
With this spirit, with this resolve, I ask you to vote for me, and I shall expect you after you have voted to work with me. Over-confidence on the Election day will bring you defeat; out of the forty thousand Electors of North Battersea, it would be a moral loss if at least twenty thousand did not solidly vote for us. The other side has elaborate preparations, and there is even a determination for some Conservatives and Liberals to combine together, and unless twenty thousand of us – that is double the number of last year – go to the Poll to vote for Labour, we shall be taking very serious risks.

Very cordially yours,

Shapurji Saklatvala.

November 26th, 1923.

Notes

Note: The India Office Records has been abbreviated in this section to IOR.

1. India and Britain

1. Spices were not merely culinary luxuries but a necessity. In the days before adequate winter fodder for cattle, animals were slaughtered in late autumn. Spices were then used to preserve the meat and to disguise the taste of any that had 'gone off'.
2. Vasco da Gama engaged an Asian pilot in East Africa to guide him across the Indian Ocean to Calicut.
3. Mughal rule in India dates from Babur's victory at the Battle of Panipat in 1526.
4. The Portuguese pursued an active policy of proselytizing the Hindu and Muslim population of India; they even introduced the Inquisition. They earned the ironical title of *'Feringee'* (from *farangi*, meaning 'frank') because they considered that as Christians they need not keep their word with the infidel. The Portuguese also introduced the policy of mixed marriages. The offspring were known as Luso-Indians or Goans.
5. The original charter was valid for 15 years, but it was renewed periodically, the last time in 1853.
6. A trading 'factory' had buildings for administration, housing the men and storing the goods.
7. India provided the Company with pepper, spices, cotton, indigo dye, sugar, silks and saltpetre (for gunpowder); in return, the Indians bought tin, lead, quicksilver, tapestries and mechanical novelties. They rejected the main English export of broadcloth as it was unsuitable for the tropical climate. In the early years the Company had to make up the shortfall in silver bullion, which earned them great unpopularity in Britain since it was considered

to be unpatriotic to spend silver bullion in foreign countries. However, the Company was able to diversify the trade with opium which was to become the most profitable item of trade. Poppies were grown in India and the opium sold to the Chinese.

8. Street names bear witness to this valuable connection with India, e.g. East India Dock Road.

9. From '*sipahi*' – an Indian soldier in European service.

10. In the early years the servants of the East India Company were encouraged to marry Indian wives or take Indian mistresses as shipping out English wives was considered expensive. Some famous names in British history trace their ancestry to Indian mothers – e.g. James Skinner (of the famous Skinner's Horse Cavalry); Lord Roberts (of Kabul fame); and Lord Liverpool (the Tory prime minister). See G. Moorhouse, *India Britannica* (Paladin, 1984), pp. 136–44; and Cedric Dover, *Half-Caste* (Secker & Warburg, 1937).

11. The War of Austrian Succession, 1744, and the Seven Years' War of 1756.

12. From the Hindi '*nawab*', meaning a prince or noble. It was also used as an honorary title, and deputies or governors in the Mughal government were known as nawabs. In England the title was used for a European who had made fortunes in the East. The word came to be used increasingly after a stage play of that name was performed in London in 1768.

13. The 'Orientalists' were a group of Englishmen, not Indians.

14. Before 1813 the East India Company had strictly forbidden any missionary activity in India.

15. Jeremy Bentham and James Mill both belonged to the Utilitarian school of thought. Mill wrote a six-volume history of India, although he himself had never visited India. His *History* was denounced as the work of a 'bigot' by many Orientalists. William Wilberforce, of abolition fame, was of the Evangelical school (the Clapham Sect), and saw the conversion of India to Christianity as 'the greatest of all causes', which he placed even 'before abolition'. He told the House of Commons debate that the Hindu gods were 'absolute monsters of lust, injustice, wickedness and cruelty. In short their religion is one grand abomination'. See G. Moorhouse, pp. 68–70; and Eric Stokes, *The English Utilitarians in India* (Clarendon Press, 1959) for more details of these two schools of Christian thought.

16. A member of the Asiatic Society, Colonel Stewart, wrote a pamphlet called *Vindication of the Hindoos, by a Bengal Officer*, in defence of the Hindu religion. See G. Moorhouse, p. 70.
17. Quoted in K. Little, *Negroes in Britain. A Study of Racial Relations in English Society* (Kegan Paul, Trench, Trubner & Co., 1947), p. 213, fn. 1.
18. The building in Whitehall, from which Indian affairs were conducted, was known as the India Office.
19. Quoted in E.J. Thompson and G.T. Garratt, *Rise and Fulfillment of British Rule in India* (Macmillan, 1934), p. 536.
20. Baring to Mallet, 25 September 1882, as quoted in Anil Seal, *The Emergence of Indian Nationalism. Competition and Collaboration in the Later Nineteenth Century* (Cambridge University Press, 1968), p. 156. The term 'Baboo' was used disparagingly by the British to denote an English-educated Indian.
21. Curzon's speech at the Delhi Durbar of 1902.
22. India and Pakistan, which was split into two wings, East and West Pakistan. In 1971 East Pakistan became the state of Bangladesh.
23. C. Kondapi, *Indians Overseas 1838-1949* (New Delhi: Indian Council of World Affairs; London: Oxford University Press, 1951); H. Tinker, *The Banyan Tree, Overseas Emigrants from India, Pakistan and Bangladesh* (OUP, 1977).
24. A labourer was bound by contract to work for five years under a small fixed wage, with a further period of five years under the same or another planter, before being allowed a free passage back to India – *if* he chose to return. The indentured Indian labourer was not only underpaid and overworked, but badly housed and sexually deprived. There was violence, and suicide rates among the labourers were high. See Hugh Tinker, *A New System of Slavery. The Export of Indian Labour Overseas 1830-1920* (published for the Institute of Race Relations, London: Oxford University Press, 1974).

2. Chattels of the Empire: Servants and Ayahs

1. Percival Spear describes the bewildering number and types of servants in India. See *The Nabobs, a Study of the Social Life of the English in 18th Century India* (Curzon Press, New Impression, 1980), pp. 52-3; see also *Memoirs of William Hickey*, ed. Alfred Spencer (Hurst & Blackett, 1913-25), Vol. IV, p. 397; Dennis

Kincaid, *British Social Life in India 1608-1937* (George Routledge & Sons Ltd, 1938), p. 83; Suresh C. Ghose, *The Social Conditions of the British Community in Bengal 1757-1800* (Leiden: E.J. Brill, 1970), p. 111. Many Europeans had their family portraits painted with their Indian servants and ayahs in the background; often Indian servants in these portraits are shown gazing at their masters/mistresses in rapt adoration. See portraits by, for example, John Zoffany (Warren Hastings, his wife and her maid; group comprising Sir Elijah and Lady Impey with their children, ayahs and servants); Van Dyck (William Fielding, Earl of Denbigh); Peter Lely (Charlotte Fitzroy); J. Reynolds (family of distinction with an ayah). See also *John Zoffany R. A. His Life and Works 1735-1810*, by Lady Victoria Manners and Dr G.C. Williamson (London, 1920).

2. Villas built in Indian style bear testimony to this. A very good example is Sezincote in Gloucestershire. Curry was first advertised at Norris Street Coffee House, Haymarket, as early as 1773. See J.M. Holzman, *The Nabobs in England, a Study of the Returned Anglo-Indians, 1760-1785* (New York, 1926), p. 88.

3. C. Dickens, *Dombey and Son*, has an Indian servant; and so has Stevenson's *Master of Ballantrae*.

4. Sophie von la Roche, *Sophie in London 1786, Being the Diary of Sophie v. la Roche*, translated by Clare Williams (London: Jonathan Cape, 1933), pp. 257 and 272.

5. *The Travels of Mirza Abu Talib Khan in Asia, Africa and Europe During the Years 1799, 1800, 1801, 1802, 1803, Written by Himself in the Persian Language*, translated by Charles Stewart (London: Longman, Hurst, Rees & Orme, 1810) Vol. I, pp. 103-4.

6. Duchess of Sermonetta [V. Caetani], *The Locks of Norbury, the Story of a Remarkable Family in the 18th and 19th Century* (John Murray, 1940), pp. 53-4.

7. *Annual Register*, 1773, pp. 110-11; Eliza Fay, an enterprising woman who travelled between India and England four times, brought back on one homeward voyage Kitty Johnson, an Indian maid. She dumped her at St Helena. See Eliza Fay, *Original Letters from India 1779-1815*, with an introduction and terminal notes by E.M. Forster (Hogarth Press, 1925), p. 242.

8. W.M. Thackeray mentions coming back from India in 1817 as a child in the company of a 'black servant', a 'Calcutta serving-man'. *The Four Georges* (Leipzig; 1861), p. 71.

9. *Memoirs of William Hickey*, ed. Spencer, Vol. II, pp. 228, 262, 275, See also J. Hecht, *Colonial and Continental Servants in the 18th Century* (Smith College Studies in History, 1954), pp. 50-4; Holzman, *The Nabobs in England*, pp. 70-91, for reasons for bringing Asian servants.

10. *Daily Advertiser*, 12 July 1777, No. 14530; *Daily Advertiser*, 3 March 1775, No. 13791; *Daily Advertiser*, 26 August 1776, No. 14255; *Morning Post and Daily Advertiser*, 11 June 1777, No. 1448.

11. *Daily Advertiser*, 21 August 1776, No. 14251.

12. Spear, p. 53.

13. *Tatler*, February 9-11 1709, No. 132; *Daily Advertiser*, 1 February 1775, No. 13765.

14. *London Gazette*, 1688, as quoted in F. Shyllon, *Black People in Britain 1555-1833* (published for the Institute of Race Relations, London: Oxford University Press, 1977), p. 11; *Daily Advertiser*, 11 June 1737, No. 1990 and 4 November 1743, No. 3993, as quoted in J. Hecht, p. 53; *Public Advertiser*, 29 May 1772, No. 11021.

15. Quoted in Eliza Fay, p. 182, Note 42.

16. Peter Fryer, *Staying Power, The History of Black People in Britain*, (London: Pluto Press, 1984), pp. 77-8; Percival Spear, p. 53 and notes 44-5 on p. 157; H.E. Busted, *Echoes from Old Calcutta Being Chiefly Reminiscences of the Days of Warren Hastings, Francis and Impey* (Calcutta: Thacker, Spink & Co., 1882), 120n; D.R. Banaji, *Slavery in British India* (Bombay: D.B. Taraporevala Sons & Co., 1933), pp. 6-8.

17. Hickey informed Auriol that 'the boy . . . being now a Christian he [Auriol] could no longer be justified, nor would the law permit him, to treat him as a slave.' *Memoirs of William Hickey*, ed. Spencer, Vol. III, p. 151.

18. *Morning Chronicle*, 17 February 1795, No. 7908; see also the *Morning Chronicle* of 6 October 1795, No. 8099, where another East Indian young man '16 years old, lame of his right foot' was being anxiously searched for. It is interesting to note the perception of the Indian languages by the Europeans. Hyder is mentioned as being fluent in the 'Moorish' language; Mrs Locke had dismissed the language as simply 'barbarous', while Sophie von la Roche thought of it as 'East Indian' which to her sounded a 'soft language'.

19. *Public Advertiser*, 16 March 1772, No. 11662.

20. *London Chronicle*, 11-14 October 1800 (LXXXVIII/6488), p. 363.

21. *Memoirs of William Hickey*, ed. Alfred Spencer, Vol. III, pp. 150–51.
22. *Report of a Meeting for the Establishment of a 'Strangers' Home' for Asiatics, Africans, South-Sea Islanders, and Others Occasionally Residing in the Metropolis*, 18 March 1855, p. 14.
23. IOR: L/P&J/2/52, No. 7/411. Agreement signed by James Murray, 22 August 1872.
24. *Morning Chronicle*, 1 April 1795, No. 7945.
25. *Morning Post and Daily Advertiser*, 31 January 1777, No. 1336; *Daily Advertiser*, 10 October 1786, No. 18053. See also *Morning Post and Daily Advertiser*, 20 November 1777, No. 1586. J. Hecht mentions more advertisements, see p. 51.
26. *Daily Advertiser*, 10 October 1786, No. 18053; *Morning Post and Daily Advertiser*, 15 October 1777, No. 1555.
27. *Report of a Meeting for the Establishment of a 'Strangers' Home'* (1855), pp. 13–14; *London City Mission Magazine*, 1858, p. 291. 16 shillings was an exorbitant sum at the time.
28. IOR: L/P&J/6/480, No. 993. Letter from Mrs Warr to Horace Walpole, dated 10 May 1898; and reply from the India Office to Mrs Warr dated 13 May 1898. Mrs Warr had not been put off so easily, *vide* her second letter of 16 May 1898.
29. *Public Advertiser*, 2 December 1786, No. 16391.
30. *Public Advertiser*, 5 December 1786, No. 10393.
31. *The Times*, 20 July 1852.
32. IOR: Home Miscellaneous Correspondence, No. 163 of 1782, p. 181.
33. IOR: L/P&J/3/1010, Public Department, No. 11, of 28 October 1835.
34. IOR: L/P&J/6/158, No. 1282.
35. The 1855 Merchant Shipping Amendment Act – to be discussed in Chapter 3.
36. IOR: L/P&J/2/49, No. 7/280, minute dated 27 January 1869; see Chapter 3 for more details of the 'Strangers' Home'.
37. Letter from Colonel Hughes to the India Office dated 12 August 1868 in L/P&J/2/47, No. 7/264.
38. Letter from George and Edward Hanlon to Colonel Hughes dated 10 August 1868 in IOR: L/P&J/2/47, No. 7/264.
39. Public No. 152 of 7 October 1868; Public No. 39 of 7 October 1868 and No. 33 dated 7 October 1868 in IOR: L/P&J/2/47, No. 7/264.

40. Act No. XIII of 1864 passed by the Governor General of India in Council: an Act to Consolidate and Amend the Laws relating to the Emigration of Native Labourers. See IOR: India Acts of 1863 and 1864.
41. No. 52 of 1869 Government of India, Home Department, Public, in IOR: L/P&J/6/158, No. 1282.
42. Letter dated 17 January 1869 from Syed Abdoollah to the India Office in IOR: L/P&J/2/49, No. 7/281.
43. Reply dated 16 February 1869 to Syed Abdoollah, and the department minute dated 27 January 1869, in IOR: L/P&J/2/49, No. 7/281.
44. For the case of topazees see letters from Colonel Hughes to the India Office dated 21 September 1871; and letter dated 4 September from Colonel Hughes to Commissioner of Emigration; letter of 6 June 1872 from the Emigration Board and letter dated 2 August 1872 in IOR: L/P&J/2/51. See also IOR: L/P&J/2/60 for the case of Greesh Chunder Dutt.
45. This was Georgii IV Cap. 80 of July 1823; Colonel Hughes to India Office dated 24 January 1879 in IOR: L/P&J/2/59, No. 7/567. In his letter dated 25 March 1879, in the same volume, Colonel Hughes pointed out that 'During the last twenty years upwards of sixteen hundred destitute natives of the East – nine-tenths of whom were natives of India – have been sheltered in this Institution . . . and sent to their homes without reference to the IO and in numerous cases it was entirely through the Law.'
46. The Merchant Shipping Act 1823 and Amendment 1855, to be discussed in Chapter 3.
47. See department minutes of 2 May 1879; 29 April 1878 in connection with the destitute and the Acts in IOR: L/P&J/2/59, No. 7/567.
48. Letter from S.B. Ivatts, dated 24 November 1870 from Dublin, to India Office in IOR: L/P&J/2/50, No. 7/345.
49. Letters dated 18 June and 29 June 1875 from Luckfield Union in IOR: L/P&J/2/55, No. 7/485.
50. Letters from Stepney Union and other correspondence in IOR: L/P&J/2/58, No. 7/562; J. Salter, *East in the West or Work Among the Asiatics and Africans in London* (London: S.W. Partridge, 1896), pp. 119–25.
51. IOR: L/P&J/2/58, No. 7/559, minute dated 23 December 1878.
52. IOR: L/P&J/6/158, No. 1282, letter dated 15 July from J.H.

Bowen and the minute dated 22 July and letter dated 23 July 1885.
53. IOR: L/P&J/2/59, No. 7/567, memo by the Political ADC dated 20 February 1879.
54. IOR: L/P&J/2/59, No. 7/567. Reply from accountant dated 6 March 1879; and the semi-official letter from Colonel Hughes dated 25 March 1879. Since the home did not differentiate between destitute sailors and 'other natives', Colonel Hughes sent 'Statistics of Working of the Home from June 1857 to December 1877'. The total number of destitute cases in the Sailors' Home was 1,605.
55. Sir Gerald Fitzgerald's memo dated 20 February 1879 in IOR: L/P&J/2/59, No. 7/567.
56. IOR: L/P&J/2/59, No. 7/567, minute from O.S. Hume dated 14 March 1879. Copies of the previous correspondence following the case of the 11 Oudhians were dispatched.
57. IOR: L/P&J/6/172, No. 432, letter dated 23 March 1886.
58. See L/P&J/6/191, No. 2122, for cases of five Punjabis; and L/P&J/6/206, No. 1185, for cases of three more Punjabis.
59. L/P&J/6/172, No. 432, memo dated 23 March 1886.
60. The committee was composed of Arthur Macpherson, secretary in the Judicial and Public Department of the India Office, and Sir Gerald Fitzgerald, the Political ADC representing the India Office, Edward Wingfield for the Colonial Office and Hugh Owen for the Local Government Board. See IOR: L/P&J/6/175, No. 781.
61. IOR: L/P&J/6/181, No. 1099a, memo of 26 July 1886.
62. IOR: L/P&J/6/207, No. 1399, letter dated 6 August 1887.
63. Monthly report submitted by the Political ADC, for April 1884. See IOR: L/P&J/3/250.
64. Henry Mayhew, *London Labour and the London Poor* (London: Griffin & Co., 1861), Vol. III, p. 406.
65. IOR: L/P&J/6/281, No. 1270, letter dated 28 August 1890.
66. IOR: L/P&J/6/281, No. 1270, letter dated 19 June 1890.
67. See for instance the case of some Burmans brought for an exhibition at Crystal Palace, IOR: L/P&J/6/435; and a few cases of destitute Asians came to the notice of the India Office from time to time. But in the main Asians took this step only as a last resort.
68. *London City Mission Magazine*, 2 July 1900, pp. 172-4. See also Kelly's Hackney and Homerton Street Directory for 1900-1901; George Sims, *Living London* (London: Cassell, 1906), Vol. III, pp. 279 and 281.

69. *London City Mission Magazine*, 1922, Vol. LXXXVII, article by A.C. Marshall, pp. 104-6.
70. *London City Mission Magazine*, 2 May 1881, p. 93.
71. Salter (1896), pp. 164-5; *London City Mission Magazine*, 1 May 1899, p. 83.
72. Memo by E.J. Pakeman, senior clerk to the Stores Department, to the Secretary of State for India, dated 4 September 1868, in IOR: L/P&J/2/47, No 7/264.
73. Quoted in *Queen Victoria's Highland Journals*, ed. David Duff (Webb & Bower, 1980), p. 217.
74. Quoted in M. Warner, *Queen Victoria's Sketch Book* (Macmillan, 1979), p. 198.
75. Queen Victoria to Lord Landsdowne, 29 March 1890, No. 22, IOR: MSS EUR D/558/I.
76. Quoted in Elizabeth Longford, *Victoria I* (Weidenfeld & Nicholson, 1964), p. 502.
77. The Queen to Lord Landsdowne, 11 July 1890, No. 28, in IOR: MSS EUR D/558/I.
78. Frederick Ponsonby, *Recollections of Three Reigns* (Eyre & Spottiswoode, 1951), p. 13.
79. Quoted in Longford, p. 536.
80. Ponsonby, p. 14.
81. Quoted in Longford, p. 536.
82. Queen to Lord Landsdowne, 29 October 1890, No. 39, in IOR: MSS EUR D/558/I.
83. Lord George Hamilton, Secretary of State for India, to Lord Elgin, Viceroy, 30 April 1897, IOR: MSS EUR F 84/126a.
84. Frederick Ponsonby to Babington-Smith, Cimiez, 27 April 1897, in IOR: MSS EUR F 84/126a.
85. Lord George Hamilton to Lord Elgin, 30 April 1897, in IOR: MSS EUR F 84/126a.
86. Lord George Hamilton to Lord Elgin, 21 February 1896; see also the memos from the Thuggee and Dacoity Department in IOR: MSS EUR F 84/126a.
87. Telegram from Secretary of State, London, to Viceroy in India, dated 30 March 1897, IOR: MSS EUR F 84/126a.
88. Telegram from Viceroy to Secretary of State dated 3 April 1897 in IOR: MSS EUR F 84/126a.
89. Frederick Ponsonby to Babington-Smith, Cimiez, dated 27 April 1897 in IOR: MSS EUR F 84/126a.

90. Lord George Hamilton to Lord Elgin, 7 May 1897, IOR: MSS EUR F 84/126a.
91. Queen to Lord Salisbury, 17 July 1897, quoted in Longford, p. 540.
92. Writing to Babington-Smith from Cimiez, on 27 April 1897, Frederick Ponsonby commented, 'If he had been kept in his proper place no harm would have been done, but as you know from being Khitmagar the Queen made him a Munshi, and then Indian Secretary, giving him at the same time the CIE.' IOR: MSS EUR F 84/126a.

3. Sailors who Filled the Gap: the Lascars

1. Lascar: this is a European adaptation from the Hindi and Persian word *lashkar*, meaning an army, a camp or a band of followers. The early Portuguese used it to mean 'soldiers', and later it came to be applied to the sailors.
2. See *Report of a Meeting for the Establishment of A 'Strangers' Home', for Asiatics, Africans, South-Sea Islanders and Others, Occasionally Residing in the Metropolis* (March, 1855), p. 19.
3. Act. 42, Geo. III Cap. 61 of 1802.
4. Letter from the Chairman and Deputy Chairman of the East India Company, to the Right Honourable Nicholas Vansittart, dated 23 February 1815, in *Copy of all Correspondence between the Commissioners for the Affairs of India, and any Other Public Body Relative to the Care and Maintenance of Lascar Sailors during their Stay in England*, 1816 (No. 279), p. 3.
5. Expenses incurred by the East India Company for the maintenance of lascars and Chinese brought to England in IOR: L/MAR/C/902.
6. Articles with the lascar crew dated 23 October 1746 serving on *Tryal Sloop* in IOR: L/MAR/B/580B (2). See Appendix I.
7. *Report from the Committee on Lascars and other Asiatic Seamen, 1814-15* (No. 471), p. 3.
8. *The Travels of Mirza Abu Talib Khan in Asia, Africa and Europe During the Years 1799, 1800, 1801, 1802, 1803, Written by Himself in the Persian Language*, translated by Charles Stewart (London: Longman, Hurst, Rees & Orme, 1810), Vol. I, pp. 33-4.
9. Joseph Salter, *The Asiatic in England: Sketches of Sixteen Years' Work Among Orientals* (Seely, Jackson & Halliday, 1873), pp. 150-51, 149.

10. Joseph Salter, *The East in the West, or Work Among the Asiatics and Africans in London* (London: S.W. Partridge & Co., 1896), pp. 127-9.
11. J. Salter, *op. cit.*, 1873, p. 150.
12. IOR: L/MAR/C/902, 26 July 1813.
13. IOR: H/MISC/163, pp. 175-85.
14. *A Letter to Archibald Macdonald Esq., on the Intended Plan for Reform in what is called the Police of Westminster*, 1784, p. 17.
15. *Public Advertiser*, 16 March 1785, No. 15854.
16. *Morning Chronicle*, 30 November and 1 December 1785 as quoted in F. Shyllon, *Black People in Britain, 1555-1833* (for the Institute of Race Relations, London: Oxford University Press, 1977), pp. 123 -4.
17. *Morning Chronicle and London Advertiser*, 26 December 1786, No. 5497.
18. Peter Fryer, *Staying Power. The History of Black People in Britain* (London: Pluto Press, 1984). Fryer has detailed the background to the settlement scheme and the fate that awaited the 350 settlers who finally embarked for Sierra Leone in April 1787. See pp. 194-202.
19. Statement of the circumstances attending the maintenance and return of lascars and Chinese, dated 11 February 1811, in IOR: L/MAR/C/902, 33 ff.
20. Letter from the Chairman and Deputy Chairman of the East India Company to the Rt. Hon. Nicholas Vansittart, dated 23 February 1815 in *Copy of All Correspondence, 1816* (No. 279), p. 3.
21. Statement of the circumstances attending the maintenance and return of lascars and Chinese, dated 11 February 1811 and 5 March 1812, in IOR: L/MAR/C/902.
22. Act. 54, Geo. III Cap. 134 of 1814. The Committee then drew up regulations for the care and return of lascars and Chinese. See Appendix in *Report from the Committee on Lascars, 1814-15* (No. 471), pp. 9-13.
23. *Lascars and Chinese: A Short Address to Young Men, of the Several Orthodox Denominations of Christians* (W. Harris *et al.*, 1814), p. 17.
24. See *Life of William Allen, with a Selection from his Correspondence* (London: Charles Gilpin, 1846), Vol. I, p. 189.
25. *Ibid.*
26. R.I. and S. Wilberforce, *Life of William Wilberforce* (1838), IV, p. 154.

27. *Life of William Allen,* Vol. I, pp. 188-9.
28. Quoted in J. Salter, (1873), pp. 4-5. T. Clarkson's letter is dated 1842, giving his recollections of the visit with William Allen to the lascar barracks. Clarkson remembered it as 'about twenty years ago', obviously a trick of the memory. See also J. Salter, (1896), p. 13.
29. Hilton Docker to John Jackson of the East India Company, dated 7 February 1814 and 28 February 1814 in IOR: L/MAR/C/902.
30. Docker's letter to the Directors of the Company dated 28 February 1814 in IOR: L/MAR/C/902.
31. Docker's letter to the Directors of the Company dated 7 February 1814 in IOR: L/MAR/C/902.
32. *The Times,* 9 December 1814, No. 9387. See Appendix II.
33. Docker's letter to the Directors of the Company dated 14 December 1814 in IOR: L/MAR/C/902. This letter is reproduced in toto as 'enclosure no: 3' in *Copy of All Correspondence, 1816* (No. 279), pp. 12-15. As already pointed out, the ideas contained in Docker's various letters of 7 February, 28 February, 5 April and 5 December 1814 form the main thesis of argument in the letter from the Chairman and Deputy Chairman to the Rt. Hon. Nicholas Vansittart.
34. Letters from Docker to the Directors of the East India Company dated 28 November 1809, 28 February 1814 and 7 February 1814 in IOR: L/MAR/C/902.
35. Docker to the Directors of the Company, letter dated 28 February 1814 in IOR: L/MAR/C/902.
36. Docker to the Directors of the Company dated 5 April 1814 in IOR: L/MAR/C/902. See also *Copy of All Correspondence, 1816* (No. 279), p. 7. The argument is emphasized by the example of the Chinese being beaten up by the Irish lumper.
37. *Report from the Committee on Lascars, 1814-15* (No. 471), pp. 4-5.
38. Instructions for the commanders of ships proceeding to England respecting the diet, management and medical care of lascars during the voyage, in IOR: L/MAR/C/902. Also the Act. 54, Geo. III Cap. 134 of 1814 laid down regulations concerning diet etc. during the voyage.
39. *Copy of All Correspondence, 1816* (No. 279), pp. 13-14.
40. *Report from the Committee on Lascars, 1814-15* (No. 471), p. 5.
41. Lt. Col. R.M. Hughes, *The Laws Relating to Lascars and Asiatic Seamen Employed in the British Merchant Service* (London: Smith,

Elder & Co., 1855), p. 5.

42. *Report from the Committee on Lascars, 1814–15* (No. 471), pp. 6–8.

43. *Copy of All Correspondence, 1816.* (No. 279), p. 16.

44. *Ibid.*, pp. 17–20.

45. Act. Geo. IV Cap. 80 of 1823.

46. *Public Advertiser*, 3 January 1787, No. 16418.

47. *Copies of All Correspondence, 1816.* (No. 279), p. 7.

48. *Lascars and Chinese* (1814), pp. 3–4, 9–10.

49. *First Report from the Committee on the State of the Police of the Metropolis* (1817), p. 195.

50. Henry Mayhew, *London Labour and the London Poor* (1861), IV, p. 366.

51. Ian Duffield, 'London's Black Transportees to Australia', paper presented to the Conference of the History of Black Peoples in London, University of London, Institute of Education, November 1984.

52. *Report of a Meeting for the Establishment of a 'Strangers' Home'* (1855), p. 23.

53. Quoted in J. Salter (1873), p. 3.

54. J. Salter (1873), p. 35. The Inspector of the Common Lodging Houses found over 30 people in this house.

55. J. Salter (1873), p. ii.

56. *Report of a Meeting for the Establishment of a 'Strangers' Home'* (1855), p. 9.

57. J. Salter (1873), pp. ii–iii; also *Report of a Meeting for the Establishment of a 'Strangers' Home'* (1855), p. 4.

58. *Report of a Meeting for the Establishment of a 'Strangers' Home'* (1855), p. 12.

59. *Ibid.*

60. *Ibid.*, pp. 13 and 23.

61. *Ibid.*, p. 9.

62. *Ibid.*, p. 9; see also J. Salter (1873), p. ii.

63. To mark the occasion, handkerchiefs with the emblem of the Strangers' Home printed on them were distributed among the guests from India, China and Africa. See the *Illustrated London News*, June 1856.

64. For eight shillings the lascars were to be provided with three meals a day, medical attendance, baths and washing facilities. See *Illustrated London News*, 28 February 1857.

65. Letter from J. Chapman, dated 3 June 1857. Church Missionary

Society Archives. See also *Report of a Meeting for the Establishment of a 'Strangers' Home'* (1855), pp. 8–11; J. Salter (1873), pp. 68–9.

66. Joseph Salter of the London City Mission was appointed missionary to the Orientals and Africans in the East End and the Strangers' Home by the Directors of the Strangers' Home. In 1876, however, the Directors appointed another missionary for the Home, and so Salter confined his work to Orientals and Africans in the docks, hospitals and elsewhere in London. He could speak Hindustani and Kiswahili. He was a prolific writer. He published reports on his work among the Orientals and Africans in the *London City Mission Magazine*. These articles were later written up in his books, *An Asiatic in England* (1873) and *The East in the West* (1896). Although generally sympathetic to the 'foreigner', his writings convey Christian prejudice of the time.

67. *Illustrated London News*, 28 February 1857.

68. J. Salter (1873), pp. 67–71.

69. *Illustrated London News*, 7 March 1868.

70. J. Salter (1873), p. 303.

71. 'Statistics of the Working of "The Home" from June 1857 to 31 December 1877' in Colonel Hughes's letter dated 27 March 1879, in IOR: L/P&J/2/59, No. 7/567.

Year	Registered inmates	Casuals	Destitute cases gratuitously provided for
1857	387	306	75
1858	354	316	126
1859	315	307	107
1860	213	75	86
1861	208	83	71
1862	367	35	62
1863	334		71
1864	279		93
1865	123		103
1866	118		45
1867	180		162
1868	126		71
1869	189		77
1870	274		69
1871	327		45
1872	256		41
1873	272		44
1874	320		49
1875	377		45
1876	295		88
1877	395		75
	5,709		1,605

72. 18 and 19 Vic. C. 91 Sections 22, 23 and 24.
73. Statistics are discussed later in the chapter. See also G. Sims, *Living London* (London: Cassell, 1906), Vol. I, pp. 81-6.
74. Lascars were paid between one-third and one-quarter of the British wages by 1914, e.g. according to Walsh, 'European crew of 46 men cost in wages £190, Indian crew of 92 men £133; in victualling the European £86, native £103. Net gain of £40 a month, about 14½%.' J. Walsh, in 'The Empire's Obligation to the Lascar' in *The Imperial and Asiatic Quarterly Review*, Vol. XXX, July-October 1910.
75. Quoted in Conrad Dixon, 'Lascars, the Forgotten Seamen' in *Working Men Who Got Wet*, proceedings of the Fourth Conference of the Atlantic Shipping Project, July 1980, Maritime History Group, University of Newfoundland (ed. R. Ommer and G. Panting). Dixon also discusses the working condition of the lascars to the present day.
76. 57 and 58 Vic. C. 60 Section 125 of 1894.
77. John Widdowson: 'Black People in Canning Town, 1900-1945', paper presented to the Conference of Black Peoples in London, November 1984, University of London, Institute of Education. See also *People Who Moved to Newham*, p. 6. (published by INSEC, the Credon Centre, London Borough of Newham.)
78. *London City Mission Magazine*, 1909, pp. 200-206: 'The Society's Work among the Lascars'.
79. *Report of the Committee on Lascars, 1814-15* (No. 471), p. 4.
80. Admission of British Empire Seamen to the Dreadnought Hospital by Decades, 1821-1901.

Decade	Lascars	UK seamen	Colonies	Total	Lascar %
1821-30	71	11,437	497	12,005	0.5
1831-40	422	19,401	667	20,490	2
1841-50	553	19,848	844	21,245	2.5
1851-60	1,269	13,225	837	15,331	8
1861-70	153	11,826	1,099	13,078	1
1871-80	281	12,295	1,007	13,583	2
1881-90	430	12,892	527	13,849	3
1891-1901	1,744	17,600	859	20,203	8

Source: Annual Reports of the Seamen's Hospital Society as quoted in C. Dixon (1980).

81. Colonel R.M. Hughes, *Laws Relating to Lascars* (1855), p. 5.
82. *London City Mission Magazine*, 1 July 1875, pp. 134-5, 137.

83. For instance, in 1906 the union passed a resolution to the effect that one lascar in every five should be able to speak English. Up to the outbreak of the First World War, Wilson demanded the language test to exclude foreign sailors.

4. Towards an Asian Community in Britain: Individuals and Interests

1. *London City Mission Magazine*, January 1867, p. 4.
2. *Ibid.*, pp. 4–16.
3. J. Salter, *The Asiatic in England: Sketches of Sixteen Years' Work Among Orientals* (Seely, Jackson & Halliday, 1873), pp. 236–9.
4. C. Kondapi, *Indians Overseas 1838–1949* (New Delhi: Indian Council of World Affairs, London: Oxford University Press, 1951). Appendix I, p. 528: 'Statement of Indian population in Overseas Country'. This estimates the Indian population in the UK in about 1932 to be 7,128. Elsewhere in the book Kondapi puts the figure of Indians in Britain at 5,000, see p. 360. See also N.V. Rajkumar, *Indians Outside India* (published by the Foreign Department of the Indian National Congress Committee, New Delhi, 1951). D. Lorimer, *Color Class and the Victorians. English Attitudes to the Negro in the Mid-nineteenth Century* (Leicester University Press, 1978), pp. 214–15, warns about the reliability of the 'Census of England and Wales in 1871'.
5. Pierce Egan, *Life in London, or the Day and Night Scenes of Jerry Hawthorn, Esq and his Elegant Friend Corinthian Tom* (Sherwood, Heely & Jones, 1821), p. 286.
6. Joseph Marryat, *More Thoughts Occasioned by two Publications which the Authors call 'An Exposure of some of the Numerous Misstatements and Misrepresentations, Contained in a Pamphlet, Commonly known by the name of Mr Marryat's Pamphlet, entitled Thoughts etc' and 'A Defence of the Bill for the Registration of Stables'* (London, 1816), pp. 99–100.
7. J. Salter, *The East in the West, or Work Among the Asiatics and Africans in London* (London: S.W. Partridge & Co., 1896), p. 152.
8. J. Salter (1896), p. 55.
9. J. Smith, *The Missionary's Appeal to British Christians on Behalf of Southern India* (1841), pp. 149, 153.
10. H.H. Montgomery, *Foreign Missions* (1902), p. 35.

11. 'F. Anstey', *Baboo Jabberjee, BA* (1897), quoted in V.G. Kiernan, *Lords of the Human Kind. European Attitudes to the Outside World in the Imperial Age* (London: Weidenfeld & Nicholson, 1969), p. 49. Cf. Peter Sellers' imitation of Indian English.
12. Henry Mayhew, *London Labour and the London Poor* (London: Griffin, Bohn & Co., 1861), Vol. IV, p. 440; and for a picture of a Hindu tract seller, see Vol. I, p. 242.
13. *Ibid.*, Vol. I, p. 241.
14. *Ibid.*, Vol. I, picture opposite p. 206.
15. *Ibid.*, Vol. IV, pp. 423-4.
16. Salter (1873), p. 221.
17. Mayhew, Vol. III, pp. 188-9.
18. Mayhew, Vol. IV, pp. 424-5.
19. Salter (1896), p. 38; *London City Mission Magazine*, January 1867, p. 9.
20. Salter (1873), p. 116.
21. Salter (1873), pp. 30-31; *London City Mission Magazine*, November 1858, p. 287.
22. Salter (1873), pp. 69-70.
23. After the Kingdom of Oudh was incorporated in the British Indian Empire, the Queen Mother came to England to plead for the Kingdom.
24. Salter (1873), pp. 69-70.
25. *London City Mission Magazine*, November 1858, p. 286.
26. Salter (1873), pp. 170-71; *London City Mission Magazine*, January 1867, p. 3.
27. *London City Mission Magazine*, January 1867, p. 13.
28. *Ibid.*
29. *Collectanea: or a Collection of Advertisements and Paragraphs from the Newspapers, Relating to Various Subjects*, compiled by D. Lysons, 223v.
30. Salter (1896), p. 41.
31. IOR: L/P&J/6/191, 1886, No. 2122.
32. *Gentleman's Magazine*, May 1805, p. 479 and January 1823, p. 80; Salter (1896), pp. 135-7.
33. *Illustrated London News*, 9 November 1889, pp. 590- 91.
34. B.M. Malabari, *The Indian Eye on English Life or Rambles of a Pilgrim Reformer* (Bombay: Apollo Printing Works, 1895), p. 228; G.M. Towler Mehta, 'Parsees in Britain', *New Community*, Vol. X, No. 2, Winter 1982, p. 244.

35. Salter (1873), p. 203.
36. *London City Mission Magazine*, August 1857, p. 217.
37. E.g. Messrs Chiragden & Godar, 451 East India Road, Poplar; 82 New Road, Whitechapel. Their advertisement carried many testimonials from various patients whom they had cured by their 'brilliant treatment of the eyes', see IOR: L/P&J/6/339, No. 241; L/P&J/6/315, No. 991 and L/P&J/6/323, No. 1066 and L/P&J/6/325, No. 1180 for oculists in Edinburgh.
38. *The Times*, 21 September 1893.
39. IOR: L/P&J/6/356, No. 1832; L/P&J/6/365, No. 77. Their advertisement showed that they had lived and worked in other countries, notably France.
40. IOR: L/P&J/6/373, No. 828; L/P&J/6/375, No. 1016. Other cases of oculists are discussed in L/P&J/6/401, No. 1264 and L/P&J/6/322.
41. *Daily Advertiser*, 5 November 1777, No. 14629.
42. Rakhal Das Halder, *The English Diary of an Indian Student 1861–62* (Dacca: The Asutosh Library, 1903), pp. 32 and 23; *Memoirs and Writings of Syed Ameer Ali*, ed. Syed Razi Wasti (Lahore: People's Publishing House, 1968), p. 24; Salter (1896), pp. 118–19.
43. Salter (1873), p. 67; IOR: L/P&J/2/49, No: 7/281, letter dated 17 January 1869.
44. R.D. Haldar, pp. 23 and 26; S.R. Mehrotra, *The Emergence of the Indian National Congress* (Vikas Publications, 1971), p. 326.
45. Memo on Anti-British Agitation Among the Natives of India in Britain. IOR: L/P/S19/168.
46. There is controversy as to whether Sake Deen Mahomed was born in 1759 or 1749. The tombstone in St Nicholas's churchyard in Brighton records his age as 101 (i.e. born in 1749). The controversy originates from Sake Deen Mahomed himself as he has given two dates in two different sources. In his book, *Travels of Dean Mahomet, A Native of Patna in Bengal, through several parts of India, while in the Service of the Honourable the East India Company*, published at Cork in 1794, he gives his birth date as 1759 (p. 5), making him 92 at his death in 1851. However, in his later work, *Shampooing or Benefits Resulting from the use of the Indian Medicated Vapour Bath*, first published in Brighton in 1822 and reaching its third edition in 1838, his birth date is recorded as 1749 (p. vi). Sir Evan Cotton who did some research on him, concluded that he was 102 and so rejected 1759 as the true date, asserting that

'if he was born in 1749 he is not likely to have joined the army before the age of 20, i.e. in 1769. Add 15 years to 1769 and we get 1784, the year in which he came to England. These dates are put out of gear if he was born in 1759.' See Sir Evan Cotton, ' "Sake Deen Mahomed" of Brighton', in *Sussex County Magazine*, Vol. 13, 1939, pp. 746–50. However, in his *Travels*, Sake Deen mentioned joining the army as a follower of Captain Baker soon after his father's death in 1769, when he was 'about 11 years old', see pp. 9 and 20.
47. *Travels of Dean Mahomet*, Vol. I, pp. 5–8.
48. *Ibid.*, pp. 9–21.
49. *Gentleman's Magazine*, Vol. 189, January–June 1851, p. 444; *Travels of Dean Mahomet*, Vol. II, pp. 90–127.
50. *Travels of Dean Mahomet*, Vol. II, pp. 127–62. This account of Sake Deen Mahomed's early career in India is based on the account given by him in his book *Travels of Dean Mahomet*. There is some mystery about his early life, again in the main compounded by himself. In his *Travels* he recorded that he joined the services of Captain Baker in 1769, when he was 'about eleven', following his fortunes in the army; he was promoted by Captain Baker in his battalion. Later, however, in his book *Shampooing*, he wrote that he had been educated 'to the profession of and served in the Company's service as a surgeon' (p. vi). Was Sake Deen Mahomed trained as a surgeon? Or had he joined the army as Captain Baker's follower when a young boy? If his earlier version is correct then he joined the army when only 'about eleven' and so could not possibly have been a surgeon. But it is quite likely that he did witness surgical operations while in the army. Surgery in the eighteenth century was merely at the barber-surgeon level, anyway. Many writers, however, relying on his version in *Shampooing* have credited him as having joined the East India Company's army as a surgeon. Sir Evan Cotton has also suggested that he was a medical student at the hospital in Calcutta and successfully treated cholera cases in the army. See *Sussex County Magazine*, Vol. 13, 1939, pp. 746–50. See also: J. Erredge, *History of Brightlemston or Brighton as I view it and others knew it* (Brighton, printed by E. Lewis, 1862), pp. 235–6; Melville Lewis, *Brighton: its History, its Follies and its Fashions* (London: Chapman & Hall, 1909), pp. 135–7; E.W. Gilbert, *Brighton Old Ocean's Bauble* (London: Methuen, 1954), pp. 70–71; C. Musgrave, *Life in Brighton from the*

Earliest Times to the Present (London: Faber, 1970), pp. 203-5; Rozina Visram, 'Sake Deen Mahomed, Shampooing Surgeon to George IV', *Dragon's Teeth*, No. 18, Summer 1984, pp. 8-9.

51. *Travels of Mirza Abu Talib Khan in Asia, Africa, and Europe During the Years 1799, 1800, 1801, 1802 and 1803, Written by Himself in the Persian Language*, translated by C. Stewart (Longman, Hurst, Rees & Orme, 1810), pp. 103-4; *Gentleman's Magazine*, Vol. 189, January-June 1851, p. 444.

52. Most writers (see note 50) suggest that Sake Deen Mahomed and his wife settled in Brighton in 1786. This is unlikely because his *Travels* were published at Cork in 1794; Mirza Abu Talib Khan met Sake Deen Mahomed in 1799 in Captain Baker's family household in Cork. 1801 is suggested here because A.B. Granville, in his book published in 1841, mentioned that 'This extraordinary man settled at Brighton 40 years ago'. See A.B. Granville, *The Spas of England, and Principal Sea Bathing Places* (London: Henry Colburn, 1841), Vol. II, p. 564. See also pp. 562-3.

53. The first indoor baths were opened in 1769 by Dr Awister, followed by the Artillery Baths and later Williams Hot and Cold Baths in 1803. See Erredge, pp. 234-5; Musgrave, p. 201.

54. *Travels of Dean Mahomet*, Vol. II, p. 42; *Shampooing*, p. vi.

55. *Shampooing*, p. vii.

56. *Ibid.*, p. vii.

57. *Ibid.*, p. 14.

58. Lord Castlereagh, Lord Canning, Lady Cornwallis, Sir Robert Peel and Lord Reay all patronized Sake Deen Mahomed. See *Shampooing*, pp. 159-86.

59. *Cases Cured by Sake Deen Mahomed, Shampooing Surgeon, An Inventor of the Indian Medicated Vapour and Sea-Water Baths*, written by the patients themselves (Brighton, 1820); his *Visitors' Book* of signatures and letters (one for the ladies' and the other for the gentlemen's names) still survives at the public reference library in Brighton. Various editions of his book, *Shampooing*, also carried many names of patients he had cured and other notices by his patients.

60. See 'Ode to Mahomet the Brighton Shampooer', in *Memoirs, and Letters and Comic Miscellanies in Prose and Verse of the late James Smith Esq.* ed. Horace Smith, in two volumes (London: Henry Colburn, 1840), pp. 356-9, Vol. I. Same ode also appears in *Shampooing*, pp. 82-9.

61. Musgrave, p. 171.
62. *Shampooing* (1822). The second edition came out in 1826, the third in 1838.
63. *Shampooing*, p. 81.
64. *Shampooing*, p. vii; Melville Lewis, p. 135.
65. Horace Smith wrote to Charles Matthews in 1828, 'To put you in good humour, I must tell you that Mahomed, yesterday, pointed out to a friend of mine a suspended crutch, which he averred to have been yours, and that he had enabled you to throw it away by shampooing you', see Melville Lewis, p. 136.
66. G.A. Sala, *Life and Adventures of G.A. Sala* (London: Cassell, 1895), p. 202.
67. *A Treatise on the Properties and Medical Application of the Vapour Bath*; see also Musgrave, p. 205.
68. *The Bath: a Concise History of Bathing, as Practised by Nations of the Ancient and Modern World, including a Brief Exposition of the Medical Efficacy and Salubrity of the Warm, Medicated Vapour, Shampooing, Shower and Douche Baths* (London: Smith, Elder & Co., 1843); *Short Hints on Bathing, with special reference to the use of the Indian Medicated Vapour Bath, with the operation of Shampooing, being the Result of the Experience of the Author and his Father Sake Deen Mahomed* (London: 7 Ryder Street, 1844).
69. Mahomed had five children: Rosanna died in January 1818 and Henry in February 1823. The three surviving sons were: Horatio, Frederick and Arthur.
70. Visitors Book of Signatures and Letters – Gentlemen's names (ii).
71. From an obituary notice printed in a Brighton newspaper: see Evan Cotton, p. 749; *Gentleman's Magazine*, Vol. 189, January–June 1851, p. 444.
72. The tombstone in St Nicholas's churchyard reads: 'Sacred to the memory of Sake Deen Mahomed of Patna, Hindoostan who died on 24th February 1851 aged 101 years and of Jane his wife who died on 26th of December 1850 aged 70 years'. It is not clear whether Jane is the same Irish girl he had eloped with in Cork. See *Guy's Hospital Reports*, Vol. LXIII, 1885-6, p. 1.
73. Akbar Mahomed was the son of Frederick, the fencing master at Brighton. By this time, Akbar was claimed to have 'English parents'. See 'In Memoriam' by James F. Goodhart and W.H.A. Jacobson, *Guy's Hospital Reports*, Vol. XLIII, p. 1.
74. *Guy's Hospital Reports*, Vol. XLIII, pp. 1-10; see also, *Dictionary*

of National Biography, Vol. XII (1921), pp. 777–8; *British Medical Journal*, 29 November 1884, p. 1099; H.C. Cameron, *Mr Guy's Hospital, 1726–1948* (Longman's, Green & Co., 1954), pp. 212, 242–5; *The Times*, 24 November 1884.

75. Some of Akbar Mahomed's articles were: 'Observations with the Sphygmograph', 'Pre-albuminuric stage of Scarlatinal Dropsy', 'Bright's Disease without Albuminuria'.

76. *Guy's Hospital Reports*, Vol. XLIII; *British Medical Journal*, 29 November 1884.

77. For information on Dr Gotla see *Bombay Chronicle*, 28 October 1927. For his signature and address in 1914 see M.K. Gandhi's letter dated 14 August 1914 in IOR: MSS EUR F 170. Dr Gotla performed the operation to remove Shapurji Saklatvala's tonsils at Highgate Nursing Home; Dr Gotla was also present at M.M. Bhownaggree's funeral in November 1933.

78. For information on Dr Pardhy see *Bombay Chronicle*, 28 October 1927.

79. R.P. Masani, *Dadabhai Naoroji, the Grand Old Man of India* (George Allen & Unwin, 1939), pp. 71 and 78; Salter (1873), pp. 295–8.

80. Panchanan Saha, *Shapurji Saklatvala, a Brief Biography* (People's Publishing House, New Delhi, 1970), p. 3. For Sir Rata Tata see *The Times*, 7 September 1918.

81. In the letter dated 14 August 1914 signed by the Asian residents in Britain and sent by M.K. Gandhi to the Secretary of State for India, six residents declared their occupation to be traders or merchants, five physicians, three barristers, and one a journalist – and many others were students. See IOR: MSS EUR F 170.

82. *Travels of Mirza Abu Talib Khan*, pp. 198–200. 'General De B____ e' most probably refers to General Benoit De Boigne. See Lester Hutchinson, *European Freebooters in Moghul India* (New York: Asia Publishing House, 1964), pp. 120–54; p. 154 refers to the marriage of De Boigne to a Persian colonel's daughter by whom he had two children, a boy and a girl – Ali Bux and Banu. The French girl that De Boigne later married was Adèle d'Osmond.

83. This study does not deal with the Anglo-Indians in England. Offspring of cross-cultural marriages were also called Indo-Britons and Eurasians. After the 1911 census the term Anglo-Indian came to be used. See also Cedric Dover, *Half-Caste* (Secker & Warburg, 1937).

84. J.C. Carr, *The Life of Sir Arthur Conan Doyle* (John Murray, 1959), p. 220.
85. For the Edalji family and case see J.C. Carr, pp. 218–36; H. Pearson, *Conan Doyle* (published for the British Publishers' Guild by Methuen, 1946), pp. 145–7; *Daily Telegraph*, January 1907. The first instalment of Doyle's 'The Case of Mr George Edalji' appeared on 11 January 1907; subsequent copies of the *Daily Telegraph* also carry letters from members of the public on the Edalji case.
86. Sometimes spelt Dhuleep Singh.
87. Runjit Singh was too old and so unlikely to have been able to bear a son. Duleep Singh was officially acknowledged as Runjit Singh's son.
88. The terms of the Treaty of Bhyrowal. Later in life, after he had seen the Koh-i-noor, Duleep Singh would in private refer to Queen Victoria as 'Mrs Fagin – a receiver of stolen property'.
89. Dalhousie to Hobhouse, 4 April 1849, as quoted in M. Alexander and S. Anand, *Queen Victoria's Maharajah Duleep Singh, 1838–1893* (Weidenfeld & Nicolson, 1980), p. 13.
90. Queen Victoria to Lord Dalhousie, 26 July 1854, as quoted in Alexander and Anand, pp. 44–5.
91. Dalhousie to Couper, 11 October 1854; Aberdeen to Queen Victoria, 26 August 1854, as quoted in Alexander and Anand, pp. 54–5.
92. Queen Victoria's Journal, 13 July 1854, as quoted in Alexander and Anand, p. 59.
93. Charles Wood to Phipps, 25 April 1859, as quoted in Alexander and Anand, p. 82.
94. See Alexander and Anand, pp. 111–12. John Lord, *The Maharajas* (Hutchinson, 1972), pp. 24–5.
95. *The Times*, 13 August 1882; see also Evans Bell, *The Annexation of the Punjab and the Maharajah Duleep Singh* (1882), which also criticized the activities of the British government in India.
96. See Alexander and Anand, pp. 167–209.
97. From Paris he kept up pressure on the India Office. He also tried making approaches to the Russians to embarrass the British government – during this period Britain was very sensitive about Russian designs on Afghanistan. Duleep Singh also married an English girl, Ada Douglas Weatherill, in May 1889.
98. IOR: MSS EUR F 143/91. Letter no. 16 from Kartar Singh in the

hospital at Milford-on-Sea, dated 24 February 1916, referred to her as 'Our King's [Runjit Singh] grand-daughter'. Censor's comment, 5 March 1916.
99. *Illustrated London News*, 17 July 1852.
100. Dalhousie to Login, 24 September 1852, as quoted in Alexander and Anand, p. 34.
101. Alexander and Anand, pp. 84–5.
102. *Ibid.*, p. 102.
103. From Horace Cockerell, Secretary to the government of Bengal, to the government of India, Foreign Department, 10 January 1879; from C. Macaulay, Secretary to the government of Bengal, to the government of India, Foreign Department, 14 February 1879. See IOR: L/P&J/7/21.

5. Early Challengers to the Empire

1. A.K. Majumdar, *Advent of Independence* (Bombay: Bharatiya Vidya Bhavan, 1963), p. 39.
2. R.C. Majumdar, *History of the Freedom Movement in India* (Calcutta: Firma K.L. Makhopadhyay, 1962), Vol. I, p. 383.
3. J.H. Bell, *British Folks and British India Fifty Years Ago: Joseph Pease and his Compatriots* (London: John Heywood, 1891), p. 60.
4. S.R. Mehrotra, *The Emergence of the Indian National Congress* (Vikas Publications, 1971), p. 16.
5. Anglo-Indian refers to Englishmen long resident in India. After the 1911 census the term applied to Eurasians, see Note 83 to Chapter 4. The Asians present were the Nawab Eckbaloo Dowlah, Prince of Oudh; the Prince Imamudin, son of Tipu Sultan; Mir Afzal Ali and Mir Karim Ali, agents in England of the Rajah of Satara; Ishanger Naorodjee (*sic*) and Hirjeebhoy Merwanjee, two young Parsis from Bombay who had come to Britain to learn shipbuilding on the Thames; and Dorabjee Mancherjee, a merchant from Bombay. See J.H. Bell, p. 65. The two Parsi shipbuilders have left a record of their visit to England. See I. Naoroji and H. Merwanjee, *Journal of a Residence in Great Britain of two years and a half* (London, 1841).
6. S.R. Mehrotra, pp. 23–4.
7. *Ibid.*, pp. 223–4.
8. *Ibid.*, p. 225.
9. *The Times*, 3 July 1917.

10. S.R. Mehrotra, p. 328. See also M.K. Gandhi, *An Autobiography, or The Story of My Experiments with Truth* (Penguin Books, 1982), p. 89.

11. See S.R. Mehrotra, pp. 324-31; M. Cumpston, 'Some Early Indian Nationalists and their Allies in the British Parliament, 1851-1906', *English Historical Review*, April 1961, pp. 279-97.

12. R.P. Masani, *Dadabhai Naoroji, the Grand Old Man of India* (George Allen & Unwin, 1939), p. 254.

13. Lalmohan Ghose, born in Krishnagar in 1849, came to England to study law at the Middle Temple. In 1873 he joined the Bar at Calcutta. He was a prominent member of the British Indian Association. In 1879 he came to England on behalf of the association to campaign for the admission of Indians into the civil service. In 1883 he agitated in England against the Ilbert Bill. He presided over the nineteenth session of the Indian National Congress in 1903. He died in October 1909.

14. *The First Indian Member of the Imperial Parliament, being a collection of the main incidents relating to the election of Mr Dadabhai Naoroji to Parliament* (Madras, 1892), p. 3.

15. For a biography of Dadabhai Naoroji, see R.P. Masani; *The Times*, 3 July 1917; *Dadabhai Naoroji, a Study* (Madras: Ganesh & Co., 1907); *Who's Who of British MPs*, Vol. II, ed. M. Stenton; *Dictionary of National Biography*, ed. S.P. Sen (Calcutta: Institute of Historical Studies, 1972), Vol. III, pp. 220-23; *India*, 6 July 1917; Rozina Visram and Audrey Dewjee, 'Dadabhai Naoroji: Britain's First Black MP', *Dragons Teeth*, No. 17, Spring 1984.

16. Cama and Co. not only traded in cotton, but also dealt in opium; Naoroji was against the opium trade and resigned on a point of principle. His own cotton company folded in 1881.

17. *Poverty and Un-British Rule in India* (London: Swan Sonnenschein, 1901). See also B.N. Ganguli, *Dadabhai Naoroji and the Drain Theory* (London: Asia Publishing House, 1965). It has been suggested that Naoroji's economic thinking was influenced by the writings and speeches of John Dickinson (1815-76), who wrote *The Government of India under A Bureaucracy* in 1852; Major Evans Bell who wrote *The Empire in 1864*, and John Bright (1811-89), of the Anti-Corn Law League.

18. 'Mr Naoroji at Plumstead', reprinted from *Poverty and Un-British Rule in India*, pp. 650-51.

19. E.g. Manmohan Ghose, a barrister, failed; so did his brother.

Surendranath Banerjee passed, but was disqualified on a trumped-up charge.

20. Quoted in R.G. Gregory, *India and East Africa. A History of Race Relations within the British Empire 1890–1939* (Oxford: Clarendon Press, 1971), p. 135.

21. *Lord Salisbury's Blackman* (Lucknow: G.P. Varma & Bros Press, 1889), *Worcestershire Echo*, p. 2. See also B.M. Malabari, *The Indian Eye on English Life or Rambles of a Pilgrim Reformer* (Bombay: Apollo Printing Works, 1895), p. 220.

22. See *Dadabhai Naoroji Correspondence*, Vol. II, Part I, *Correspondence with D.E. Wacha*, edited with an introduction and notes by R.P. Patwardhan (Bombay: Allied Publishers Private Ltd, 1977), p. xxx.

23. Total percentage of the poll: 57.1. F. Duncan polled 65.2 per cent with Naoroji taking 34.8 per cent.

24. Finsbury Central constituted Clerkenwell district with its watch and jewellery trade. It also included Muswell Hill with its 'detached villas', where 5 per cent of the electorate lived. See Henry Pelling, *Social Geography of British Elections* (Macmillan, 1967).

25. At the first count Naoroji had a majority of only three; Colonel F.T. Penton, his opponent, filed a petition and a recount was ordered. The majority was then raised to five. Narrow majorities and recounts were a common feature at Finsbury: F.T. Penton himself had previously won the seat by five votes.

26. Lord Salisbury's speech in *Lord Salisbury's Blackman*, p. 1.

27. *Ibid., Newcastle Leader*, p. 1.

28. *Ibid., Star*, pp. 6–7.

29. *Ibid., Glasgow Mail*, p. 15; *Star*, p. 11.

30. *Ibid., Accrington Times*, p. 17.

31. *Ibid., Bristol Mercury*, p. 22.

32. *Ibid., Warrington Examiner*, p. 84.

33. *Ibid., Graphic*, p. 86; *Daily News*, p. 31.

34. *Ibid., Figaro*, p. 20.

35. *Ibid., Echo*, pp. 9–10.

36. *Ibid., Hawk*, p. 43; see also *Land and Water*, p. 25.

37. *Ibid.*, Lord Salisbury's apology, pp. 32–3.

38. *Ibid., The Times*, pp. 63–5.

39. *Ibid., St James Gazette*, p. 3.

40. *India and Mr Dadabhai, MP: an Open Letter to her Most Gracious*

Majesty Victoria, Queen Empress of India, by Fair Play (1893).
41. R.P. Masani, pp. 231 and 234.
42. William Digby noted: 'Though bearing so strongly Indian a name, Mr Naoroji is to all intents and purposes an Englishman as well as an English subject. His long residence in this country and his mastery of our tongue, added to his English appearance, take away any objection which might occur to his not being an Englishman.' See R.P. Masani, p. 265.

An eye-witness account of the Holborn election noted that 'he has the appearance and the manner of a cultivated English gentleman, his face a shade or two off colour, perhaps, but not darker than many an Australian', see R.P. Masani, p. 243. See also the comment in the *Pall Mall Gazette*, as quoted in R.P. Masani, p. 243.

43. See Naoroji's manifesto to the electors of Holborn division, 19 June 1886. During the 1892 election, Naoroji supported the 'Newcastle Programme'. See his election address to the electors of Central Finsbury.
44. *The Times*, 26 June 1886; Masani, pp. 238-9.
45. See C.L. Parekh, p. 303 for Naoroji's speech at the meeting held on 27 June 1886, in the town hall Holborn: 'Standing as I do here, to represent the 250,000,000 of your fellow subjects in India, of course, I know thoroughly well my duty: for if I am returned by you, my first duty will be to consult completely and fully the interests of my constituents.'
46. In the final ballot held on 15 August 1888, Naoroji polled 49 votes, Richard Eve 45 and F.A. Ford 23. The Secretary to the Association confirmed Naoroji's selection by congratulating him on his victory. See R.P. Masani, p. 258; *Mr D. Naoroji and Mr Schnadhorst* (London, 1892), p. 3.
47. Schnadhorst to Naoroji, 18 August 1888 in IOR: MSS EUR D 767/1; *Mr D. Naoroji and Mr Schnadhorst*, pp. 4-5.
48. Schnadhorst to Digby, 18 August 1888 in IOR: MSS EUR D 767/1; *Mr D. Naoroji and Mr Schnadhorst*, p. 5.
49. *Lord Salisbury's Blackman*, p. 64.
50. Arnold Morley of the London Liberal Radical Union asked Naoroji on 22 March 1889 to go to arbitration, and Schnadhorst also joined in the suggestion. See *Mr D. Naoroji and Mr Schnadhorst*, p. 8. This despite the fact that an earlier motion for arbitration had been thrown out.

51. Interview with F.A. Ford, in the *Finsbury and Holborn Guardian*, 23 May 1891. See IOR: MSS EUR D 767/6.

52. Correspondence between Digby and Schnadhorst. See R.P. Masani, p. 271.

53. Masani, p. 271; *Mr D. Naoroji and Mr Schnadhorst*, p. 13.

54. Naoroji to Digby, 23 April 1891, in IOR: MSS EUR D 767/1; see also Naoroji to Digby, 25 May 1891; for the statement in the *Weekly News & Chronicle* see R.P. Masani, p. 272; IOR: MSS EUR D 767/4; and *Mr D. Naoroji and Mr Schnadhorst*, p. 14.

55. Naoroji to Digby, 26 March 1892, IOR: MSS EUR D 767/1. The pamphlet was entitled: *Mr D. Naoroji and Mr Schnadhorst* (London, 1892).

56. Naoroji to Digby, 29 April 1892, IOR: MSS EUR D 767/1.

57. *First Indian Member of the Imperial Parliament*, p. 14.

58. *Ibid., The Times*, p. 111.

59. *Ibid., Bristol Times*, p. 112.

60. *Ibid., St Stephen's Review*, p. 114.

61. *Ibid., Pall Mall Gazette*, p. 115.

62. *Ibid., Scottish Leader*, p. 114.

63. For details see Address to his Fellow Electors in Central Finsbury, July 1895, by Dadabhai Naoroji. Appendix IV.

64. H. Tinker, *A New System of Slavery. The Export of Indian Labour Overseas 1830-1920* (published for the Institute of Race Relations by Oxford University Press, London, 1974), pp. 201 and 303.

65. Turnout: 71.5 per cent. W.F.B. Mussey: 3,588, 56.3 per cent; Naoroji: 2,783, 43.7 per cent.

66. Turnout: 72.1 per cent. H. Myer (Lib.): 2,162, 44.1 per cent; W. Houghton Gastrell (Con.): 1,904, 38.4 per cent; Naoroji (Ind. Lib.): 733, 14.7 per cent; F.W. Honer, (Ind. Con.): 108, 2.2 per cent.

67. I am grateful to Lord Chitnis for this information on his grandfather.

68. The appreciative citizens of Bombay presented to the electors of Finsbury a wooden casket containing an album of photographs of Indian life. The casket is still in the possession of the Islington libraries, Finsbury local history collection.

69. *The Times*, 3 July 1917.

70. *The Comet*, Lagos, Nigeria, 3 July 1937. I am grateful to A. Dewjee for giving me this reference.

71. R.P. Patwardhan, pp. xxxiii–xxxiv; see also Naoroji, *The Rights of Labour* (1890).

72. Masani, p. 451.
73. *The Late Dadabhai Naoroji on Swaraj. Presidential Address at the Calcutta Congress 1906* (Bombay Home Rule Series, No. 6, published by S.G. Banker for the Home Rule League, Bombay); see also C.F. Andrews, *The Rise and Growth of the Congress in India* (Allen & Unwin, 1938), p. 211; R.P. Patwardhan, p. xxxiv.
74. R.P. Masani, p. 370.
75. For details see *Dictionary of National Biography*, 1931–1940, ed. L.G. Wickham Legg (London: Oxford University Press, 1949); *Who's Who of British Members of Parliament*, ed. M. Stenton and S. Lees (Brighton: Harvester Press, 1978), Vol. II, 1886–1918, p. 32; *The Times*, 15 November 1933; B. Kosmin, 'London's Asian MP's: the Contrasting Careers of Three Parsee Politicians', paper presented to the Conference of the History of Black Peoples in London, University of London, Institute of Education, 1984.
76. *The Times*, 15 November 1933.
77. *The Times*, 15 November 1933; see also *British Parliamentary Election Results 1885–1918*, compiled and edited by F.W.S. Craig (Macmillan, 1974), p. 5. The sitting MP was Howell, who came from a working-class background. The constituency was also against Irish and Jewish immigration.
78. *Lord Salisbury's Blackman*, pp. 63–5.
79. Hamilton to Elgin, 2 April 1897, Hamilton correspondence, as quoted in A.K. Majumdar, Appendix VI, pp. 368–9.
80. R.P. Masani, p. 370.
81. *The Times*, 15 November 1933.
82. *The Times*, 14 November 1895.
83. *The Times*, 15 November 1933.
84. *The Times*, 14 November 1895.
85. *The Times*, 15 November 1933. The obituary notice is headed 'An Indian Imperialist'; the Dictionary of National Biography describes him as a 'sound and practical Imperialist'.
86. Speech by Lord Harris at the complimentary dinner to mark Bhownaggree's victory at Bethnal Green, see *The Times*, 14 November 1895. Among the influential Tories present was Sir Lepel Griffin.
87. Bhownaggree was unanimously adopted by the constituency.
88. *Eastern Argus*, 4 July 1895.
89. Obituary notice in *Bethnal Green News*, 18 November 1933.
90. See Earl of Meath's speech backing Bhownaggree, *Eastern Argus*,

29 June 1895.
91. *Eastern Argus*, 3 August 1895. Explaining his success at Bethnal Green, Bhownaggree commented that it was due to 'a large number of lady friends who canvassed, and explained and corrected such mis-statements as that I was an "alien" and a "foreigner" and that I knew nothing of English life and political work, which were made by the opposition party to prejudice the electors against me'.
92. *Eastern Argus*, 4 May 1895.
93. F.W.S. Craig (1974), p. 5. Number of electors: 7,431. Turnout: 67.6 per cent. Bhownaggree: 2,591, 51.6 per cent; Howell: 2,431, 48.4 per cent.
94. *Bethnal Green News*, 18 November 1933.
95. F.W.S. Craig (1974), p. 5. Number of electors: 8,012. Turnout: 69.9 per cent. Bhownaggree: 2,988, 53.4 per cent; H.L.W. Lawson: 2,609, 46.6 per cent.
96. *The Times*, 15 November 1933.
97. R.P. Masani, p. 370.
98. *The Times*, 15 November 1933.
99. H. Tinker (1974), p. 303.
100. *The Times*, 15 November 1933.
101. *Morning Leader*, 29 August 1905.
102. F.W.S. Craig (1974), p. 5. Total number of electors: 7,734. Turnout: 80.9 per cent. Sir E.A. Cornwall (Lib.): 4,127, 66.0 per cent; M.M. Bhownaggree: 2,130, 34.0 per cent.
103. Gowers to Seton, 19 May 1916. IOR: L/P&J/6/1443, No. 2322.
104. Gowers to Seton, 19 May 1916. Minute by T.W.H. (Sir Thomas Holderness) IOR: L/P&J/6/1443, No: 2322.
105. Both Sant Nihal Singh and S.M. Mitra were ruled out, Sant Singh because he might not be wholehearted enough and Mitra because he did not carry much weight. See IOR: L/P&J/6/1443, No. 2322. Note by A. Hirtzel dated 20 May 1916 and note by E. Younghusband, dated 20 May 1916; Gowers to Dumbell, 24 June 1916.
106. F. Younghusband to Seton, 1 June 1916; Seton to Sir T. Holderness, 1 June 1916, in IOR: L/P&J/6/1443, No. 2322.
107. See minute by T.W.H. (Sir Thomas Holderness) in IOR: L/P&J/6/1443, No. 2322.
108. Sir M.M. Bhownaggree, KCIE (formerly MP for Bethnal Green Northeast), *The Verdict of India* (Hodder & Stoughton, 1916).

109. S. Caselee to Gowers, 17 October 1916 in IOR: L/P&J/6/1443, No. 2322.
110. Bhownaggree to Dumbell, 27 October 1916 in IOR: L/P&J/6/1443, No. 2322.
111. From Seton to Bhownaggree, 8 November 1916 in IOR: L/P&J/6/1443, No. 2322; also from the Home Department Delhi to Seton, 12 December 1916, IOR: L/P&J/6/1443, No. 2322.
112. *The Times*, 15 November 1933.
113. The death occurred at his London home, 177 Cromwell Road, Earl's Court.
114. Ameer Ali, 'India and the New Parliament', in *The Nineteenth Century*, August 1906, reprinted in *Memoirs and Other Writings of Syed Ameer Ali*, ed. Syed Razi Wasti (Lahore: People's Publishing House, 1968), p. 236.
115. Ameer Ali's address read at the Third Annual Session of the All-India Muslim League held in Delhi, in 1910, in Matiur Rahman, *From Consultation to Confrontation. A Study of the Muslim League in British Indian Politics, 1906-1912* (London: Luzac & Co. Ltd., 1970), p. 163.
116. Ameer Ali's address read at the Delhi session, 1910, quoted in M. Rahman, p. 164.
117. Ameer Ali's family traced their ancestry to the Prophet Muhammad. His family had come to India in 1739 with Nadir Shah.
118. For an outline of his life see: *The Times*, 4 August 1928; *Memoirs and Other Writings of Syed Ameer Ali*, pp. 5-129; *Heroes of Our Freedom Movement, Syed Ameer Ali*, produced by the Department of Films and Publications, government of Pakistan, Karachi, 1970; *Dictionary of National Biography, 1922-1930*, ed. J.R.H. Weaver (Oxford University Press, 1937).
119. In 1884 Ameer Ali had married in London, Isabella Ida, daughter of Heyman Konstan. When he retired, they lived in Sussex and also had a house in Cadogan Place, southwest London.
120. His portrait by Oswald Birly is in the Privy Council Office, Downing Street, London.
121. The Muslims had taken a long time to adjust to their loss as the ruling power before the British conquered India. Their educational awakening began with Syed Ahmad Khan and Aligarh College.

122. *Memoirs and Other Writings of Syed Ameer Ali*, p. 44.
123. Report of the Committee of the Central National Muhammadan Association, 15 April 1883; in Rahman, p. 3.
124. *Heroes of Our Freedom Movement*, p. 8.
125. *Ibid.*, p. 6.
126. Ameer Ali, 'India and the New Parliament', in *The Nineteenth Century*, August 1906, in *Memoirs and Other Writings*, p. 236.
127. *Ibid.*
128. Ameer Ali was a regular contributor to *The Times* and the *Nineteenth Century*.
129. *Memoirs and Other Writings*, pp. 75–6.
130. *The Times*, 26 December 1908.
131. *Memoirs and Other Writings*, pp. 80–81.
132. See the Aga Khan's letter in *The Times*, 21 May 1909. Also the Aga Khan's *Memoirs*.
133. Quoted in M. Rahman, p. 153.
134. See *Memoirs and Other Writings of Syed Ameer Ali*, pp. 105–18.
135. Ameer Ali, 'The Anomalies of Civilization' in the *Nineteenth Century*, in *Memoirs and other Writings of Syed Ameer Ali*, pp. 302–18.
136. Some of his authoritative publications include: *The Spirit of Islam*; *A Critical Examination of the Life and Teachings of Muhammad Woman in Islam*; *Muhammadan Law*; *Islam*; *A Short History of the Saracens*; *The Legal Position of Women in Islam*; see pp. 351–2 in *Memoirs and Other Writings of Ameer Ali*.
137. *The Times*, 4 August 1928.
138. *The Times*, 4 August 1928.
139. K.C. Ghose, *The Roll of Honour: Anecdotes of Indian Martyrs* (Calcutta: Vidya Bharati, 1965), p. 159.
140. For instance, Vivekananda opposed the social westernization of Indians: 'We must grow according to our nature . . . If you find it impossible for the Europeans to throw off the few centuries of old culture which there is in the West, do you think it is possible for you to throw off the culture of shining scores of centuries?'
141. Shayamaji Krishnavarma commented that 'the only methods which can bring the English government to its senses are the Russian methods'. *Indian Sociologist*, Vol. III, No. 12, quoted in S.R. Wasti, *Lord Minto and the Indian Nationalist Movement 1905 to 1910* (Clarendon Press, 1964), pp. 89–90.
142. Bal Gangadhar Tilak published *Kesari*, the influential Marathi

paper. The revolutionary movement in India first came to notice with two annual festivals: the Sivaji and Ganpati celebrations. See the *Report of the Committee appointed to investigate Revolutionary Conspiracies in India* (London, 1918), No. 9190, known as the *Rowlatt Report*, IOR: L/PARL/2/444.

143. In the USA a large number of Indians were active in revolutionary politics; the movement was organized from San Francisco by Har Dyal, with *Ghadr* as its organ; in New York the movement received the support of Irish nationalists. In Tokyo it was started by Mahomed Barakatullah.

144. S.R. Rana had a jewellery business in Paris. Madame Cama was Mrs Bhikaji Rustom Cama, the daughter of Sorabji Framji Patel of Bombay. She was educated in Bombay and spoke several languages fluently. She was married to Rustom Cama, the son of K.R. Cama, the Parsi reformer. She edited *Bande Mataram* from Geneva and kept up its publication till 1914. She lived in Paris; travelled between the USA, France and London. She died in Bombay in 1937. In official intelligence reports she was referred to as the 'notorious' Mrs Cama, whose programme was 'frankly revolutionary and murderous'. The authorities considered her a 'quarrelsome lady'. See *Indian Agitators Abroad*, compiled by the Criminal Intelligence Office, Simla, November 1911, IOR: V/27/262/1.

145. Dhanajay Keer, *Savarkar and His Times* (Bombay: A.V. Keer, 1950), p. 34.

146. Krishnavarma was amongst the first Indians to attend Oxford; in tribute to his mentor, Herbert Spencer, he founded the Herbert Spencer lectureship.

147. J.C. Ker, *Political Troubles in India, 1907–1917* (Calcutta: Superintendent of Government Printing, 1917), p. 170.

148. Quoted in V.N. Datta, *Madan Lal Dhingra and the Revolutionary Movement* (New Delhi: Vikas Publishing House, 1978), p. 9.

149. IOR: L/PARL/2/444, *the Rowlatt Report*, p. 11.

150. See *Indian Agitators Abroad* compiled in the Criminal Intelligence Office, Simla, November 1911, IOR: V/27/262/1; *Memo on the Anti-British Agitators among the Natives of India in England*, compiled by the Thugee and Dacoity Dept, IOR: L/P/S19/168 for biographical details of those connected with the Revolutionary Movement. (These are, of course, from the 'Intelligence' angle.)

151. *The Times*, 23 May 1908; *Memo on the Anti-British Agitators in England*, IOR: L/P/S19/168.
152. *The Times*, 23 May 1908. This interpretation was later reiterated by the official reports. See IOR: L/PARL/2/444, the *Rowlatt Report*; J.C. Ker, and *Memo on the Anti-British Agitators in England*, IOR: L/P/S19/168. Shyamaji Krishnavarma in his letter to *The Times*, 2 June 1908, pointed out that he had left London 'fully seven weeks before the question appeared in the Newspaper and in the Parliamentary proceedings of 30 July 1907'.
153. See Mr Rees's question for the 1908 session of parliament in IOR: L/P&J/6/871, No. 156; see also L/P&J/6/891, No. 3430.
154. Quoted in V.N. Datta, p. 11.
155. J.C. Ker, p. 174.
156. This is how Sir Valentine Chirol referred to it. See Dhanajay Keer, p. 9.
157. See *The Times*, 23 May 1908; *Memo on Anti-British Agitation in England*, IOR: L/P/S19/168.
158. The printed invitation card to the 51st Anniversary celebration read: 'To commemorate the Anniversary of the Indian National Rising of 1857. A Meeting of Indians in England will be held at India House, 65 Cromwell Avenue, Highgate, on Sunday, the 10 of May 1908, at 4 p.m. precisely. You and all your *Indian* friends are invited.' See *The Times*, 23 May 1908; *Memo on Anti-British Agitation in England*, IOR: L/P/S19/168.
159. Mr Chatterji in his toast reminded the gathering that 'the future of the country depended on their political emancipation'; while Dr Pereira emphasized that 'the idea of blood was repulsive to educated men, but it was only by blood that India could be freed'. See J.C. Ker, p. 170.
160. See *The Times*, 23 May 1908.
161. These were circular enamelled badges with the 'Bande Mataram' flag in the centre, and words in the memory of 1857 Martyrs.
162. See *Memo on Anti-British Agitation in England*, IOR: L/P/S19/168.
163. *Rowlatt Report*, IOR: L/PARL/2/444; and *Memo on Anti-British Agitation in England*, IOR: L/P/S19/168.
164. *Memo on Anti-British Agitation in England*, IOR: L/P/S19/168; also see letter from the government of India to Viscount Morley, Secretary of State for India, dated 4 March 1909 in India Home

(Political) Proceedings in IOR: POS 5945.

165. Leaflets such as 'A Grave Warning', which warned that the government securities were worthless, and suggested that the public withdraw their securities. 'Oh Martyrs' was another leaflet and the British authorities were convinced that it was the work of Krishnavarma because of the 'French type' print. They believed it was posted from London because the copy of the *Daily News* in which they had been wrapped had '65 Crom' written on it. See J.C. Ker; *Rowlatt Report*, IOR: L/PARL/2/444; *Memo on Anti-British Agitation in England*, IOR: L/P/S19/168, and letter from the government of India to Viscount Morley, Secretary of State for India, dated 4 March 1909 in India Home (Political) Proceedings, IOR: POS 5945.

166. *Rowlatt Report*, IOR: L/PARL/2/444; J.C. Ker.

167. Letter from the government of India to Viscount Morley, Secretary of State, dated 4 March 1909 in India Home (Political) Proceedings, IOR: POS 5945.

168. See the weekly reports by the Director of Criminal Intelligence in India Home Department (Political) Proceedings, IOR: POS 8962; see also J.C. Ker; *Memo on Anti-British Agitation in England*, IOR: L/P/S19/168; *Indian Agitators Abroad*, compiled in the Criminal Intelligence Office, Simla, IOR: V/27/262/1.

169. Letter dated 8 May 1909, demi-official from J.H. Du Boulay to Sir Harold Stuart; telegram from the Viceroy to the Secretary of State, dated 15 May 1909 and from the Secretary of State to the Viceroy of 19 May 1909 in India Home (Political) Proceedings, IOR: POS 5945. Ganesh Savarkar was arrested for the Nasik murders. See *Rowlatt Report*, IOR: L/PARL/2/444.

170. Dr Kaikhusro Lalcaca, aged 45, was for many years a medical practitioner in Shanghai, China. He was on a visit to London. After his murder, a memorial fund was started in Bombay, to which the Indian government contributed, to recognize his 'heroism'. See India Home Department (Political) Proceedings, IOR: POS 8962.

171. J.C. Ker, p. 81. The 'grudge' referred to, it was alleged, went back to 1895 when after Wyllie was appointed in Udaipur, he was instrumental in removing Krishnavarma from the service of Udaipur state. See J.C. Ker, p. 170. See also India Home Department (Political) Proceedings, IOR: POS 8962; *Memo on Anti-British Agitation in England*, IOR: L/P/S19/168; and

Rowlatt Report, IOR: L/PARL/2/444.

172. *The Times*, 17 July 1909; J.C. Ker, p. 180.

173. When Dhingra was arrested, a statement was found in his pocket explaining the reason for his action. The police suppressed it. Savarkar and his friends at India House tried their best to have the statement printed in the English newspapers. Eventually, with the help of Garnett, the statement was printed in the *Daily News* of 18 August 1909. For the statement see: *Daily News* 18 August 1909; also J.C. Ker, pp. 179–80; weekly reports from the Director of Criminal Intelligence for 14 August 1909, in IOR: POS 8962; Datta, p. 41. The statement was also printed as a leaflet and smuggled into India.

174. J.C. Ker, p. 179.

175. Weekly report of the Director of Criminal Intelligence, 31 July 1909 in India Home Department (Political) Proceedings, IOR: POS 8962. In this report Koregaonkar is mentioned as encouraging Dhingra with the words, '*Aji, jao na, kya karte ho*' ('Well, go on, what are you doing').

176. Weekly report of the Director of Criminal Intelligence, 7 August 1909 in India Home Department (Political) Proceedings, IOR: POS 8962.

177. J.C. Ker, p. 183.

178. *Ibid.*, p. 183.

179. *Ibid.*, pp. 187–94.

180. This was Ameer Ali's view. See V.N. Datta, p. 73. At a public meeting of some Indian residents held in Caxton Hall (with the Aga Khan in the chair and Bhownaggree, among others, present) a resolution was passed condemning Dhingra's action. Dhingra's own brother, Bhajan Lal, disassociated himself from the act. At another meeting on 3 July at which S.N. Bannerjea presided, similar resolutions were passed. See weekly report from the Director of Criminal Intelligence, 31 July 1909, in India Home Department (Political) Proceedings, IOR: POS 8962. Gokhale, a moderate leader of the Indian National Congress, too, at a meeting in Poona denounced the philosophy of the bomb; Mahatma Gandhi was also critical of violence. See Datta, pp. 70–74.

181. J.C. Ker, p. 180; weekly report from the Director of Criminal Intelligence, 31 July 1909, in India Home Department (Political) Proceedings, IOR: POS 8962.

182. V.N. Datta, *Madan Lal Dinghra*, pp. 74–8.

183. Demi-official from Colonel J.R. Dunlop Smith to H.A. Stuart, 8 July 1909, in India Home (Political) Proceedings, IOR: POS 5945.

184. Letter dated 7 July 1909 from the brothers of Dhingra. They attributed his eccentricity to the fact that his education in India had been interrupted, and pointed as evidence of this to his running away to sea as a lascar for six months. Dhingra was educated at Municipal College, Amritsar, and then sent to Government College, Lahore. Within a few months, his father had him removed from the college and put him to business. It was only after the brothers had pleaded with the father that Madan Lal Dhingra was sent to England to study mechanical engineering at London University. He came to England in 1906. See India Home (Political) Proceedings, IOR: POS 5945.

185. See the letter of Dhingra's brothers, dated 7 July 1909 in India Home (Political) Proceedings, IOR: POS 5945.

186. Madan Lal's father was Rai Sab Ditta Mal, a civil surgeon. One brother was a barrister, another a medical officer, yet another a health officer, and the eldest was engaged in business. See India Home (Political) Proceedings, IOR: POS 5945.

187. Letter from Dhingra's brothers, dated 7 July 1909; also the letter of Chiman Lal Dhingra published in C & M Gazette in May 1908. See India Home (Political) Proceedings, IOR: POS 5945. See also the comment by Dunlop Smith dated 7 July 1909.

188. See the two letters dated 4 July 1909 from Dhingra's father to Dunlop Smith, in India Home (Political) Proceedings, IOR: POS 5945. Also the letter dated 7 July 1909 from the brothers of Dhingra.

189. See report from the Director of Criminal Intelligence for 3 July 1909, and the report for 31 July 1909, in India Home (Political) Proceedings, IOR: POS 5945; also J.C. Ker, p. 181.

190. Weekly report from the Director of Criminal Intelligence dated 7 August 1909, in India Home Department (Political) Proceedings, IOR: POS 8962.

191. Weekly report from Director of Criminal Intelligence, 23 July 1909, in India Home Department (Political) Proceedings, IOR: POS 8962.

192. Statement of Dhingra. See J.C. Ker, pp. 179–80, and India Home Department (Political) Proceedings, IOR: POS 8962.

193. Quoted in V.N. Datta, pp. 39–40.

194. See V.N. Datta, pp. 74-5; letter dated 23 August 1909 from Ponsonby, Secretary to the King, to Lord Morley in IOR: MSS EUR D 573/49.
195. See the India Councils Act, 1909.

6. Soldiers of the Empire in Two World Wars

1. An Indian escort was requested for the marriage of Princess Victoria Mary of Teck. See Queen Victoria to Lord Lansdowne, 11 May 1893, IOR: MSS EUR D/558/I.
2. Dadabhai Naoroji, Chairman, at the Annual Conference of the London Indian Society, Westminster Town Hall, 28 December 1898.
3. S.D. Pradhan, 'Indian Army and the First World War', in *India and World War I*, ed. Dewitt C. Ellinwood and S.D. Pradhan (New Delhi: Manohar Publications, 1978), p. 51. See also Philip Mason, *A Matter of Honour. An Account of the Indian Army, Its Officers and Men* (Jonathan Cape, 1974), p. 405.
4. D.C. Ellinwood and S. D. Pradhan, pp. 56 and 215.
5. Naoroji's speech and A.A. Khan's supporting motion at the Annual Conference of the London Indian Society, Westminster Town Hall, 28 December 1898.
6. See Dewitt C. Ellinwood, 'The Indian Soldier, the Indian Army and Change', in Ellinwood and Pradhan, p. 199.
7. The 27 largest Indian princely states maintained armies.
8. *Cambridge History of India*, Vol. VI: *Indian Empire 1818-1858*, ed. H.H. Dodwell; and *The Last Phase 1919-1947*, edited by R.R. Sethi (Delhi: S. Chand & Co., 1964), p. 477.
9. Quoted in *India and the War* with an introduction by Lord Sydenham of Combe (London: Hodder & Stoughton, 1915), pp. 68-9.
10. Quoted in *India and the War*, pp. 63-5.
11. M.K. Gandhi to the Undersecretary of State for India, dated 14 August 1914 and reply, IOR: MSS EUR F 170. See also M.K. Gandhi, *An Autobiography or The Story of My Experiments with Truth* (Penguin Books, 1982), pp. 316-18.
12. The sentiment was expressed by the Aga Khan. See *India and the War*, pp. 68-9.
13. Quoted in *India and the War*, p. 55.
14. British Isles including

Channel Isles	6,184,416
India	1,401,350
Canada	640,886
Australia	416,809
New Zealand	220,099
South Africa	136,070
Newfoundland and Labrador	11,922

See Krishna G. Salini, 'The Economic Aspect of India's Participation in the First World War', in Ellinwood and Pradhan, p. 144.

15. *India's Contribution to the Great War* (Calcutta: Superintendent of Government Printing, 1923), in Ellinwood and Pradhan, pp. 143–53. See also Parliamentary Papers, House of Commons, 1918, Vol. 18.

16. For India's role in the First World War, see P. Mason, *Cambridge History of India*, Vol. VI; Sir Charles Lucas (ed.), *The Empire at War* (OUP, 1921-6), Vol. V; B. Mollo, *The Indian Army* (Blandford Press, 1981); Sant Nihal Singh, *India's Fighters: Their Mettle, History and Services to Britain* (London, 1914).

17. Soldiers of the Empire who died in the First World War (Army Museum figures):

British Isles	702,410
India	64,449
Australia	59,380
Canada	57,843
New Zealand	18,711
South Africa	7,121
Colonies	507

18. The Indians won 12,908 honours in all; see *India's Contribution*, quoted in Ellinwood and Pradhan, p. 199. See also Khan Bahadur Colonel Sardar Asghar Ali, *Our Heroes of the Great War* (Bombay, 1922).

19. P. Mason, p. 41.

20. Massia Bibikoff, *Our Indians at Marseilles* (London, 1915), pp. 11-12; *The Times History of the War*, p. 322. The Indians themselves noticed this warm welcome. Nanak Singh wrote: '. . . the women of this place are very pleased to see us, like opening flowers. They shake hands with our men when they disembark and attempt to feed them from their own pocket.' Letter dated 15 February 1915, IOR: MSS EUR F 143/84, Extracts from Censored Mails, letter 17. Another wrote: 'We left for Paris on 12

July and arrived there on the 13th at 5 p.m. Along the route from the station to the camp vast crowds of people were collected whose welcome to us was beyond description. They cheered us and shed flowers over us', letter from — of Sialkot Cavalry brigade, dated 6 August 1916, IOR: MSS EUR F 143/92, Further Extracts (256), letter 1.

21. For Indian involvement on the Western Front, see *The Times History of the War*, Ch. XLI; P. Mason, Ch. XVII.
22. It has been suggested that more Indians suffered from frostbite and pneumonia than soldiers from Europe. In a letter dated 7 September 1915, J.T. Kusat mentioned that: 'Last year more people from Hindustan died of pneumonia than as a consequence of the war', IOR: MSS EUR F 143/85, Extracts from Censored Mails.
23. Report of 12 months' working of the Indian mail censorship, by E.B. Howell. IOR: MSS EUR F 143/84, Extracts from Censored Mails.
    Typescripts of these extracts from the letters in English translation together with the weekly reports by E.B. Howell, the censor of Indian mails, are lodged at the India Office Library and Records. Two copies of these extracts are available: (i) as part of the Military Records, under the classification L/MIL/5/825–828. These are bound volumes. (ii) as part of the Sir Walter Lawrence Papers, under the European Manuscripts Classification, MSS EUR F 143/83–100 (for letters from the European theatre of war). These are unbound folders. Sir Walter Lawrence was in charge of Indian wounded in England. Not only were Indian soldiers' letters from the front censored, but so were their letters written from English hospitals. See also Mulk Raj Anand, *Across the Black Waters* (Jonathan Cape, 1940), a novel describing Indian soldiers' experiences in the First World War.
24. From a Muslim, dated 8 October 1916, IOR: MSS EUR F 143/92, Further Extracts (276), letter 26.
25. Comment by E.B. Howell, dated 6 March 1915; see also letters 13 and 15, IOR: MSS EUR F 143/83, Extracts from Censored Mails.
26. From Khan Bhadur, dated 17 June, IOR: MSS EUR F 143/84, Extracts from Censored Mails, letter 1.
27. From Ludar Singh, dated 22 July 1915, IOR: MSS EUR F 143/84, Extracts from Censored Mails, letter 28.
28. A Jat remarked that 'no-one considers rifles now-a-days'. Letter

dated 5 September 1916, IOR: MSS EUR F 143/92, Further Extracts (273), letter 21.

29. See note appended to E.B. Howell's report, dated 23 January 1915, IOR: L/MIL/5/825, pt I, ff. 1–185, Extracts from Censored Mails.

30. Report by E.B. Howell, dated 23 January 1915, IOR: L/MIL/5/825, pt I, ff. 1–185, Extracts from Censored Mails.

31. German soldier's letter published in *Frankfurter Zeitung*, and quoted in *The Times History of the War*, p. 350.

32. An English soldier's letter dated 22 October 1915, IOR: MSS EUR F 143/86, Extracts from Censored Mails (843/848), letter 74.

33. Memo by James Willcocks, Commander of the Indian Army corps, dated 6 July 1915, IOR: MSS EUR F 143/77.

34. *Neuve Chapelle, India's Memorial in France 1914–1918* (Hodder & Stoughton, 1927).

35. From a Hindu student, dated 28 January 1915, IOR: L/MIL/5/825, pt I, ff. 1–185, Extracts from Censored Mails.

36. From a Muslim, Mohammed Ali Bey, IOR: MSS EUR F 143/84, Extracts from Censored Mails, letter 106.

37. Ali Mohammad Khan, 20 May, IOR: MSS EUR F 143/83, Extracts from Censored Mails, letter 7.

38. See letter from a Pathan dated 3 March 1915, 'Fight well and bravely that the name of India may not be disgraced', IOR: MSS EUR F 143/83, Extracts from Censored Mails, letter 27. And another wrote: 'Our regiment has exhibited great bravery. The fame of the Garhwalis is now higher than the skies. One of the Garhwalis, a Havildar, has won the VC' dated 15 March 1915, IOR: MSS EUR F 143/83, Extracts from Censored Mails, letter 58.

39. The King's message to the Indian troops, quoted in P. Mason, p. 414.

40. From a Sikh, Jan Phuma, dated 1 December 1915, IOR: MSS EUR F 143/88, Extracts from Censored Mails (921/925), letter 30.

41. A Pathan wrote, 'Pray for me always. I do not know whether I shall be alive when this letter reaches you', letter dated 19 January 1915, IOR: L/MIL/5/825, pt I, ff. 1–185, Extracts from Censored Mails. A Garhwali wrote, 'In a few days you will hear that in our country only women will be left. All the men will be finished here',

IOR: L/MIL/5/825, pt I, ff. 1-185, Extracts from Censored Mails.

42. E.B. Howell's report dated 23 January 1915, IOR: L/MIL/5/825, pt I, ff. 1-185, Extracts from Censored Mails.

43. Letter addressed to the King from Milford on Sea, dated 25 May 1915, IOR: MSS EUR F 143/83, Extracts from Censored Mails, letter 28. The V.C. Mir Dast also made this request when presented to the King, see letter from Haider Khan, a Pathan, dated 20 July 1915, IOR: MSS EUR F 143/84, Extracts from Censored Mails, letter 1; and from Yusuf Khan dated 25 August 1915, IOR: MSS EUR F 143/85, Extracts from Censored Mails (644), letter 1.

44. From a Muslim, Abdul Karim, dated 14 October 1915, IOR: MSS EUR F 143/86, Extracts from Censored Mails (batch dated 16 October 1915), letter 60. The writer in despair mentioned that he had been waiting for a year for the war to end, but all he saw was that it was getting worse. A parcel containing the nut *bhailawa*, was found; experiments showed that the juice applied on the skin produced irritation, which could produce sores. See censor's comment, dated 6 November 1915, IOR: MSS EUR F 143/87, Extracts from Censored Mails.

45. See a British ASC Motor driver to his fiancée in England, dated 20 January 1915 and the censor's comment in IOR: L/MIL/5/825, pt I, ff. 1-185, Extracts from Censored Mails. See also letter from Yusuf Khan, dated 6 October 1915, IOR: MSS EUR F 143/86, Extracts from Censored Mails (batch dated 11 October 1915), letter 6.

46. From a Jat, Gunga Ram, May 1915, IOR: MSS EUR F 143/83, Extracts from Censored Mails, letter 41.

47. From a Punjabi Muslim, Khan Mohammad, 10 May, IOR: MSS EUR F 143/83, Extracts from Censored Mails, letter 30.

48. From Khan Muhammad, dated 17 May 1915, IOR: MSS EUR F 143/83, Extracts from Censored Mails, letter 4.

49. Comment by E.B. Howell, dated 29 May 1915, IOR: MSS EUR F 143/83, Extracts from Censored Mails.

50. From Mian Ahmad Sirdar Khan, 27 May 1915, IOR: MSS EUR F 143/83, Extracts from Censored Mails, letter 39. See also letter from a Punjabi Muslim, Fateh Ahmad, IOR: MSS EUR F 143/84, Extracts from Censored Mails, letter 4.

51. Indian General Hospital, Mont Dore, Bournemouth; Indian

Convalescent Home, Barton, New Milton; Pavilion and Dome Indian General Hospital, Brighton; York Place Indian General Hospital, Brighton; Kitchener Indian General Hospital, Brighton; Lady Hardinge Hospital, Brockenhurst; Royal Victoria Hospital, Netley.

52. Some Indian students obtained medical appointments as house surgeons and house physicians. Some distinguished themselves, e.g. Drs R.N. Cooper, G.C. Chatterjee, and Cawas Homi. See Indian Students Department Reports (printed by HMSO), IOR: V/24/832. See also IOR: MSS EUR F 143/100 for a photograph of some Indian doctors who were granted commissions in the Indian Medical Service in recognition of their services in the war.

53. Report by E.B. Howell, dated 3 February 1915, IOR: L/MIL/ 5/825, pt I, ff. 1-185, Extracts from Censored Mails.

54. Censor's report for 31 July 1915 and letter 19 from a Sikh in Canada; see also censor's report for 9 August 1915, in IOR: MSS EUR F 143/84; and his report dated 13 February 1916 in IOR: MSS EUR F 143/90, Extracts from Censored Mails.

55. Note by E.B. Howell, dated 23 January 1915, IOR: L/MIL/5/825, pt I, ff. 1-185, Extracts from Censored Mails.

56. See *A Short History in English, Gurmukhi and Urdu, of the Royal Pavilion Brighton and a Description of it as a Hospital for Indian Soldiers* (1915). IOR: MSS EUR F 143/94, pp. 5-8.

57. J.N. Macleod, CIE, IMS, Commanding Officer in charge of the Pavilion Hospital, to Sir Walter Lawrence, dated 3 December 1914, IOR: MSS EUR F 143/66.

58. See *The Times*, 16 October 1915 for a full-length report of the cremation ceremony at the burning ghat, near Patcham.

59. Janet Gooch, *A Short History of Brighton General Hospital* (London: Phillimore & Co., 1980), pp. 106-11.

60. *A Short History* (1915), IOR: MSS EUR F 143/94.

61. J.N. Macleod to Sir Walter Lawrence, 1 September, 1915, IOR: MSS EUR F 143/66.

62. See Rozina Visram, 'The First World War and the Indian Soldiers', paper presented to the Conference on the History of Black Peoples in London, University of London, Institute of Education, November 1984.

63. E.g. 'Britain Prepared'; 'The Battle of the Somme', see IOR: L/P&J/6/1424, No. 240.

64. *A Short History* (1915), IOR: MSS EUR F 143/94, pp. 4 and 7.

65. *A Short History* (1915), IOR: MSS EUR F 143/94, p. 5.
66. J.N. Macleod to Sir Walter Lawrence dated 30 March 1915, IOR: MSS EUR F 143/66.
67. *A Short History* (1915), IOR: MSS EUR F 143/94, p. 17.
68. Letter dated 5 July 1915, IOR: MSS EUR F 143/77.
69. A postcard bearing a Christian inscription was found enclosed in a letter of a sepoy being sent to a friend in India. See letter from E.B. Howell, to General Sir Edmund Barrow, Military Secretary, India Office, dated 15 January 1915, IOR: L/MIL/5/825, pt I, ff. 1-185, Extracts from Censored Mails.
70. E.B. Howell to Sir Edmund Barrow dated 3 February 1915, IOR: L/MIL/5/825, pt I, ff. 1-185, Extracts from Censored Mails.
71. Report by E.B. Howell, dated 11 October 1915, IOR: MSS EUR F 143/86, Extracts from Censored Mails.
72. *A Short History* (1915), IOR; MSS EUR F 143/94, pp. 13-18; *Daily Telegraph*, 23 August 1915; *Observer*, 23 August 1915; *Sussex Daily News*, 23 August 1915.
73. Letter from J.N. Macleod to Sir Walter Lawrence, dated 17 March 1915: 'The Indian Army I believe is all right but needs to be kept *warmed* up with the news like this last fight [Neuve Chapelle]. It is the cold and the damnable trench work that paralyses them ... Could not a bulletin be specially published for Indian hospitals at short intervals in which the doings of the Regiments by name could be given? ... Glowing accounts of the doings of their bhais [brothers] would hustle many of these young fellows back to have another go at the "dushman [enemies] of their Sahibs" ', IOR: MSS EUR F 143/66.
74. See IOR: MSS EUR F 143/75 for a selection of such letters from *Akbar i Jang*.
75. From a Muslim, Amerbhai, dated 30 April 1915, IOR: MSS EUR F 143/83, Extracts from Censored Mails, (batch dated 8 May 1915), letter 16.
76. From a Punjabi Muslim, Ghulam Muhiyudin, dated 5 May 1915, IOR: MSS EUR F 143/83, Extracts from Censored Mails, letter 43.
77. From a Sikh, Ranjit Singh, dated 10 November 1915, IOR: MSS EUR F 143/87, Extracts from Censored Mails (886/891), letter 27.
78. Report from E.B. Howell, dated 16 January 1915, IOR: L/MIL/5/825, pt I, ff. 185, Extracts from Censored Mails.

79. See comment in *Akbar i Jang*, letter 13, IOR: MSS EUR F 143/75; also letter dated 5 August 1915, from a Sikh in IOR: MSS EUR F 143/84, Extracts from Censored Mails, letter 36.

80. Report on the visit of convalescent Indian troops to London, October-November 1915, by Major P.G. Shewell, IOR: MSS EUR F 143/66.

81. Report on the visit of convalescent Indian troops to London, October-November 1915, by Major P.G. Shewell and extract of the letter from R.C. Volker, dated 14 October 1915, IOR: MSS EUR F 143/66.

82. See letter from Fitzgerald to Sir Walter Lawrence, dated 14 July 1915, IOR: MSS EUR F 143/66.

83. Specially relating to European women and men of subject races. See Chapter 1.

84. Letter from Sir Shapurji Broacha dated 2 July 1915 and letter from Fitzgerald to Sir Walter Lawrence, dated 14 July 1915, IOR: MSS EUR F 143/66.

85. Letter from Sir Alfred Keogh to Sir Walter Lawrence, dated 15 January 1915, IOR: MSS EUR F 143/66.

86. Note on a visit by ladies, letter dated 13 January 1915 from R.J. Dunlop Smith to Sir Walter Lawrence; letter dated 14 January 1915 from Holderness to Sir Lawrence; letter from Sir Walter Lawrence to Sir Alfred Keogh dated 14 January 1915; and letter dated 15 January 1915 from Sir Alfred Keogh to Sir Walter Lawrence, IOR: MSS EUR F 143/66.

87. Report by E.B. Howell, dated 19 June 1915, IOR: MSS EUR F 143/83, Extracts from Censored Mails.

88. See K. Ballhatchet, *Race, Sex and Class Under the Raj. Imperial Attitudes and Policies and their Critics, 1793-1905* (London: Weidenfeld & Nicolson, 1980).

89. Report from E.B. Howell, dated 26 June 1915, IOR: MSS EUR F 143/84, Extracts from Censored Mails.

90. Letter 18, dated 15 February 1916, and E.B. Howell's report dated 28 February 1916, IOR: MSS EUR F 143/90 (139), Extracts from Censored Mails.

91. From a Parsi, dated 16 January 1915, IOR: L/MIL/5/825, pt I, ff. 1-185, Extracts from Censored Mails.

92. Report by E.B. Howell, dated 30 January 1915, IOR: L/MIL/5/825, pt I, ff. 1-185, Extracts from Censored Mails.

93. From a Parsi, dated 23 January 1915, IOR: L/MIL/5/825, pt I,

ff. 1–185, Extracts from Censored Mails.
94. The report by E.B. Howell, dated 19 June 1915, IOR: MSS EUR F 143/83, Extracts from Censored Mails.
95. A Report on the Kitchener Indian Hospital, Brighton, by Colonel Sir Bruce Seton, IOR: MSS EUR F 143/82.
96. Quoted in Janet Gooch, p. 106.
97. A Report on the Kitchener Indian Hospital, Brighton, by Colonel Sir Bruce Seton, IOR: MSS EUR F 143/82.
98. *Ibid.*
99. From a Maratha Brahmin, J.H. Godbole, dated 11 November 1915, IOR: MSS EUR F 143/87, Extracts from Censored Mails (886/891), letter 47.
100. From J.H. Godbole, dated 14 December 1915, IOR: MSS EUR F 143/89, Extracts from Censored Mails (1/6), letter 24.
101. Quoted in C. Musgrave, *Life in Brighton from the Earliest Times to the Present* (London: Faber, 1970), p. 371.
102. From a Hindu, Mithan Lal, dated 2 December 1915. The writer further explained that in India they had been led to believe that the daily work of the storekeeper 'would not take up more than three hours' a day and after the work they would be free to 'wander where we pleased'. But he found 'on all sides there is barbed wire and a sentry stands at each door, who prevents us from going out', IOR: MSS EUR F 143/88, Extracts from Censored Mails (921/925), letter 44.
103. From a Sikh, Bhan Singham, dated 28 July 1915, IOR: MSS EUR F 143/84, Extracts from Censored Mails, letter 21.
104. From a Pathan, Gulam Shah, dated 5 August 1915, IOR: MSS EUR F 143/84, Extracts from Censored Mails, letter 1; from a Pathan, Nur Baz Khan, dated 28 October 1915, IOR: MSS EUR F 143/87, Extracts from Censored Mails (860/865), letter 3; from a Pathan, IOR: MSS EUR F 143/83, letter 1; and from a Muslim, Gulam Haider, letter 27.
105. From a Dogra, Sepoy Hoshanki, IOR: MSS EUR F 143/85, Extracts from Censored Mails (684), letter 57.
106. Letter dated 27 October 1915, IOR: MSS EUR F 143/83, Extracts from Censored Mails (860/865), letter 60.
107. A report on Kitchener Indian Hospital, Brighton by Colonel Sir Bruce Seton, IOR: MSS EUR F 143/82.
108. Janet Gooch, p. 109; letter from JUSTITIA, of Leamington, IOR: MSS EUR F 143/96.

109. Report by E.B. Howell, dated 31 July 1915, IOR: MSS EUR F 143/84; and report dated 11 September 1915, IOR: MSS EUR F 143/85, Extracts from Censored Mails.

110. *A Short History* (1915), IOR: MSS EUR F 143/94, p. 16. See also extract from the report of the Secretary of State, Austen Chamberlain, to Sir Walter Lawrence, 11 July 1915, IOR: MSS EUR F 143/66.

111. See letter from a Pathan, Subadar Mahammad Azim, dated 4 June 1915, IOR: MSS EUR F 143/83, Extracts from Censored Mails, letter 16.

112. From a Punjabi Muslim, Havildar Abdul Rahman, May 1915, IOR: MSS EUR F 143/83, Extracts from Censored Mails, letter 17.

113. From Bishan Singh, dated 14 May 1915, IOR: MSS EUR F 143/83, Extracts from Censored Mails, letter 31.

114. Report by E.B. Howell, dated 29 May 1915, IOR: MSS EUR F 143/83, Extracts from Censored Mails.

115. From a Pathan, dated 27 June 1915, IOR: MSS EUR F 143/84, Extracts from Censored Mails, letter 4.

116. From a Punjabi Muslim, dated 23 June 1915, IOR: MSS EUR F 143/84, Extracts from Censored Mails, letter 26.

117. Letter from a 'Muhammadan Native Officer', IOR: L/MIL/5/825, pt I, ff. 1-185, Extracts from Censored Mails.

118. From Muhammad Khan, dated 14 February 1916, IOR: MSS EUR F 143/90, Extracts from Censored Mails (135), letter 12.

119. From a Hindu of Western Punjab, dated 28 August 1915, IOR: MSS EUR F 143/84, Extracts from Censored Mails (286/A/8), letter 28.

120. Dewitt C. Ellinwood, 'The Indian Soldier, The Indian Army, and Change 1914-1918' in Ellinwood and Pradhan, p. 202; also S.D. Pradhan, 'The Sikh Soldier in the First World War', in Ellinwood and Pradhan, p. 223.

121. Hindustani Muslim, Abdul Hakim, dated 5 January 1916, IOR: MSS EUR F 143/89, Extracts from Censored Mails (20/2/5), letter 30.

122. From Ram Jewan Singh, Kitchener Hospital, dated 30 September 1915, IOR: MSS EUR F 143/86, Extracts from Censored Mails (batch dated 2 October 1915), letter 66.

123. From Ram Jivan Singh, Barton on Sea, dated 1 November 1915, IOR: MSS EUR F 143/87, Extracts from Censored Mails

(860/865), letter 59.
124. From a Pathan dated 10 September 1916, IOR: MSS EUR F 143/92, Further Extracts (265), letter 1.
125. Letter dated 16 March 1916, IOR: MSS EUR F 143/92, Further Extracts (151), letter 32.
126. From a Sikh dated 18 January 1915, IOR: L/MIL/5/825, pt I, ff. 1–185, Extracts from Censored Mails; and a Hindu sub-assistant surgeon, IOR: L/MIL/5/825, pt 1, ff 1–185, Extracts from Censored Mails.
127. From a Sikh dated 18 January 1915, IOR: L/MIL/5/825, pt I, ff. 1–185, Extracts from Censored Mails.
128. From a Pathan dated 10 September 1916, IOR: MSS EUR F 143/92, Further Extracts (265), letter 1.
129. From a Hindu sub-assistant surgeon, IOR: L/MIL/5/825, pt I, ff. 1–185, Extracts from Censored Mails.
130. Report by E.B. Howell, dated 11 December 1915, IOR: MSS EUR F 143/88, Extracts from Censored Mails.
131. From a Hindu sub-assistant surgeon, IOR: L/MIL/5/825, pt I, ff. 1–185, Extracts from Censored Mails.
132. From a Maratha Brahmin, J.H. Godbole, 16 November 1915, IOR: MSS EUR F 143/87, Extracts from Censored Mails (886/891), letter 47.
133. From a Pathan dated 10 September 1916, IOR: MSS EUR F 143/92, Further Extracts (265), letter 1.
134. S.D. Pradhan, 'The Sikh Soldier in the First World War' (interview with war veterans), in Ellinwood and Pradhan, p. 222.
135. From a Sikh, Sub Hukam Singh, 1915, IOR: MSS EUR F 143/87, Extracts from Censored Mails, (886/891), letter 24; and a Dogra, Sant Ram, dated 6 September 1915, IOR: MSS EUR F 143/85, Extracts from Censored Mails (684), letter 59.
136. From Ram Jewan Singh, dated 26 September 1915, IOR: MSS EUR F 143/86, Extracts from Censored Mails (batch dated 2 October 1915), letter 67.
137. From a Punjabi Muslim, dated 19 January 1916, IOR: MSS EUR F 143/89, Extracts from Censored Mails (65/70), letter 4.
138. S.D. Pradhan, 'The Sikh Soldier in the First World War' (interview with Sikh war veterans), in Ellinwood and Pradhan, p. 224.
139. From a Rajput, dated 26 August 1916, IOR: MSS EUR F 143/92, Further Extracts (269), letter 19.

140. For India's role in the Second World War see: *The Official History of the Indian Armed Forces in the Second World War, 1939-45,* ed. B. Prasad (Combined Inter-Services Historical Section, India and Pakistan 1956), Vols I-IV; J.G. Elliott, *A Roll of Honour: The Story of the Indian Army 1939-1945* (Cassell, 1965).

141. For the Indian Armies in Italy, see J.G. Elliott, Chapters 14 and 15; *The Tiger Triumphs: the Story of the Three Great Divisions in Italy* (HMSO, 1946); *A Gurkha Brigade in Italy: the Story of the 43 Gurkha Lorried Brigade* (India: War Department Directorate of Public Relations; Bombay: Times of India Press, c. 1946); F. Majdalany, *Cassino: Portrait of a Battle* (Longman, 1957).

142. This section on Noor Inayat Khan is based on Jean Overton Fuller, *Madeleine, The Story of Noor Inayat Khan* (London: Victor Gollancz, 1952); see also by the same author, *Born for Sacrifice: The True Story of Madeleine, Heroic British Secret Agent in Paris* (Pan Books, 1957). See also M.R.D. Foot, *SOE. An Outline History of the Special Operations Executive 1940-46* (BBC Publications, 1984), pp. 138-40, and 178 for photograph.

143. Jean Overton Fuller (1952), p. 27.

144. *Jataka Tales* comprise a cycle of about 500 legends symbolizing the various incarnations of Buddha.

145. Jean Overon Fuller (1952), p. 60.

146. *Ibid.,* p. 60.

147. *Ibid.,* p. 68.

148. *Ibid.,* p. 118.

149. *Ibid.,* Appendix I, p. 188.

150. *Ibid.,* Appendix I, p. 188.

151. *Ibid.,* Appendix I, pp. 188-9.

7. Radical Voices

1. *Indian Agitators Abroad,* compiled in the Criminal Intelligence Office, Simla, 1911, IOR: V/27/262/1. According to this report, Saklatvala was carrying on business in 1910 at 19 Brazenose Street, Manchester.

2. See Cecil Kaye, *Communism in India, with Unpublished Documents from National Archives of India (1919-1924),* compiled and edited by Subodh Roy (Calcutta: Editions Indian, 1971), p. 364. See also David Petrie, *Communism in India 1924-1927,* ed. with

introduction and notes by M. Saha (Calcutta: Editions Indian, 1972), p. 377.

3. *Indian Agitators Abroad*, compiled in the Criminal Intelligence Office, Simla, 1911, IOR: V/27/262/1.
4. For biographical details see *Dictionary of National Biography 1931–1940*, ed. L.G. Wickham Legg (Oxford University Press, 1949); *The Herald Book of Labour Members*, ed. S.U. Bracher (1922); *Dictionary of Labour Biography*, VI, ed. Joyce M. Bellamy and J. Saville (1982); *Daily Herald*, 19 April 1923; *The Times*, 17 January 1936; and Panchanan Saha, *Shapurji Saklatvala, a Brief Biography* (New Delhi: People's Publishing House, 1970).
5. D. Petrie, p. 377; Documents, pp. 34–7, 51. C. Kaye, p. 364; Documents, pp. 54, 85, 237.
6. *The Times*, 17 January 1936.
7. *Clapham Observer, Tooting and Balham Times*, 23 May 1924.
8. For Battersea politics, see Richard Price, *An Imperial War and the British Working Class* (London: Routledge & Kegan Paul, 1972); Barry Kosmin, 'Political Identity in Battersea', in *Living in South London, Perspectives on Battersea 1871–1981*, Sandra Wallman and Associates (published for the LSE by Gower Press, 1982); 'A Pilgrimage to Battersea', Malcolm M. Thomson, in the *British Weekly*, 11 December 1924.
9. Ian Duffield, 'The Dilemma of Pan-Africanism for Blacks in Britain, 1760–1950', paper presented to the International Conference on the History of Blacks in Britain, Institute of Education, 1981; see also Peter Fryer *Staying Power* (London: Pluto Press, 1984), p. 352; Barry Kosmin, 'London's Asian MPs: The Contrasting Careers of three Parsee Politicians', paper presented to the Conference on the History of Black Peoples in London, Institute of Education, 1984.
10. William S. Sanders's political career began in Battersea in 1888, at the age of 17, under John Burns. He had been one of the first secretaries of the Battersea League. He was recruiting officer during the war, and after the First World War worked at the ILO in Geneva.
11. *1922 Election* Turnout

		56.6 per cent
Saklatvala (Lab.)	11,311	50.5 per cent
H.C. Hogbin (Lib.)	9,290	41.6 per cent
V.C. Albu (Ind. Lib.)	1,756	7.9 per cent

1923 Election Turnout		62.4 per cent
H.C. Hogbin (Lib.)	12,527	50.4 per cent
Saklatvala (Lab.)	12,341	49.6 per cent

12.
1924 Election Turnout		73.1 per cent
Saklatvala (Com.)	15,096	50.9 per cent
H.C. Hogbin (Const.)	14,554	49.1 per cent

13. *Daily Graphic*, 7 December 1923.
14. *Daily Herald*, 19 April 1923.
15. *Daily Graphic*, 30 October 1924.
16. *British Weekly*, 11 December 1924.
17. *Daily Graphic*, 30 October 1924.
18. *British Weekly*, 11 December 1924.
19. 'The Battle of Battersea', by Saklatvala in the *Communist*, 25 November 1922.
20. *British Weekly*, 11 December 1924.
21. *Daily Express*, 7 July 1927.
22. *Daily Herald*, 11 May 1929. See also *Daily Worker*, 13 October 1931; *The Times*, 3 June 1929; and the *Daily Worker*, 23 and 24 October 1931.
23.
1929 Election Turnout		69.7 per cent
W. Sanders (Lab.)	13,265	37.8 per cent
A. Marsden (Con.)	10,833	30.8 per cent
Saklatvala (Com.)	6,554	18.6 per cent
T.P. Brogan (Lib.)	4,513	12.8 per cent

1930 Election (Glasgow, Shettleston) Turnout		59.2 per cent
J. McGovern (Lab.)	10,669	42.9 per cent
W. Templeton (Con.)	10,303	41.2 per cent
J.M. McNicol (SNP.)	2,527	10.1 per cent
Saklatvala (Com.)	1,459	5.8 per cent

1931 Election (Battersea North): Turnout		67.6 per cent
A. Marsden (Con.)	18,688	55.4 per cent
W. Sanders (Lab.)	11,985	35.6 per cent
Saklatvala (Com.)	3,021	9.0 per cent

24. See Foreword by R. Palme Dutt, in P. Saha, p. viii.
25. *Daily Herald*, 3 December 1923.
26. *Daily Express*, 12 August 1925; *Daily Chronicle* 28 November 1923.
27. *Evening Standard*, 26 November 1923; *Daily Telegraph*, 1

151 to 155*273*

December 1923.
28. *Daily Chronicle*, 28 November 1923.
29. *Daily Telegraph*, 28 November 1923.
30. *Daily Chronicle*, 28 November 1923.
31. *Daily Telegraph*, 28 November 1923.
32. *Evening News*, 1 December 1923; *Evening Mail*, 1 December 1923. Saklatvala had indeed issued his supporters with a warning in the form of a leaflet, advocating 'a fair hearing' to all. See *Daily Chronicle*, 1 December 1923; and the leaflet itself in the Local History Collection, Battersea Reference Library.
33. *Morning Post*, 15 September 1925.
34. See Saklatvala's letter of resignation in the *Evening News*, 17 September 1925.
35. *Sunday Worker*, 20 September 1925. The family's life style was very frugal. I am grateful to Miss Sehri Saklatvala for giving me this information.
36. *Daily Express*, 12 August 1925. The MPs who withdrew were Robert Bird, MP for West Wolverhampton; Peter MacDonell, MP for Isle of Wight; H.C. Woodcock, MP for Everton.
37. *Evening News*, 17 September 1925.
38. *Daily Graphic*, 18 September 1925; *Daily Herald*, 18 September 1925.
39. *Evening News*, 17 September 1925.
40. *Birmingham Mail*, 18 September 1925.
41. *Daily Herald*, 18 September 1925.
42. *Daily Telegraph*, 19 September 1925.
43. *Sunday Worker*, 20 September 1925.
44. *Daily Worker*, 21 February 1926.
45. *Manchester Guardian Weekly*, 22 November 1929.
46. *Star*, 1 July 1927.
47. During the Mosleyite movement of the thirties, the family of Saklatvala suffered attacks because of his Communist sympathies. I am grateful to Miss Sehri Saklatvala for this information.
48. *Westminster Gazette*, 4 May 1926; *The Times*, 5 May 1926.
49. See *Sunday Worker*, 27 November 1927. The reporter wrote: 'If one wants to know the cruelty of British rule in India it is only necessary to sit in the House and listen to the daily list of complaints put forward by members regarding what is happening in that country. The very first question asked in the House on Monday was by Harry Day on the cultivation of opium poppy in

India. [This was the most lucrative British trade with China.] He
was calmly informed, by Earl Winterton, that no fewer than 71,057
acres were utilized for that purpose in 1926! Dozens of questions
are asked each week about the treatment meted out to political
prisoners in Indian prisons. For example, Mr Montague raised the
question of the people who committed suicide in prison. He was
followed by George Hall who protested against the practice of
chaining prisoners, and he quoted the 1926 report of the Bombay
Jail Department which shows that flogging of prisoners has
increased!'

50. Quoted in *Condition of India*, M. Whately, V.K. Krishna Menon
and others (India League Publications, 1934), p. 245.
51. *Parliamentary Debates*, Vol. 186, 9 July 1925, pp. 705–19.
52. *Parliamentary Debates*, Vol. 191 (1926), p. 84.
53. *Parliamentary Debates*, Vol. 159 (1922).
54. *Daily Telegraph*, 31 August 1925. For the comment by Philip
Sassoon, see P. Saha, p. 59.
55. E.g. 'The Indian Round Table Conference', Saklatvala, the *Labour
Monthly*, December 1930.
56. Quoted in P. Saha, p. 19.
57. *Bombay Chronicle*, 21 February 1927; also 15 January, 16 January,
19 January 1927.
58. *Bombay Chronicle*, 24 January 1927.
59. *Bombay Chronicle*, 29 January 1927.
60. *Bombay Chronicle*, 1 March 1927.
61. *Bombay Chronicle*, 10 February 1927. See also his open letter to
Gandhi.
62. *Bombay Chronicle*, 17 January 1927; 5 February 1927.
63. *Bombay Chronicle*, 24 January 1927.
64. *Daily Sketch*, 6 August 1927.
65. See *Indian National Herald*, 15 January 1929, under the title,
' "Johukum" meeting taken by surprise', by Arthur Field. Press
cuttings from the British and Indian newspapers are available in
bound volumes for easy reference at the Battersea Reference
Library, Local History Collection.
66. *Daily Worker*, 18 January 1936.
67. Pen portrait by Herbert Bryan in *Bombay Chronicle*, 23 January
1927.
68. Quoted in P. Saha, p. 101; see also Appendix 5 in Saha's book for
all the tributes to Saklatvala.

69. *The Times,* 17 January 1936.
70. *Daily Herald,* 19 April 1923.
71. For an outline of Menon's biography, see the *Observer,* 30 November 1974; *Daily Telegraph,* 7 October 1974; *The Times,* 7 October 1974; *Dictionary of National Biography,* ed. S.P. Sen (Calcutta: Institute of Historical Studies, 1972), Vol. III, pp. 98-101; T.J.S. George, *Krishna Menon, A Biography* (London: Jonathan Cape, 1974); and E. Lengyel, *Krishna Menon* (New York: Walker & Company, 1962).
72. One leading MP informed George: 'There is no use our trying to pretend that we are above all that.' See T.J.S. George, p. 150.
73. From A.H. Joyce, Information Department, to Sir F.H. Puckle, British Embassy, Washington, dated 21 October 1946, in IOR: L/I/1/1457.
74. Between 1934 and 1936, 19 volumes were brought out. In the first two years the titles in the Twentieth Century Library series included: J.A. Hobson, *Democracy;* N. Bentwich, *The Jews;* N. Mitchison, *The Home;* J.H. Driberg, *The Black Races;* Ralph Fox, *Communism;* W. Holtby, *Women.* See also the Twentieth Century Library, edited by V.K. Krishna Menon (1934-6).
75. See Selwyn and Blount's Topical Books, V.K. Krishna Menon (1934).
76. For a background on Penguin and Pelican Books see *Penguins: A Retrospect 1935-51* (Penguin Books, 1951); *The Penguin Story 1935* (Penguin Books, 1956).
77. *The Times,* 7 October 1974. Among the Pelicans brought out by Menon were: G.D.H. Cole, *Practical Economics;* E. Halevy, *A History of English People in 1815;* J.B.S. Haldane, *The Inequality of Man;* Roger Fry, *Vision and Design;* H.G. Wells, *A Short History of the World* (first issued as a Penguin).
78. Quoted in T.J.S. George, p. 55.
79. Quoted in E. Lengyel, p. 82.
80. T.J.S. George, p. 63.
81. Menon wrote articles for the London *New Statesman and Nation* and New York *Nation;* the British dailies received many letters from him.
82. Some of the pamphlets written by Menon and issued by the India League include: 'Why Must India Fight?' (1940); 'Britain's Prisoner' (1941), 'A National Government of India' (1942). See also *Unity of India, Collected Writings,* edited by Menon (1941).

83. Quoted in T.J.S. George, pp. 65–6.
84. See *Condition of India*, M. Whately, V.K. Krishna Menon *et al.* (India League Publications, 1934).
85. *Ibid.*, p. 245.
86. *Ibid.*, pp. 182–3.
87. *Observer*, 6 September 1959.
88. See IOR: L/I/1/1457; and letter dated 18 July 1947 from the Earl of Listowel to Rear-Admiral Viscount Mountbatten of Burma. Mountbatten Papers, in *The Transfer of Power* (HMSO, 1983), Vol. XII, p. 251. It was in Tory Party circles that he was so regarded.
89. *Observer*, profile, 30 November 1947.
90. *Camden Journal*, 10 May 1974.
91. *North London Press*, 28 January 1955; *Camden Journal*, 10 May 1974; Minutes of the Proceedings of a Special Meeting of the Council of the Metropolitan Borough of St Pancras held on 28 January 1955, for the purpose of conferring the Honorary Freedom of the Borough upon V.K. Krishna Menon. See also the Council Minutes 1934–47.
92. *Camden Journal*, 10 May 1974; Minutes of the Proceedings of the Special Meeting, 28 January 1955.
93. See George, p. 128.
94. *The Times*, 7 October 1974.
95. Quoted in George, p. 137.
96. Viceroy's Personal Report No. 12, dated 11 July 1947, L/PO/6/123, ff. 168–77; and letter from Rear-Admiral Viscount Mountbatten of Burma to Krishna Menon dated 10 July 1943, Mountbatten Papers, in *Transfer of Power*, Vol. XII, pp. 96 and 70.
97. Letter from Professor D.V. Glass and Mrs Ruth Glass in *The Times*, 18 October 1974.
98. Minutes of the Proceedings of a Special Meeting, 28 January 1955.
99. *Camden Journal*, 6 December 1974, No. 5667; see also *Camden and St Pancras Chronicle*, 18 March 1977.

8. Princes, Students and Travellers

1. All visitors to Britain, students or princes, must have written letters to their families. However, only a few select records in English are available to us. For the diaries kept by the princes see:

*Diary of the late Rajah of Kolhapoor during his visit to Europe in
1870*, ed. E.W. West (London: Smith Elder & Company, 1872);
Journal of a Visit to England in 1883, Bhagvat Sinh Jee Thakore
Saheb of Gondal (Bombay: Education Society's Press, 1886). For
students' writings, see: J. Nowrojee and H. Merwanjee, *Journal of
a Residence of two years and a half in Great Britain* (London:
William H. Allen, 1841); Rakhal Das Haldar, *The English Diary of
an Indian Student 1861–62* (Dacca: The Asutosh Library, 1903);
M.K. Gandhi, *An Autobiography, or the Story of my Experiments
with Truth* (Penguin Books, 1982); S. Satthianadhan, *Four Years in
an English University, together with a complete guide to Indian
Students proceeding to Great Britain* (Madras: Srinivasa, Varada-
chari & Co., 1893); D.F. Karaka, *I Go West* (Michael Joseph,
1938): Cornelia Sorabji, *India Calling. The Memoirs of Cornelia
Sorabji* (London: Nisbet & Co., 1934). For visitors see: B.M.
Malabari, *The Indian Eye on English Life or Rambles of a Pilgrim
Reformer* (Bombay: Apollo Printing Works, 1895); T. Rama-
krishna, *My Visit to the West* (London: T. Fisher & Unwin, 1915);
see Kripalani, *Rabindranath Tagore, a Biography* (Calcutta: Visva-
Bharati, 1980), for his various visits; also R. Tagore, *Letters to a
Friend*, edited with two introductory essays by C.F. Andrews
(George Allen & Unwin, 1928).

2. Rammohun Roy was a linguist with a knowledge of Arabic,
Persian, Sanskrit, Bengali and English; he also mastered Hebrew,
Latin and Greek. As a social reformer, he had campaigned for the
abolition of sati and widow remarriage. He was the founder of the
Brahmo Samaj. He also campaigned for press freedom, having
established two newspapers himself; as an educationist he published
the first Indian grammar and dictionary of the Bengali language.
He also championed the cause of Irish peasants against absentee
landlords, and of Latin America against Spanish imperialism.
When he heard that a constitutional government had been set up in
Spain in 1823, he celebrated this event by a public dinner in
Calcutta town hall and declared, 'Ought I to be insensible to the
sufferings of my fellow creatures wherever they are, or however
unconnected by interests, religion or language?'

3. Sophia Dobson Collet, *Life and Letters of Rajah Rammohun Roy*,
ed. Biswas and Ganguli (Calcutta, 1962), pp. 310–11.

4. Quoted in *Raja Rammohun Roy, A 150th Death Anniversary
Tribute*, ed. Subhas Chopra and Premen Addy (issued by the

Indian High Commission, London), p. 19.

5. Quoted in Collet, p. 312. Rammohun Roy took a great interest in the passge of the Reform Bill in 1832. See his letter to William Rathbone in Mary Carpenter, *The Last Days in England of the Rajah Rammohun Roy* (Calcutta, 1915), pp. 87–8.

6. Quoted in Collet, p. 326.

7. See Appendix IX in Collet, pp. 501–4.

8. See Mary Carpenter, pp. 168–71.

9. See Collet, pp. 365–6. In 1872 an inscription was added. See also *Rammohun Roy, Commemoration of the 150th Anniversary of his Death in Bristol on 27 September 1833* (issued in Bristol). His portrait painted by H.P. Briggs, 1832, is in the City of Bristol Museum and Art Gallery.

10. *Journal of the National Indian Association*, November 1871, No. 11, p. 244.

11. Princes were invited for both the Golden and Diamond Jubilee of Queen Victoria; and for the coronations of Edward VII and George V.

12. The first princely heir to be educated wholly in Britain was Rajendra of Cooch Behar. He started at a prep school in Farnborough, then went to Eton and Oxford. However, official policy preferred 'young native chiefs' to be educated in India, see Memo 2 July 1916, IOR: L/PS/11/75.

13. See *Diary of the Late Rajah of Kolhapoor*, p. 144.

14. For a coverage of Indian princes' visits to Britain, see Kusoom Vadgama, *India in Britain* (London: Robert Royce, 1984).

15. Instructions dated 12 October 1872 to O.J. Burne, the first Political ADC, IOR: L/PS/3/352.

16. John Lord, *The Maharajahs* (London: Hutchinson, 1972), p. 61.

17. Alan Ross, *Ranji Prince of Cricketers* (Collins, 1983), see illustration opposite p. 64.

18. David R. Allen, *A Song for Cricket* (Pelham Books, 1981), pp. 50–54.

19. Ranji is the author of *The Jubilee Book of Cricket* (Blackwood, 1897) and *With Stoddart's Team in Australia* (James Bowden, 1898).

20. Quoted in Ross, p. 77. For more information on Ranji, see the biography by Ross; see also *Ranji, a Centenary Album*, ed. Vasant Raiji (Bombay: Seven Star Publications, 1972).

21. Quoted in J. Lord, pp. 160–61.
22. Lord Curzon to Lord George Hamilton, Secretary of State for India, 18 July 1900, IOR: MSS EUR F 111/159.
23. Curzon to Hamilton, 27 August 1902, IOR: MSS EUR F 111/161.
24. Curzon to Hamilton, 29 August 1900, IOR: MSS EUR F 111/159; Curzon to Hamilton, 18 July 1900, IOR: MSS EUR F 111/159; and Summary of Proceedings of the Government of India in the Foreign Department during the Viceroyalty of Lord Curzon, January 1899–1905, Native States, IOR: MSS EUR F 111/541.
25. See Summary of the Proceedings of the Government of India in the Foreign Department during the Viceroyalty of Lord Curzon, January 1899–1905, Native States, IOR: MSS EUR F 111/541. See also circular letter from W.J. Cuningham to Local Governments, 24 August 1900 in IOR: Select documents on the History of India and Pakistan, Vol. IV, edited by C.H. Philips. Document 10, pp. 424–5.
26. Curzon's minute on the Native States, dated 29 February 1904, IOR: L/P&S/7/163, No. 694.
27. From Lord George Hamilton to Curzon, 1 October 1900, MSS EUR F 111/159.
28. Curzon to Hamilton, 15 November 1901, MSS EUR F 111/160.
29. IOR: L/P&J/2/24, No. 3/174.
30. E.g. IOR: L/P&J/6/165, No. 2167, dated 1885 about a Brahmin woman student at Oxford; IOR: L/P&J/2/38, memo on two Parsi students, the Sorabji sisters, Pheroze and Mary, dated 1879; IOR: L/P&J/6/355, No. 1697, dated 1893 about a Muslim student at Oxford, who had first come for public school education; IOR: L/P&J/6/315, dated 1892 about a government scholar; and High Commissioner for India, Indian Students' Department Reports (printed by HMSO), IOR: V/24/832 (these reports cover the period 1916–40). See also IOR: L/P&J/6 and L/P&J/11 files for identity certificates issued to students going to Europe. For student diaries see Note 1.
31. One student at Cambridge reckoned that in the early 1890s there were about 207 students in England, with 30 at Cambridge and only 9 at Oxford. See Satthianadhan, p. 21.
32. For instance, in the 1921–2 session London University had 450 students, while another 647 were at the various Inns of Court;

Edinburgh had 140.

33. For statistics of students in British universities see: Anonymous: 'Indian Students in England', *Journal of the National Indian Association*, January 1885, No. 169, pp. 1–9; Indian Students' Department Reports, IOR: V/24/832.

34. Demi-official from C.J. Lyall, India Office to H.H. Risley, Secretary to the Government of India, Home Department, dated 7 August 1903, IOR: MSS EUR F 111/281.

35. C.J. Lyall to H.H. Risley, 7 August 1903, IOR: MSS EUR F 111/281.

36. D.W. Douthwaite, Steward of Gray's Inn, to Sir Curzon Wyllie, Political ADC, dated 15 December 1902, IOR: MSS EUR F 111/281.

37. Sir Owen Burne (ex-Political ADC) to Sir Curzon Wyllie, 18 May 1903, IOR: MSS EUR F 111/281.

38. D.W. Douthwaite, Steward of Gray's Inn to Sir Curzon Wyllie, dated 15 December 1902; note by W.R. Hamilton, India Office, in IOR: MSS EUR F 111/281.

39. The opinion consulted included both English and Indian residents in England. The Indian opinion was represented by M.M. Bhownaggree, the Tory MP for Bethnal Green 1895–1905; and Romesh C. Dutt, retired ICS, and President of Indian National Congress for the 1899 session.

40. See Minute by Curzon, 6 September 1903, IOR: MSS EUR F 111/281.

41. Indian Students' Department Reports; IOR: V/24/832.

42. See the First Annual Report of the National Indian Association, held at the Athenaeum, Bristol, 24 November 1871; see also Haldar, p. xvi.

43. First Annual Report of the NIA; Indian Students' Department Records, IOR: V/24/832.

44. The *Handbook* dealt mainly with courses and examinations at the various universities in Britain and the finances needed by students for the courses offered; Cornelia Sorabji wrote very warmly of the help given to her by 'Miss Manning' of the NIA on her first arrival in England. See her letters to her family for the year 1889, IOR: Cornelia Sorabji Collection, MSS EUR F 165.

45. Report of the Political ADC, Gerald Fitzgerald, 5 April 1884, IOR: L/P&J/3/250.

46. Indian Students' Department Reports, IOR: V/24/832.

47. *Edinburgh Indian Association 1883*-1983, Centenary Brochure, p. 13.
48. Indian Students' Department Reports, IOR: V/24/832.
49. *Ibid.*
50. Gandhi, p. 56. Gandhi made several visits to England: first as a law student in 1887 to 1890 (age 18); he was also in England during 1914; and later for the Round Table Conference in 1931, when he was enthusiastically received in the East End of London and by the mill workers of Lancashire.
51. J. Nowrojee and H. Merwanjee, pp. 34 and 91; Gandhi, p. 84.
52. D.F. Karaka, p. 34.
53. Cornelia Sorabji in *India Calling*, p. 52.
54. See Nowrojee and Merwanjee (in Britain during 1838-41), pp. 35 and 451-2; Haldar (in Britain during 1861-2), pp. xvi and 85; Satthianadhan (in Britain during 1890s), p. 49; Karaka (in Britain in the 1930s), p. 34.
55. Satthianadhan, p. 47.
56. K.R. Shirsat, *Kaka Joseph Baptista: Father of Home Rule Movement in India* (Bombay: Popular Prakashan, 1974), p. 10 (Baptista was at Cambridge in 1894-9); Karaka, pp. 49 and 182.
57. J. Nowrojee and J. Merwanjee, p. 110.
58. Indian Students' Department Reports, IOR: V/24/832; Karaka, pp. 36 and 175-6.
59. Karaka, pp. 42 and 170-71.
60. Indian Students' Department Reports, IOR: V/24/832.
61. Quoted in Karaka, p. 192.
62. Quoted in Kripalani, p. 291.
63. Nowrojee and Merwanjee, pp. 24, 29, 30 and 98; B.M. Malabari (in Britain 1890), pp. 28-9, 46, 229; Thakore Saheb of Gondal (in Britain 1883), pp. 28-30; Haldar, p. 166.
64. Rajah of Kolhapoor, p. 57; Thakore Saheb of Gondal, p. 30.
65. B.M. Malabari, pp. 76, 155, 217; see also Thakore Saheb of Gondal, p. 171.
66. Thakore Saheb of Gondal, p. 99.
67. Malabari, pp. 85-7.
68. Malabari, pp. 123-4, 126.
69. Malabari, p. 13.
70. Satthianadhan, pp. 95-6.
71. Malabari, p. 220.
72. Thakore Saheb of Gondal, pp. 176-7; Malabari, pp. 65-7.

73. Malabari, p. 67.
74. Tagore: *Letters to a Friend*, pp. 87, 90; see also Malabari, p. 220.
75. Cornelia Sorabji in *India Calling*, p. 7.
76. *Purdah nasheen* = 'sitting behind the curtain'.
77. See Lady Hobhouse's letter to *The Times*, 12 June 1889 and the list of subscribers, IOR: Cornelia Sorabji Collection, MSS EUR F 165.
78. Cornelia Sorabji in *India Calling*, p. 38.
79. Letter to her family dated 4 February 1892, IOR: Cornelia Sorabji Collection, MSS EUR F 165.
80. Cornelia Sorabji in *India Calling*, p. 28; see also letter to her family dated 8 May 1892, IOR: Cornelia Sorabji Collection, MSS EUR F 165.
81. Letter to her family dated 16 June 1892, IOR: Cornelia Sorabji Collection, MSS EUR F 165. See also letter dated 26 May 1892.
82. Cornelia Sorabji in *India Calling*, p. 35.

9. Into the Twentieth Century: Indian Influences in Britain

1. See N.V. Rajkumar, *Indians outside India* (published by the Foreign Department of the India National Congress, All-India Congress Committee, New Delhi, 1951), Statement I.
2. D.R. Prem, *The Parliamentary Leper. A History of Colour Prejudice in Britain* (Aligarh: Metric Publications, 1965), p. 6.
3. D. Wood, 'The Immigrant in the Towns', in *Coloured Immigration in Britain*, by J.A.G. Griffiths *et al.* (published for the Institute of Race Relations, London: Oxford University Press, 1960), p. 38.
4. James Mowat, *Seafarers' Conditions in India and Pakistan* (Mowat Report), (International Labour Organization, Geneva, 1949), p. 19; see also C. Dixon,'Lascars, the Forgotten Seamen', in *Working Men Who Got Wet*, Proceedings of the Fourth Conference of the Atlantic Canal Shipping Project, July 1980, Maritime History Group, University of Newfoundland, (ed. R. Ommer and G. Panting).
5. C. Kondapi, *Indians Overseas 1838-1949* (New Delhi: Indian Council of World Affairs, London: Oxford University Press, 1951), p. 360. Some doctors of Indian origin from countries like the West Indies were also to be found practising in Britain.
6. I am grateful to Dr Hingorani, an eye specialist in Harley Street, for this information. See also Elsie Goldsmith-Gooding, *A Man of*

Vision, Dr R. Hingorani (printed by D. Kirston, Essex); and D.R. Prem, p. 7.

7. D. Hiro, *Black British White British* (Pelican, 1975), p. 104.
8. I am grateful to Victor Kiernan for this information.
9. John De Witt, *Indian Workers' Associations in Britain* (published for the Institute of Race Relations, London: Oxford University Press, 1969), p. 45.
10. See Yule and Burnell's *Glossary of Anglo-Indian Colloquial Words and Phrases* (1886). The alternative title for this work is *Hobson-Jobson*. See also *Common Indian Words in English*, compiled and edited by R.E. Hawkins (OUP, India).
11. Council Meeting Minutes, 29 April 1948. See also *Daily Telegraph*, 23 October and 31 October 1975.
12. D.R. Prem, p. 8.
13. Dictionary of National Biograply, ed. S.P. Sen (Calcutta: Institute of Historical Studies, 1972), Vol. IV, pp. 245-6.
14. *The Times*, 7 September 1918.
15. E. Cotton, 'Sake Deen Mahomed of Brighton', *Sussex County Magazine*, Vol. 13, 1939.
16. John Widdowson, 'Black People in Canning Town: 1900-1945', paper presented to the Conference of the History of Black Peoples in London (University of London, Institute of Education, 1984); see also *People who Moved to Newham* (published by INSEC, the Credon Centre, London Borough of Newham), p. 6.

Suggestions for Further Reading

A formal bibliography is not included in this book. Readers who wish to obtain more information about a particular theme, topic or individual will find the relevant information in the notes.

The following short list is for general guidance.

Peter Fryer, *Staying Power. The History of Black People in Britain* (London: Pluto Press, 1984). This is a scholarly work covering the history of black people in Britain from the Roman times to the present. However, its main focus is on people from Africa and the Caribbean.

Kusoom Vadgama, *India in Britain. The Indian Contribution to the British Way of Life* (London: Robert Royce, 1984). This book, principally of extracts from contemporary newspapers and reports, and of photographs, concentrates on the Indian nobility in Britain.

Three other works, dealing with Asians in Britain after 1947, are also recommended:

Hamza A. Alavi, *Pakistanis in Britain* (London: London Council of Social Services, 1963).

Rashmi Desai, *Indian Immigrants in Britain* (published for the Institute of Race Relations, London: Oxford University Press, 1963).

Amrit Rao Wilson, *Finding a Voice. Asian Women in Britain* (London: Virago, 1978).

Index

Indian Home Rule Society, 193
Indian languages: influence on
English, 193; see also Bengali,
Gujerati, Gurmukhi, Hindi,
Hindustani, Urdu
Indian National Congress, 8, 79,
81, 90–5 passim, 99, 142, 144,
155, 157, 161, 163, 164, 166–
7, 178, 190, 195, 211–13;
British Committee, 81–2, 89;
see also Indian nationalist
movement
Indian National Rising (1857),
7, 8, 104, 106, 109, 115
Indian nationalist movement, 8–
9, 10, 64, 91, 97, 137–9, 139,
144, 154–8, 162, 186; in
Britain, 76–92, 102–12, 145,
179–80; co-operation with
Irish nationalists, 77–8, 254n.
143; in USA, 254n. 143; see
also Indian National Congress
Indian navy in Second World
War, 139
Indian Parliamentary
Committee, 89, 93
Indian Seamen's Association,
146
Indian Social Club, 97
Indian Sociologist, 103, 104–5,
105, 109
Indian Students' Union and
Hostel, 181
Indian Voluntary Aid
Contingent, 115, 123
Indian Women's Education
Association, 181
Indian Workers' Association,
192
Indians in Britain: beggars, 18,

19, 24, 36, 48, 50, 57–8, 59,
60; businessmen, 69–70, 77;
conjurer, 61; entertainers, 21–
2, 61, see also musicians;
hawkers, 192; impressions of
Britain, 182ff., 193; linguists,
63; merchants, 56; migration
to Britain after 1946, 192–3;
ministers of religion, 70, 71,
196; musicians, 57, 58–9, 59–
60, 60; nobility, 10, 26, 56, 59,
71–5, 169, 172–7; oculists, 62–
3; professional people, 56, 63–
71, 177–8, 184–9, 191–2, 195;
sailors, see lascars; seamen, see
lascars; secret agents in
Second World War, 139, 140–
3; servants, 9, 11–33, 55, 56,
58, 59, 60, 62, 169, female, 12,
13, 14, 16, 17, 28; slaves, 13–
15; snake charmer, 61;
soldiers, 9, 69, 73, 97, 106,
107, 113–39, 176–7; street
traders, 57–8, 60, 60–1, 190;
'topazees' (cleaners), 24; see
also ayahs, lascars, students,
women
Indo-Chinese war (1962), 167
Indo-Egyptian Nationalist
Association, 106
International Medical Congress
(Copenhagen, 1884), 68
International Socialist
Congresses: Amsterdam
(1904), 91; Stuttgart (1907),
103
Inter-Parliamentary Union, 152,
153
Ireland, 110, 156; Home Rule,
77–8, 82, 86, 90

Public Advertiser, 18–19, 37
Puddukotta, Rajah of, 176
Punjab, 25, 53, 71, 72, 73, 85,
  155, 192; Duleep Singh,
  Maharajah of the, 49, 71–3,
  74
Punjabis, 61, 191
Purcell, Albert Arthur, 163
Putney, 14
Pymmes House (Edmonton), 74

Quakers, 163
Queen Victoria Seamen's Rest
  (Poplar), 196

racism and race prejudice, 5–7,
  8, 33, 56–7, 59, 60–1, 70–1,
  75, 82–5, 127, 138, 151, 160,
  171, 174, 182–4, 193
Rajputs, 114, 138
Ramnagaur, Battle of, 64
Ramus, Mrs, 15
Rana, S. R., 103, 109
Rangoon 30
Ranjitsinhji, K. S., afterwards
  Maharajah the Jam Saheb of
  Nawanagar, 173–4
Ratcliffe Highway, 16, 17, 39
Reay, Donald James Mackay,
  eleventh Baron, 79
Red Sea, 116
Reform Club, 102
Regulating Act (1773), 4
Religious Society of
  Zoroastrians, 61
Rhemon, Abdool, 60
Rhodesia, 178
Richmond trial of oculists
  (1893), 62–3
Ripon, George Frederick

Samuel Robinson, first
  Marquess of, 73, 81, 87
Roche, Marie Sophie von la, 11
Round Table Conference
  (1931), 177
Roy, Rajah Rammohun, 76,
  169–71, 180, 277–8 n. 2
Royal Air Force, 141
Royal College of Physicians, 68,
  69
Royal College of Surgeons, 68,
  69
Royal Commission on Finance
  (1895), 89
Royal Cornwall Infirmary
  (Truro), 69
Royal Navy, 25, 34, 52
Royal Society of Arts, 92
Royal Sussex County Hospital,
  67, 68
Rukhmibai Committee, 92
Russell, Bertrand Arthur
  William, third Earl, 163
Russell, Dr Richard, 65
Russia, 102, 110, 145–6, 158

Saeed, Monshee Mahomet, 63
Saheb, Thakore, Rajah of
  Gondal, 184, 185, 186
Sahib, Nana, 106
sailors, see lascars
Sailors' Magazine, 48
St George's Hanover Square, 90
St George's-in-the-East, 28, 48
St Giles, 39
St Marylebone, 28
St Mary's Hospital, 68
St Pancras, 160, 165, 166, 194;
  Arts and Civic Council, 165
St Stephen's Review, 88